Cecil Tr...
Washington Senators

Cecil Travis of the Washington Senators

The War-Torn Career of an All-Star Shortstop

ROB KIRKPATRICK

foreword by Dave Kindred

Best wishes,

Rob Kirkpatrick

McFarland & Company, Inc., Publishers

Jefferson, North Carolina, and London

LIBRARY OF CONGRESS CATALOGUING-IN-PUBLICATION DATA

Kirkpatrick, Rob, 1968–
Cecil Travis of the Washington Senators : the war-torn career of
an all-star shortstop / Rob Kirkpatrick; foreword by Dave Kindred.
p.   cm.
Includes bibliographical references and index.

ISBN 0-7864-2113-4 (softcover : 50# alkaline paper)

1. Travis, Cecil.
2. Baseball players— United States— Biography.
3. Washington Senators (Baseball team : 1886–1960)
I. Title.
GV865.T69K57   2005   613.7'01'9 — dc22   2005018504

British Library cataloguing data are available

On the cover: Cecil Travis in the late 1930s (*Sporting News*)

Manufactured in the United States of America

*McFarland & Company, Inc., Publishers
Box 611, Jefferson, North Carolina 28640
www.mcfarlandpub.com*

For Cameron

Acknowledgments

I would like to thank Carolyn Cary of the Georgia Historical Society; Joey Elger of the Southern League; Frank Ceresi and Carol McMains of FC Associates; and Mickey Vernon, the excellent first baseman of the Washington Senators. These individuals kindly aided me in my research for this book. In addition, I would like to express my appreciation to the staff of the National Baseball Hall of Fame and Museum in Cooperstown, New York.

Special thanks go to Mariah Krok, who provided invaluable help in the consolidation of archival material.

I am indebted to Dave Kindred for providing the foreword to this book.

And I would like to thank my family for their encouragement and support.

Table of Contents

Foreword

by Dave Kindred

The Sporting News

Of Ted Williams' many virtues, one of the most appealing was his generosity to other baseball players. Maybe it was born of his military service, maybe of his loneliness. Whatever its origins, it was real. He treated players as brothers in arms. That said, it is important to know that some brothers in arms were more equal than others. For if Theodore Samuel Williams admired all players, even pitchers, he loved only the hitters.

On a November day in 1994, we talked about hitting for a story in *The Sporting News*. Williams was dealing with the effects of a stroke that impaired his vision and a fall that bruised a shoulder. Yet as he sat by his pool in Herndon, Florida, Williams turned his hands around the handle of an imaginary bat and saw an imagined pitch coming from knuckleballer Hoyt Wilhelm.

It was not the usual knuckleball. Williams suddenly became 25 years old, not 76. He shouted, "Fast ball!"

He all but leaped from his chair to get at that blessed thing.

"Boom! Line drive to right field!"

Then came a smile and words soft with remembered pleasure.

"I don't think I ever saw another fast ball from Hoyt Wilhelm."

In the way that good interviews often go, one thing reminded Williams of another. I had succeeded Shirley Povich as the *Washington Post* sports columnist. Williams had managed the Senators in Povich's day. Somehow those connections prompted Williams to drop into the conversation a name only vaguely familiar to me.

"I'm not so sure Cecil Travis doesn't belong in the Hall of Fame," Williams said. "He was just as good a hitter as John Olerud is today, only

1

he did it longer. But in World War II, he got frozen feet and his career went boom."

On returning home to Atlanta, I studied the *Baseball Encyclopedia*. Of course, Williams was right. A serious Hall of Fame argument could be made for Cecil Travis, a quiet man whose remarkable life and career are here so wonderfully told in *Cecil Travis of the Washington Senators*.

Travis hit .314 in 12 seasons at shortstop and third base for the Senators. In 1941, the year Williams hit .406, Travis was No. 2 in the American League at .359; he had more hits, 218, than any A.L. player would get in a season for the next 36 years.

In the '41 All-Star game, Travis started alongside six men who would go to the Hall of Fame: Ted Williams, Joe DiMagggio, Bill Dickey, Joe Cronin, Bobby Doerr, and Bob Feller.

From Travis's first full season, 1934, through his last before entering the U.S. Army, 1941, he was one of the A.L.'s three outstanding shortstops. Joe Cronin of Boston hit .300 in those eight seasons, Luke Appling of Chicago hit .326, and Cecil Travis hit .327. Of those three, only Travis has not yet been called to Cooperstown.

After reading the statistics, I called my friend and mentor, Shirley Povich, who wrote about the Senators for a half-century, befriended Walter Johnson, and had the astonishing ability to interrupt his own golf swing and explain how Goose Goslin used to tomahawk line drives off pitches over his head.

"What a sweetheart Cecil Travis was, a kind and modest gentleman," said Povich, himself a kind and modest gentleman. "A left-handed hitter, slapped at the ball, used the whole ballpark. Everyone said, 'Lucky hitter, lucky.' He'd get five hits and they'd say, 'Lucky.' He was 'lucky' for 10 years."

Then Shirley surprised me.

"Cecil's still alive," he said, "and he lives down there by you."

The *Baseball Encyclopedia* listed Travis's birthplace as Riverdale, Georgia. So I visited him. He was 81 years old, tall and lean, alert, alive, and happy to be remembered fondly by Williams and Povich.

As he sat in an easy chair in his living room, feet up on a stool, he told me about his first day in a big league ballpark: "It was the middle of May, 1933. Ossie Bluege had gotten hurt, so the Senators needed an infielder in a hurry. I was in Chattanooga when they called and they said get on a train to Washington right now.

"I was 19 years old. The train took all night to get from Chattanooga to Washington. I got there at 12:30 and went straight to the ballpark. I guess I didn't have time to get scared. When I got there they were already taking batting practice. Somebody said, 'You're playing today.'"

Rob Kirkpatrick tells us that the teenage shortstop stepped off the train that day and slapped out five hits in seven at bats as the Senators beat Cleveland, 11–10, in 12 innings.

So began a career that, save for World War II, might have taken Travis to Cooperstown. Not that he would ever say such a thing. As a GI marching through Europe in the winter of 1944, Travis suffered frostbite on two toes of his left foot. Though he came back to play two full seasons and part of another, he was not the runner or hitter he had been. After two mediocre seasons and part of another, he retired in 1947. He was 34.

Of that winter in '44, here's all Travis said to me: "Durn cold, whew." He refused to use the frostbite as explanation for his decline as a player. "That didn't have nothing to do with it." He insisted he had simply lost the edge of youth. "You didn't have to be off but just a hair and you couldn't play."

Rob Kirkpatrick's great achievement with this meticulously researched book is the reminder that Major League Baseball has been built on the accomplishments of men we should not forget. As Ted Williams knew that, so does Rob Kirkpatrick, who now comes to give Cecil Travis the full measure of respect he has long been due.

Introduction

> Conrad looked about; the old man also had a McDonald's cup over his mouth. Then he put that one down behind a framed sepia-toned picture of a baseball player named Cecil Travis and picked up another one and tilted it back to his lips. The sweet smell of brown whiskey, bourbon or rye, spread through the room.
>
> —*A Man in Full*, Tom Wolfe

This passing mention of Cecil Travis is a nice touch on the part of Tom Wolfe. It makes sense that Conrad Hensley, the idealistic father of two in Wolfe's 2001 Atlanta-set opus, would come across a picture of this ball player as he rummages through the offerings of the Hello Again antique shop. Travis, who hails from the Atlanta suburb of Riverdale, Georgia, has been a local celebrity for decades. One can make a case that, aside from Ty Cobb, Travis—a three-time All-Star and holder of a .314 career batting average—is the best hitter to ever come out of the state of Georgia.

Wolfe's allusion is doubly fitting in that Travis, like the old picture of him found in the antique store, has been largely forgotten by subsequent generations of fans. In his day, Travis was considered a pure hitter—a left-handed player with Roy Hobbsesque hitting ability and a natural opposite-field stroke that sent drive after drive into the spacious outfield gap at Griffith Stadium in Washington, D.C., where he played for all twelve of his major league seasons. From 1931, the year he began his career as a pro with the minor league Chattanooga Lookouts, to his peak season in 1941, only once did Travis fail to hit at least .300. (In 1939, the season in which he lost — depending on various accounts— anywhere from twenty and thirty pounds to a mysterious disease, he posted an "off" year of .292.) He was such a natural, pure hitter that he told a Senators coach who claimed to have stolen pitching signs from the opposition not to bother feeding him this information; he didn't need it. Was he being arrogant?

5

No—Travis simply knew how to hit. After the 1941 season, his ninth season in Washington, Travis possessed a career mark of .329 and seemed destined for the Hall of Fame.

But then came World War II, and Travis, like many players throughout the nation, went off to war. He lost the better part of four seasons while serving in the uniform of Uncle Sam and returned to the United States in 1945 after having served in the European Theater. He suffered frostbite in two of his toes while his unit, the 76th Infantry Division, marched through a brutal European winter en route to Germany, and many have pointed to this affliction to explain what happened in his postwar career. Travis himself denies that his frostbitten foot had anything to do with it—he has written it off to a loss of "timing" that came from not facing major league-caliber pitching for 3½ years—but it is undeniable that Travis was not the same player upon his return to baseball near the end of the 1945 season. Unlike players such as Ted Williams and Joe DiMaggio, who were able to resume their stellar careers after serving in the military, Travis never got it back after his years away from the game. After posting decidedly uncharacteristic averages in the mid-to-low .200s from 1945 to 1947, the soft-spoken man from Georgia called it quits and, eventually, returned to raise livestock on the Riverdale farm where he had lived as a boy. And in the superficial flow of history, Travis—once regarded as one of the best and purest hitters in the game—was soon largely forgotten.

The first seeds of inspiration for this book were planted by a newspaper article that I read back in the summer of 1991. The article, which appeared in the *USA Today Baseball Weekly* under the headline, "Travis was a silent hit in '41 season," discussed how neither Ted Williams (of the historic .406 season) nor Joe DiMaggio (of the 56-game hitting streak) had led the league in hits that season. Instead, the player who had led both leagues in hits in 1941 was someone I had never heard of. Here was the quintessential trivia question. Odds were that most people who remembered the 1941 season, or who at least knew about the feats of the Splendid Splinter and the Yankee Clipper from fifty years before, would never guess that another player had been that season's hit leader.

I asked my father (who grew up following the careers of World War II–era players) if he remembered Travis, and he did not. In a strange way, this pleased me; it seemed to confirm that I had encountered one of those rare nuggets of trivia. The *Baseball Weekly* article had explained how Travis's career pretty much ended when he went off to serve his country. When I consulted my *Baseball Encyclopedia*, I discovered just how good

Travis had been prior to the war. He was more than just an answer to a trivia question; he was a player who might very well have been on his way to the Hall of Fame were it not for the interruption of world affairs.

For me, this seemed to transform Travis's career into the level of myth. The legends of many of our culture's heroes, it seems, were born in some sort of premature ending — in the loss of what might have been. One wonders, for example, what creative heights bluesman Robert Johnson might have reached were it not for his mysterious death in 1938 in Greenwood, Mississippi. How much more would Jimi Hendrix have transformed the electric guitar if not for his drug-related death at the age of 27? How many Oscars might James Dean have won if he had not died in a car accident before his twenty-fifth birthday?

The pondering of unrealized potential is not limited to those who legends who met an early mortality. Sports fans debate endlessly about the achievements that certain players could have achieved on different teams or in different situations. Football fans may long wonder how many Super Bowls Dan Marino might have won if he'd had a Barry Sanders in his backfield. Similarly, baseball historians might ask: What fame might Travis have achieved if he had played for a pennant contender in Boston or New York? And what feats could he have accomplished in the years lost to war?

Travis, though, does not regret having never played in the World Series (he came close in 1933, when he was not eligible for the postseason roster). He does not regret having played in small-market city for a notoriously frugal team president. Instead, he seems content, a man in full, having led a life in which baseball was just one stage, one that he remembers fondly from the porch of his Riverdale farmhouse, on the same land where he was born more than nine decades ago.

In researching Travis, I was pleasantly surprised to learn of the many fascinating aspects of his life and career. He tied a major league record with five hits in his very first major league game. He was a three-time All-Star who played with and against some of the game's all-time greats. He saw Lou Gehrig play his final game and was in person to hear the Iron Horse's unforgettable farewell speech; that same year, Travis was selected to participate in an all-star exhibition in Cooperstown, New York, where he witnessed the dedication of the National Baseball Hall of Fame and Museum. Ted Williams used to talk his ear off about hitting, and in the classic 1941 All-Star contest, Travis's "take out" slide at second base kept the game alive and allowed Ted Williams to hit his famous home run, a blast that one writer described as an irreplaceable moment in the game's golden age. Travis also faced Satchel Paige in an historic wartime exhibition, and the battle between the two players served as an important step in early movements to integrate the game.

A player who spoke softly with his mouth but loudly with his bat, Travis was once voted the umpires' favorite player. He also was the favorite player of a young Griffith Stadium scoreboard operator who, one day, became the commissioner of Major League Baseball. He played baseball in front of two United States presidents, Roosevelt and Truman. And when the Washington Senators held "Cecil Travis Night" in the summer of his final season, a rising general named Dwight D. Eisenhower was on field to pay his respects.

In reading Travis's story, one also reads the story of baseball from days gone by. One reads about a time when St. Louis was the westernmost baseball city, when road trips meant spending hours in noisy train compartments. It was an era in which players annually negotiated for one-year contracts, when baseball teams experimented with night baseball.

Travis's story is also the story of baseball in the nation's capital. Long before the days of lucrative merchandise deals and television contracts, Clark Griffith juggled salaries while running a baseball franchise that often failed to draw large crowds during the Depression years. Reporters like Shirley Povich of the *Washington Post* wrote with humor and hope, frustration and veneration, of the beloved home team Senators. And the rest of the league bemoaned the fate of a city that was, as the saying went, "first in war, first in peace, and last in the American League."

Finally, in reading Travis's story, one understands why he is first in the heart of those dwindling few who remember his career. If I have one hope for this book, it is that more people will become familiar with the life and career of this great player. Travis deserves to be remembered by this generation and by future ones. He deserves to be remembered not just as a natural hitter with a .314 career average, but also as a man who showed that the measure of a player's life can be taken both on and off the diamond.

Rob Kirkpatrick
Fall 2005

1

In the Shadow of
Kennesaw Mountain

To many baseball fans, the name *Kennesaw Mountain* conjures up images of the wild-eyed commissioner with the surname Landis who has been both credited with saving the game of baseball after the 1919 Black Sox scandal and vilified for opposing the integration of the game. In fact, Kenesaw Mountain Landis (who spelled his first name with just one *n*) got his monolithic nickname from a twin-humped mountain in Georgia.

The name *Kennesaw* is derived from the Cherokee *Gah-nee-sah*, meaning "cemetery" or "burial ground"—a fitting origin, given the battle that would one day take place there. Standing near Marietta, Georgia, Kennesaw Mountain housed a Confederate signal station during the Civil War. In one of many stops along what historian Bruce Canton called the "macabre dance" between Major General William Tecumseh Sherman and General Joseph E. Johnston of the Confederate army, Sherman led an attack on Johnston's forces near Kennesaw on June 27, 1864. As Sherman paused to ponder the site of what would turn out to be one of the most costly episodes of his famous charge to the sea, he noted, "the summits were crowned with batteries, and the spurs were alive with men busy in felling trees, digging pits, and preparing for the grand struggle impending. The scene was enchanting; too beautiful to be disturbed by the harsh clamor of war."[1]

Sherman mistakenly thought that Johnston had stretched his forces in the region too thin. The resulting Northern offensive would be known as the Battle of Kennesaw Mountain. Of the estimated 4,000 military casualties from the battle, only 1,000 were on the Confederate side. At least one of those 1,000 Confederate soldiers felled in the bloody battle bore the surname of Travis. It was an era when generations grew up on the same land, and the Travises had lived in northern Georgia since Revolutionary times.[2]

A descendant of the Confederate solder, James B. Travis lived and worked a 200-acre farm in Riverdale, a small farming town which lies 12 miles out of Atlanta and two counties south of Kennesaw Mountain. In 1901, at the age of 39, James married a woman named Ada, 10 years his junior. According to census data from 1910, James and Ada Travis raised 10 children: five boys and five girls. Cecil, the youngest of the clan, would grow up to become one of the best baseball players to ever come out of the state of Georgia.

Cecil Howell Travis was born on the Travis farm on August 8, 1913. On the day of his birth, a 16-page edition of the *Atlanta Constitution* carried a cover story on the lurid trial of Leo Frank, the 29-year-old supervisor at the National Pencil Factory in Atlanta who was charged with the rape and murder of Mary Phagan, a 13-year-old employee at the factory. Earlier in the year, the *Atlanta Constitution* had carried a story in which a brothel owner named Nina Formby claimed that a man named "Leo" had telephoned her and demanded a room for himself and a young girl, telling her, "It's a matter of life and death." Although many witness testified that Frank, a Cornell University graduate and president of the Atlanta chapter of the B'Nai B'rith, was home entertaining friends at the time of the rape and murder, Frank would be found guilty and sentenced to death by hanging. The following June, governor John Slaton, who believed that Frank was innocent, commuted Frank's sentence to life in prison. But on August 16, a group called the Knights of Mary Phagan — which later re-christened themselves as an order of the Ku Klux Klan — kidnapped Frank from his jail cell, drove him to Fey's Grove on the outskirts of Marietta, and lynched him in the early morning of August 17.

Expressing a sentiment at the heart of the war in which Cecil's ancestor had lost his life, a *Macon Telegraph* editorial addressed the gruesome turn of events, saying, "The men who lynched Leo Frank went ahead with clear consciences. It would never have happened had the rest of the nation left this state to mind its own business."[3] The rest of the nation reacted with outrage. The *San Francisco Bulletin* said, "Georgia is mad with her own virtue, cruel, unreasoning, blood thirsty, barbarous. She is not civilized. She is not Christian. She is not sane." The *Chicago Tribune* concluded, "The South is a region of illiteracy, blatant self-righteousness, cruelty and violence." The *Boston Post* asked: "Is Georgia in America?"[4]

Nina Formby later recanted her story, claiming that Atlanta police detectives had gotten her drunk and coerced her testimony against Frank. The state of Georgia posthumously pardoned Leo Frank in 1986.

Cecil Travis, a man who would one day serve as an important symbol in the efforts to integrate baseball, was born 12 miles away from Atlanta, on the 200-acre farm in Riverdale on which the Travis family raised livestock and grew cotton. Now officially a city, Riverdale was then, as one Travis interviewer has described, "little more than a marker on the road in the farming community."[5] The town was named after Spratin Rivers, a local landowner who had provided right-of-way to the railroad.

Like his five older brothers, Cecil grew up working on his family's rural Riverdale estate. On the 1930 Census, James Travis's sons (ranging from Cecil, 16, to Emery, 30) were registered as being single and, simply, "laborers" on the farm. (Interestingly, in the field for "Occupation," Cecil's mother, Ada, was originally listed as a "housewife," but

A young Cecil Travis, looking wide-eyed and cherubic early in his career. (Transcendental Graphics)

the census worker crossed that out and wrote "none."[6]) "I naturally had my share of farm work to do ... but being the youngest of the children, escaped much of the hard work," Travis later remembered.[7]

"[T]here wasn't as much to do as there is today," he said of farm life in Riverdale. Baseball was one pastime for Travis, and his brothers played amateur ball, as well. "All we did was play ball. Didn't matter if we use rocks or sticks just as long as we were playing. I just learned the game by playing it."[8] He even used spare moments during chores to refine his hitting technique: "Instead of chopping cotton, I'd pick up rocks and whack 'em with my hoe."[9]

Travis attended Bethsaida Elementary School[10] and then, in 1927, began his courses at the Fayetteville High School. It was there that he first developed a serious interest in baseball. One of his teachers, Roy Hodgson, had been an athlete at the University of Georgia. Hodgson formed a baseball team in Travis's freshman year and "coached the youngsters and placed them in the lineup where he believed them most suited."[11] Travis hit from the left side but threw right-handed, and Hodgson had Cecil play the shortstop, the position where the best players on youth teams are often placed. Travis was tall and thin, even lanky, with an unusual body type for a middle infielder, but Hodgson saw knew baseball and saw talent in the young player. So Travis played shortstop that year and developed an affinity for the position.

The school stopped fielding a team after that one season, but Cecil was able to play during the summer months, in between his farm chores. "I had the baseball bug and cut work short to go to Fayetteville whenever there was a game."[12] The Flint River League was an amateur league that featured games between teams from such towns as Jonesburg, Fairburn, and Fayetteville, for whom Cecil played.

While playing in the Flint River League, Cecil began to display the natural hitting ability that would distinguish him throughout his pro career. Legend of the sweet-swinging kid from Riverdale first grew out of this amateur league. Cecil graduated in the spring of 1930, and he was offered scholarships to three local colleges: Georgia Tech University, the University of Georgia, and Oglethorpe University.[13] He initially planned to go to Georgia Tech — and even had a room all set at the school — until he met a man named Kid Elberfeld.

"They ran a baseball school in 1931 in Atlanta, and some of the fellas that played on the Jonesburg team, they went up there to the school and told Kid Elberfeld about me playing against them," Travis recounted 60 years later.[14] Elberfeld, an ex-major leaguer, was president of Tubby Walton's Baseball University in Atlanta. The school was named after William Hewlett "Tubby" Walton. Tubby Walton was as large, jovial man known amongst Atlanta sandlots for his good nature. He once ran a café named Tubby's Home-Cooked Meals, which he had to shut down when he realized he was giving away more meals through the back door of the café than he was selling to paying customers. Walton was what was known then as a "bird dog," or freelance scout. He developed young players at his "university" and then shopped their rights to professional teams. He also ran a touring team, Tubby Walton's Firecrackers, which gave his students a chance to refine their playing skills.

Once, Walton had informed Elberfeld that he'd discovered "a little boy that can hit a curve ball."

"Ain't no boy can hit a curve ball, Bird," Elberfeld replied.

"This boy kin. Look a little like a Indian and kin hit a curve ball."

Elberfeld told him to bring the player to the school, which in truth consisted of a "skin diamond and a chicken-wire backstop" in Almand Park. Elberfeld later remembered: "I got this pitcher who was sorta mean. Later got in jail. I tole him to knock this Indian down and then curve him. This mean boy low-bridged him, then that Indian-looking boy hit the next curve 10 miles." The "Indian-looking boy" was named Luke Appling. Elberfeld accepted Appling to the school, and later he got Appling signed to a pro contract for the Atlanta Crackers of the South Association.[15] Appling would go on to a Hall of Fame career as a shortstop in the Majors.

Walton also had the distinction of discovering Johnny Mize, the future Hall of Famer slugger. When he first saw Mize playing in the North Georgia hills, Walton claimed that Mize "flogged a line drive that hit a hickory tree 500 feet from home, so hard hickor' nuts kept falling for five minutes."[16]

The circumstances of Travis's discovery were similar to that of Appling's. A student of the school, a boy named Leroy Waldrop, told Walton that he knew "a boy out in Clayton County that could hit anybody."

"Ain't nobody kin hit anybody, Leroy," the Walton responded.

"This boy kin," the youth asserted, "but he can't get away." He then explained the commitment that Cecil had to his family and the farm. Intrigued, Walton told Waldrop to bring Travis to the school at nine o'clock the next morning, and that Travis would be a guest of the school while Waldrop gave him a look.

The next morning, Waldrop brought Travis, who showed up wearing tennis shoes and white duck pants. Walton greeted the youth and told him to pick out a bat hit and swing at some pitched balls. While Walton noted that the rest of his students would always choose models bearing the signatures of their favorite players— Babe Ruth, Al Simmons, Jimmie Foxx — Travis simply picked up a random bat and strode to the plate to face a pitcher named Hugh Casey, an ex-con who'd done time on a chain gang. Walton remembers: "I told ol' Hughie to bear down, and this lean ol' plowboy hit a line drive off him, and kept hitting 'em."[17] And "that boy hit every mean thing that ex-con could throw at him."[18]

But could he field? Unfortunately, that week had seen so much rainfall that the school's diamond had been rendered unusable for any substantial fielding practice. So Elberfeld took Cecil to his home in Atlanta. He had Cecil stand at one end of his living room, and from the other end, Elberfeld hit grounders to Travis over a rug surface. Apparently, Travis evidenced enough skill in fielding ground balls in a domestic setting. Both Elberfeld and Walton were thrilled at the chance to have Cecil as a prized pupil at their struggling school.

Travis also felt that he had found his true calling. He would later recount:

> I had a good mind to go there on my own hook, but at the time was torn between two emotions. First, I had an ambition to become a professional ball player; second, I had the choice of going to one of three colleges. It was a difficult decision to make, but I finally decided to take a chance with Walton and Elberfeld and try to make my own money.[19]

Not surprisingly, Travis's family was reluctant to see Cecil turn down a chance to attend college on a scholarship — and at a time when the nation's economy was reeling from the effects of the great stock market crash that had occurred in October 1929. "My parents were not enthused," Travis admitted. "I think they and my siblings were ready to carry me off to Georgia Tech."[20] Despite the standing scholarship offer from Georgia Tech, the 17-year-old Travis had the two men accompany him back to Riverdale and talk to his father. As they drove up the hill that led to the Travis farm, Cecil reportedly said, "Mistuh Walton, get Pa to let me plow and play baseball, too."[21]

Walton and Elberfeld met with James Travis on the porch of his the Travis house and told him about their baseball school. They brought with them a contract that would give Travis a scholarship to the Tubby Walton school. In exchange for the scholarship, Travis the player would essentially become the property of the school. The elder Travis sat in his rocking chair and closely read the contract.

"It sounds like he's joining the chain gang," he commented.

"It does sound like that," Walton admitted, "but they'll pay him for his work. They don't pay on the chain gangs."[22]

Seventeen-year-old Cecil signed the contract and returned to Atlanta with Walton and Elberfeld. Elberfeld took it upon himself to tutor Cecil personally. Kid Elberfeld had been known as "The Scrappy Kid" during his playing days, which, as H.G. Salsinger noted, was "no mean distinction since at the time major league rosters were filled with gents who made pugnacity their main virtue."[23] In fact, legend has it that Elberfeld used to file the spikes of his cleats in order to make them more dangerous to fielders when attempting to tag him out or turn double plays.

Elberfeld, perhaps seeing something of himself in Cecil, taught the third base position to the youngster. Unfortunately, the school was due to close for the season in only a couple of days. But Elberfeld saw potential in Travis, and he took him to visit a number of Southern Association teams, including the Atlanta Crackers and the Little Rock Travelers, shopping the youngster's talents.

It was the spring of 1931, and in Elberfeld's hometown of Chattanooga, the Lookouts farm team was about to begin training for the upcoming season. Elberfeld took Cecil under his wing and arranged for him to work out with the Lookouts team. Travis would remember:

> Elberfeld made me feel right at home. In fact, he took me to his home, where I had my meals and slept. During the evenings Elberfeld talked nothing but baseball to me. He was a third baseman and a shortstop in his day and he gave me many pointers that helped me a great deal. Even when I was working out with the Lookouts, Elberfeld frequently called me to one side and corrected a fault, or told me how to do a certain thing.[24]

Cecil was just one of 108 fresh, young students of the Tubby Walton school whom Elberfeld had brought to Chattanooga for a tryout that spring. But Cecil showed enough standout ability in his workouts to make a favorable impression on Lookouts manager Bert Niehoff and team president Joe Engel. They gave Elberfeld a $200 finder's fee and signed Travis to a contract with Chattanooga.

Cecil was still green to the world of professional ball, and Niehoff already had a third baseman named Rube Lutzke. So Niehoff gave him the option of either sitting the bench with the Lookouts or playing for a semi-pro team in Newport, Tennessee, where Travis could gain more playing time. Travis remembered: "I told them as long as they'd pay me, I'd rather go up there and play, so I went up there and played."[25] So Travis went north to Newport, with Niehoff's promise that the youngster would get another chance with the Lookouts before the end of the 1931 season.

According to Travis's later recollection, he hit .400 mark while playing shortstop at Newport that summer.[26] But he was not getting paid while playing for the semipro team. Discouraged, Travis considered going home to Riverdale and giving up thoughts of playing pro ball. But before he could, Niehoff made good on his promise and recalled Travis to the Chattanooga squad in August.

In the summer of 1931, as Connie Mack's Philadelphia Athletics and the hard-nosed St. Louis Cardinals were running away with the American and National Leagues, respectively. Travis took advantage of his second chance in Chattanooga. The 18-year-old collected 15 hits in 35 at bats for an average of .429. Travis's run was a brief flurry at the end of a minor league season, but it foretold the rapid rise of one of the game's next great hitters.

2

The Chattanooga Kid

Following Travis's impressive professional debut, he began to generate interest within baseball circles, even if not everyone got his name right. One newspaper article on "Cecil Travers" quoted Engel, who praised his prize pupil's talents. "He can hit through a dime," Engel raved. "Several times he was called upon to hit on the hit-and-run play, and each time he came through. That batting mark of .428 in the Southern Association is worthy of a trial on any big league team."[1] (Another article in 1932 referred to him as "Cecil Tavis.")[2]

In January, though, Engel went to the nation's capital to meet with Clark Griffith, the president of the Washington Senators. *The Washington Post* noted that Engel's "system seems to be to dig up baseball talent for the Washington Club and then to try to coax President Clark Griffith to turn over these discoveries to his Southern Association outfit." Thus, Engel scouted players for the big club but also liked to be able to keep them on the Lookouts roster for a time. Apparently, Engel was successful in the latter, as Travis was retained by Chattanooga for the upcoming 1932 season. The *Post* noted, "With respect to Travis, he is only a youngster in his teens, and, although being tapped as having natural ability, is still considered at least two years away from the majors."[3]

Professional baseball in Chattanooga dated back to 1885, when the city had fielded a team as one of the charter members of the Southern League of Professional Baseball Clubs. (The Southern Association had formed out of the ruins of the Southern League, which folded in 1899.) The original Chattanooga franchise moved to Montgomery, Alabama, in 1902, but in 1910 the Southern Association franchise in Little Rock, Arkansas, relocated to Chattanooga and became the Lookouts.

In 1932, the Chattanooga Lookouts put together a season that its fans would remember for years to come. The starting staff had two pitchers, Alex McColl and Clyde Barfoot, who recorded 20-win seasons, while Leon

Petit and Walter "Duster" Mails won 18 and 17 games, respectively. But the strength of that year's team was its lineup, which included six full-time starters who hit .322 or better, including right fielder Johnny Gill (.344, 120 RBI), left fielder Joe Bonowitz (.350, 85 RBI) and first baseman Harley Boss (.338, 99 RBI). Playing in his first full season as a pro, Travis collected 203 hits (was one of four Lookouts to collect 200 hits), and his average — which was either .356 or .362; there is a discrepancy in the official statistics — led the team. (See Appendix I for an explanation of an apparent error in the official statistics recorded for Travis that season.) He led the league with 17 triples and also added three home runs (his first as a pro). While batting in the bottom half of the potent lineup, Travis knocked in 88 runs in 152 games.

The race for the 1932 Southern Association title was a two-team affair, with Chattanooga and Memphis battling down to the wire. A key point of controversy involved the replaying of a postponed game between Chattanooga and last-place Knoxville. The league president ruled that the game should be made up, but the president of Memphis club protested, most likely wanting to deny the rival Lookouts an extra game with the league's cellar dwellers. Major League commissioner Landis was brought in, and he ruled that the game, which had been scheduled in Chattanooga, should be replayed, and the Knoxville team rushed to Chattanooga to make up the game on September 9. The Lookouts won 12–4, and then they traveled to Memphis for the team's final two scheduled games. Chattanooga swept both games, and the team's 3–0 victory in the final game clinched the league flag. Ironically, Memphis won 101 games that season — three more games than the Lookouts — but Chattanooga played five fewer games and was awarded the championship based a better winning percentage:

	W	L	PCT.
Chattanooga	98	51	.658
Memphis	101	53	.656
Little Rock	77	75	.507
Nashville	75	78	.490
Birmingham	68	83	.450
New Orleans	66	84	.440
Atlanta	62	90	.408
Knoxville	60	93	.392

Back then, the winner of the Southern Association faced the Texas League champions in the "Dixie Series." Chattanooga emerged triumphant in a five-game series with Beaumont. In the series winner, the powerful Lookouts lineup rapped out 12 hits. Travis, batting sixth, went one for two with a sacrifice and also recorded three assists at third base. It was the first Southern Association title and first Dixie Series title for Chattanooga.[4]

Travis, who turned 19 that August, carved a niche for himself with his fine play that season. Many felt Travis to be the best third baseman to play in the Southern Association in years. Some fans gave him the nickname the "Pie," after Pittsburgh Pirates third baseman Pie Traynor, a future Hall of Famer.[5] That November, *The Washington Post* did a feature story on Travis. Dubbing Travis a "Brilliant Prospect," the article identified him as the one player that stood out in a crop of young hopefuls within the Senators organization:

> He is Cecil Travis, still in his teens and a standout this year with the Chattanooga team.... So capable did this youngster perform in the Southern during the past season he now seriously is regarded in local baseball circles as being just the lad to groom as successor to Ossie Bluege at third base for the Griffmen.... He not only took care of his position in gratifying style, but swatted in exceedingly impressive fashion and, although a mere lad, displayed a notable degree of coolness and poise in the most testing situations....

The article acknowledged that the "juvenile Geawgian" still had to improve his defense, such as fielding bunts and charging slow grounders, but noted that these skills would improve with coaching and practice, and concluded that Travis's natural talent with the bat would propel him far in the organization.[6]

Naturally, some onlookers remained skeptical regarding the youngster's promise. One writer pointed out:

> In the minors, a hitter may face big league pitching once or twice a weak. In the majors he faces big league hurling every day. That's the difference. [Incumbent third baseman Ossie] Bluege still can hit 20 points under Travis and be more valuable man to the Nats. His is the poetry of motion, the pinnacle of art, and if there's a better fielding third baseman in the league, it's William Kamm, the peer of 'em all.[7]

Indeed, winning the third base job with the parent club would be a mighty task as Ossie Bluege had established himself as perhaps the best glove in the Majors at the hot corner. Furthermore, the same article named Bob Boken, not Travis, as the organization's best prospect. Boken, a lanky middle infielder whom Washington owner Clark Griffith had recently purchased from the Kansas City Blues, fielded ground balls "like a big leaguer to the manner born." Boken, though, faced perhaps an even bigger challenge, as the Senators infield already included player-manager Joe Cronin (also a future Hall of Famer) at shortstop and a fine second baseman in Buddy Myer.[8]

Still, many prognosticators speculated that Travis was being groomed as Bluege's ultimate successor at the hot corner in Washington. *Post* writer Bob Considine said Travis was "young, strong, coming along with the momentum of a runaway Mack truck"[9] and wrote: "Contrary to the general notion he's not a slugging hitter, in the proper sense of the word. He punches his bingles [*sic*] well and, if you believe Joe [Engel], can hit the lobe of the Goddess of Liberty's ear on a dime placed 100 yards from the plate."[10]

Travis reported to Biloxi, Mississippi, on February 28 to attend spring training for the Washington Senators in 1933. Prior to Travis's arrival, the item of highest interest in the Senators camp seems to have been the stories that catcher Moe Berg was telling teammates of his time in Japan as a baseball ambassador and instructor the previous year. Berg delighted his camp rookies with stories of how he had become adept at eating with chopsticks. One rookie was heard to say, "Just think—chopsticks."[11] Berg was one of the most enigmatic characters on the Senators, if not in all of baseball. Biographer Nicholas Dawidoff notes: "Travis didn't know quite what to make of Berg, and neither did anybody else on the ball club."[12] Berg had the reputation of eccentrically smart, and a saying went that he could speak in 12 languages but hit in none of them. In November 1934, Berg—a career .243 hitter—would go to Japan as part of an "all-star" team of major leaguers. While in Tokyo, Berg allegedly acted as a spy on behalf of the United States and shot footage that later aided U.S. bombers in World War II.

On Travis's much-awaited first day in camp, half the players on the field stopped what they were doing to watch curiously as Travis participated in a pepper drill. He then took his place at third for fielding practice. The *Post* reported, "He made a couple of stops that caused the batter [Nick Altrock] to drop his bat, lift his cap and scratch idly at his collection of mauve dandruff." (Altrock, in his last year as a player, would later become famous for his clownish antics as a coach.) The article also noted that Travis had "a beautiful throwing arm [and] gets the ball away from him with one of those motions that start the instant the grounder hits his gloves." Travis also did well in charging bunts, but Cronin noticed that Travis was "getting off the bag too quickly" on steals, so the player-manager took the position to model the correct timing. The 19-year-old from the small Georgian crossroads town sounded surprisingly relaxed on his first day in a major league camp. When asked about the chances of getting sent back down to Chattanooga, he displayed a confidence that was uncharacteristic of his famously humble nature: "I'll be up here some day, anyhow."[13]

The team began batting practice on March 2. "The center of all eyes was Cecil Travis, the much discussed rookie slugger, the first time he sauntered to the plate," wrote Bob Considine. Travis sent a drive back at pitcher Jack Russell, knocking Russell down. "Travis really hits the ball," Considine remarked.[14] The only pitcher who gave Travis trouble that first day was Paul Lines, who threw with an underhanded "submarine" style. One reporter asked Travis if he had hit cleanup for the Lookouts championship team, and the modest Travis seemed surprised. "No, seventh," he pointed out.[15]

In the spring training games, Travis—who carried a .360 career average as a professional into camp—showed himself to be, as one commentator said, "a solid hitter who fears no pitcher."[16] The Senators faced the minor league Atlanta Crackers before 129 people in Mobile, Alabama, on March 11, and Travis stroked two hits, including an RBI-single in the first inning. But in the bottom of the first, Travis failed to glove a ball off the bat of Atlanta's Red Barron, and two runs scored on the play. The *Post* said, "Of the rookies, Boken and [Cliff] Bolton looked good enough to step right into regular service. Travis was visibly shaky throughout the proceedings."[17]

Earlier in camp, Cronin gave Travis a closer look in infield practice and noticed that Travis had a hitch in his throwing motion, waiting until he had shifted his weight to his left leg and lifted his right before throwing. Travis's reputation as a shaky fielder would dog him throughout the exhibition season, especially in comparison to the veteran Bluege. "Young Cecil Travis, one of the flashiest kids ever to don a Washington bloomer, was carrying on in swell style the other day. He fielded spectacularly, threw across the field with great speed, if a little awkward.... Then Ossie [Bluege] relieved him. Everything that Travis unconsciously made hard, Ossie gathered in with the ease of an artist. He caught and threw the ball with one smooth rolling motion that—coming close on the heels of the performance of a most promising rookie—made the kid look like a sandlotter." The reporter concluded: "We take Ossie too much for granted."[18]

At the end of March, Washington traveled to Atlanta for two more games against the Crackers, and the day before the two-game series, Cronin announced that Travis would relieve Bluege at third in the fifth inning of the first game and then play the entire second game. It was a good public relations move for the club, who would then attract fans of Travis, the pride of the Atlanta of suburb Riverdale. The Washington club historically did not attract great numbers to its gates, and had drawn just over 370,000 fans in 1932, so spring exhibitions were often viewed not just as preseason practices but also as additional revenue opportunities.

After Travis's Georgia homecoming, he experienced another one of sorts when the team traveled to Chattanooga for an exhibition with the Lookouts on April 2. Travis wowed his old fans by knocking a double off the right field fence. But he also committed an error and, perhaps more tellingly, was upstaged by Boken on the final play of the game. With the Senators winning 11–4, a Chattanooga hitter sent a grounder into the hole between third and short. Travis missed it, but Boken — with whom Travis was battling for the final utility infield position on the roster — ranged behind Travis to gather in the ball and throw to first to end the game.

Although that one particular play probably did not decide Travis's fate, it probably made management's decision all the more easy. The team decided that Travis's fielding was not ready for the majors, and after the game, the club announced that Travis would remain in Chattanooga, as he was being farmed out to the Lookouts for another year's seasoning. But the parent team said it would keep Travis on "24 hours recall" in case anything happened to Bluege.[19]

Travis, who had predicted he would be up with the parent club one day or another, did not know just how soon that would happen.

Without Travis, the Washington Senators began the 1933 season in a promising fashion. The "Nationals," or "Nats," as the home papers in the nation's capital dubbed them, won 16 of their first 27 games. But the injury bug bit the team — and, in particular, its infield — as Myer, Bluege and Boken were all sidelined by mid–May. Suddenly, the team was in dire need of Travis's services. He was recalled by the Senators and ordered to meet the team in Washington for its game on May 16 with the Cleveland Indians.

"It was just so sudden," Travis remembered later. He had to hop an overnight train to nation's capital. Once he arrived at Union Station, the hopeful, skinny 19-year-old standing six feet tall might have looked at bit like a wide-eyed Jimmy Stewart in *Mr. Smith Goes to Washington* as walked outside and flagged a taxi cab to Griffith Stadium. "I got the call and went straight to Washington. I got to the ballpark at around 12:30 that afternoon and by one o'clock I was playing."[20] Cronin wrote Travis into the sixth spot in the lineup, playing third base for the home team. "It was the biggest thrill," he said later. "I was only 19 years old and I'm playing with the players that I had only read about."[21] Travis, who had spent his entire youth in the South during an era when the major league play extended only as far south as the District of Columbia (and only as far west as St. Louis), had never seen a major league game until the one he played in that day.

It is also likely that Travis had never seen anything like the spacious grounds of Griffith Stadium. After the 1930 major league season had seen unprecedented offensive numbers, a number of clubs moved their fences back. The left field wall at Griffith had been relocated to 407 feet from home plate. Dead center was 421 feet from home plate, while the power alley in right-center seemed to touch the horizon at a distant 457 feet. (Famed columnist Furman Bisher has described the park as being "as big as Rhode Island."[22]) To make things even more daunting for hitters, even the comparatively shallow right field stands were protected by a 30-foot high wall. In short, the stadium was not designed for home run hitters. But this would suit Travis, who was made for hitting line drives—"blue darters," as they were called back then — not home runs.

If the signing of Travis was straight out of Ring Lardner, then the story of his big league debut is something out of Bernard Malamud. In his first major league at bat, Travis bounced a grounder into the hole on the right side. First baseman Ed Morgan fielded it, but when starter Belve Bean was late in covering first, Travis reached safely for an infield single. In his next at bat, he sent a sharp liner into center for a single. He lined a single into center in his third at bat, as well. In his fourth at bat, he looped another single into shallow center. In his fifth, he lined an opposite-field single into left field. Travis' bid for a sixth hit was thwarted by a scoring error, as he reached base on an error by second baseman Bill Cissell. In Travis's final at bat, he was retired when Indians ace Mel Harder, who was forced into a relief role as the game went into extra innings, knocked down a shot back to the box and threw him out at first. But by then, Travis had written his name in the record books. He was the first player since Fred Clarke in 1894 to recorded five hits in his first Major League game, and the first player ever to record hits in his first five at bats.[23]

Washington won the game 11–10 in 12 innings. Travis scored three runs and shone in the field as well. Cleveland manager Roger Peckinpaugh had shrewdly ordered his first batter of the day, Dick Porter, to test Travis with a bunt down the third base line. Travis reacted with catlike reflexes, scooped up the ball and threw out Porter by two steps. Later in the game, Earl Averill attempted a bunt Travis's way, but Travis also fielded that chance successfully, and Peckinpaugh and the Indians attempted no more bunts toward third the rest of the game. *Post* writer Shirley Povich wrote, "Travis filled Ossie Bluege's shoes in a manner that threatens to give Bluege a prolonged rest."[24] It was the beginning of what would be a long and distinguished career for the Georgia native.

It was a wild affair as both teams combined to break a major league record by using 11 pitchers in the 12-inning game. The box score for the game read as follows:

CLEVELAND	AB	R	H	WASHINGTON	AB	R	H
RF Porter	6	2	2	1B Kuhel	8	1	5
SS-2B Bennett	6	0	2	LF Manush	6	1	2
CF Averill	6	1	1	RF Goslin	5	0	2
2B Cissell	6	1	1	SS Cronin	7	0	2
SS Knickerbocker	0	0	0	CF Schulte	7	1	1
1B Morgan	5	2	1	3B Travis	7	3	5
3B Kamm	6	1	1	2B Myer	6	2	3
LF Vosnik	5	1	4	C Sewell	7	2	5
C Spencer	6	1	3	P Stewart	2	1	1
P Bean	0	0	0	P Burke	0	0	0
P Connally	1	1	1	P Weaver	0	0	0
PH Ferrell	1	0	0	PH Harris	1	0	0
P Craighead	0	0	0	P Russell	0	0	0
PH Powers	1	0	0	P McAfee	0	0	0
P Brown	0	0	0	PH Rice	1	0	1
P Harder	0	0	0	P Crowder	0	0	0
				PH Bluege	0	0	0
				PR Kerr	0	0	0
Team	32	10	16	Team	37	11	27

Joe Kuhel, who also had five hits in the game, actually overshadowed Travis as the hitting star of the day. The Washington first baseman had a triple, a home run, and singled in the winning run in the bottom of the twelfth, giving pitcher General Crowder and the Senators a victory. But no one would soon forget the prolific debut of the left-handed hitter who had been banished to the minors just over a month before. *Post* writer Frank Young speculated:

> Ossie Bluege's injured knee must have improved in leaps and bounds as the Nats' regular third sacker sat on the bench and saw Rookie Cecil Travis field flashily and crack out five hits in seven trips to the tee.... If Travis continues showing anywhere near the form he did yesterday, Bluege can take as long a rest as he desires.[25]

Travis started the next day against Cleveland, as did Crowder, rushed back after his emergency relief appearance the day before. Crowder courageously outdueled the Indians' Wes Ferrell and Senators won 3–2. Travis went two for three and reached base a third time when he was hit by a pitch; more importantly, he figured in two of the team's three runs. In the sixth inning, Travis showed good decorum by knocking in his manager, Cronin, from second with a single — Travis first RBI in the bigs. Later in the inning, Travis crossed the plate with an insurance run on Luke Sewell's single.

The Nats lost the final game of the series, 6–5, and Travis managed only one hit in five times up. He also made his first mistake of note in the field when he got in Cronin's way on a ground ball and prevented the shortstop from making the play. Still, Travis had made a name for himself, and the caption to a *Post* photo of Travis and Boken celebrated the third baseman as having "scintillated" at third while compiling a .533 average in the Cleveland series.[26]

In taking two of three from Cleveland, Washington pulled into second place in the American League. Bluege, who could have played the series if necessary, was back in the lineup during the team's next series against Chicago. But he aggravated his leg in his first game back, and Travis was forced back into the lineup. He and Boken were guests on the "Radio Joe" show on WMAL on May 24 (though one wonders if the quiet Travis made for good radio). Boken also saw time at third base in Bluege's absence. By the end of May, papers in Chattanooga anticipated Travis's return to the Lookouts squad, but Cronin disputed this. "Until Bluege is back again and in normal shape, I'm going to keep Cecil right here."[27] But Bluege was back soon enough, and Travis was sent back to Chattanooga following the team's 4–3 victory over Boston on June 4.

The Senators burned through the month of June, winning 15 of 16 games and jumping over the New York Yankees into first place; the team never looked back. Washington was having its finest season since its championship year of 1924. The club had two 20-game winners in 1933, Crowder (24–15) and Earl Whitehill (22–8), and all four staff starters finished with double figures in wins and ERAs under 4.00. Jack Russell came out of the bullpen to add 12 wins and 13 saves. The Washington offensive attack, meanwhile, had six starters with averages of .295 or better, led by Heinie Manush (.335, 115 runs, 95 RBI) and Joe Kuhel (.322, 89 runs, 107 RBI). Player-manager Cronin hit .309 while scoring 89 runs and knocking in 118. At the end of August, the Senators were 82–44 and securely atop the American League standings.

Meanwhile, Travis was putting together another fine season in Chattanooga. In only 129 games, he notched 129 hits, scored 80 runs, and knocked in 74 while hitting at a .352 clip. It came as little surprise when he was recalled by the club and rejoined the Senators for its game on September 6. In the final month, Cronin used him at third to give the veteran Bluege occasional day of rest as the Senators eyed World Series play. On September 21, a Thursday afternoon crowd of 20,000 at Griffith Stadium saw Lefty Stewart outduel the Browns' Bump Hadley 2–1, and the Senators clinched the pennant. Cronin and his club celebrated in the stadium clubhouse. Charles Alexander records that:

After the clubhouse merrymaking, bachelor Joe Cronin donned his street clothes and dashed across the field, trailed by a posse of adoring women. Expecting to find his automobile waiting behind a door in the right field fence, the Senators' young manager found nothing, ran to the center field fence and through another door, finally reached his automobile on Fifth Avenue, and sped away from his female pursuers.[28]

Washington's home team fell just one win short of 100 victories in 1933. In the regular season finale, the Philadelphia Athletics shut down the Senators 3–0 in 11 innings. After the A's had broken through for three runs in the top of the eleventh, the Senators sent Nick Altrock, its 57-year-old coach, to the plate to pinch hit with two outs. Philadelphia pitcher Babe Walberg called the outfielders in, and his infielders crowded around the mound. Walberg served up a hittable pitch to Altrock, who bounced it weakly back to Walberg. The pitcher fielded the ball, ran to the baseline, and waiting for Altrock. The coach circled around Altrock via the dugout steps and ran to first base, but he was called out for running out of the baseline. It was an ignoble ending to a distinguished regular season.

Travis appeared in 18 games during the season, recording 13 hits (12 singles and one double) in 43 at bats for a .302 average. He played third base in 15 games, compiling a respectable .974 fielding percentage. In the two-part tryout with the Senators in 1933, he showed the same natural hitting ability as he had in the minors. Unfortunately, since Travis was not on the team's roster on September 1, he would not be eligible for the World Series, in accordance with Major League rules. Nevertheless, Cronin and the Senators players voted that Travis should get a $500 share of the team's World Series pot. A full share of approximately $5000 would go to players on the winning team, with nearly $3200 going to players on the losing team.

In the 1933 World Series, the Senators faced off against the New York Giants. New York had had a fine season as well, going 91–61 in senior circuit play. Outfielder Mel Ott had led the Giants attack with 23 home runs and 103 RBI, while first baseman Bill Terry had led the team with a .322 average. The team's best player, though, was southpaw screwball pitcher Carl Hubbell, who went 23–12 and added five saves while compiling a microscopic 1.66 ERA. Hal Schmacher (19–12, 2.16 ERA), Freddie Fitzsimmons (16–11, 2.90 ERA) and Roy Parmelee (13–8, 3.17 ERA) had rounded out an impressive starting four, and Hi Bell (6–5, 2.05 ERA, five saves) and Dolf Luque (8–2, 2.69 ERA, four saves) provided strong support out of the pen.

In game one of the series, played at New York's Polo Grounds on October 3, Hubbell befuddled the Nats' bats, limiting them to just five hits and three unearned runs. Mel Ott tied a series record by going four for four;

Buddy Myer also tied a record by committing three errors, and New York won 4–2. Washington was held to just five hits in the second game, as well, which the Giants also won on the strength of a six-run outburst in the sixth inning.

The series moved to Washington on October 5, and President Franklin Roosevelt braved a steady rainfall to watch Senators pitcher Whitehill toss a 4–0 shutout. But Hubbell, who after the series would be named the National League's Most Valuable Player of 1933, pitched an 11-inning complete game to outduel Washington's Monte Weaver, 2–1. Hubbell's remarkable performance was not even his best of the season. Back on July 2, he had gone 18 innings against the vaunted St. Louis Cardinals lineup while not allowing a walk and striking out 12.

In game five of the series, Mel Ott gave the Giants another dramatic victory by homering in the tenth-inning, and New York took the game 4–3 and the series 4–1.

It was a disappointing end to a fine season. Not unnoticed in the Senators' series loss was the performance of Bluege, who managed only two hits in 16 at bats for an average of .125. Speculation soon began regarding the smooth swinging third baseman from Georgia that the team had waiting in its wings.

3

Rookie Season

"Pity the poor rookie who goes South with the Washington Ball Club. The 1934 cast of the Nats is not scheduled to vary in any particular from the 1933 campaigners," wrote *Washington Post* columnist Shirley Povich as the Senators' roster players and hopefuls headed to Biloxi for spring training. Povich's observation stood to reason for a club whose starters had won the American League pennant the previous season. The one sure change in the Nats' lineup would be in right field; in the offseason, Washington had traded Goose Goslin to Detroit for Jonathan Stone, who had topped 100 runs and RBI two years before, and who would take Goslin's spot in the outfield. As for the younger players, Povich warned: "A rookie's chance of breaking into the Washington line-up in 1934 is no better than the proverbial Chinaman's chance."[1]

Nevertheless, most onlookers expected Cecil Travis to present a formidable challenge to Ossie Bluege, the incumbent third baseman. Washington fans were still abuzz over the hitting prowess that Travis had displayed during his brief stint with the club in 1933. Bluege, who had turned 33 just after the World Series, was still recognized as one of the finest fielding third sackers in the game, but his average had dipped to .280 in 1933, and he had "failed to hit the size of his chapeau" against the Giants in the World Series. Clark Griffith and Joe Cronin, both Travis fans, were nevertheless reluctant to anoint Travis the team's new third baseman based less than 50 plate appearances from the previous season. Plus, Travis had yet to prove that he could play defensive on a major league level. "Bluege can give his young rival cards, spades and big casino and still outfield him around the bag," wrote Povich. "Unless there is a crying need for hitting from the third baseman Bluege will remain on the job."[2]

For many fans, though, the young Georgian was the team's Great Young Hope, and it was clear that management saw Travis as the ultimate successor to Bluege at third. Cronin began to tutor the youngster in some of the subtleties of playing the infield, such as how to avoid getting spiked by sliding baserunners. And even though Travis seemed to have a natural talent for getting base hits, management encouraged Travis to start using a lighter bat. Beginning with his major league debut, when only one of his five hits had been pulled to the right side, Travis had acquired a reputation as being a light, opposite-field hitter. Of his 13 hits in 1933, only one (a double) was for extra bases. Cronin hoped that Travis would develop into a more powerful hitter with the ability to drive balls into the cavernous gaps in the Griffith Stadium outfield.

Travis performed well in the team's exhibition season. On March 23 against the Cleveland Indians, Travis hit a triple and — perhaps more encouragingly for the club — twice fielded ground balls and began around-the-horn double plays. Speculation began on Travis's earning the third base job. One article noted that Joe Cronin would not rest on the team's pennant-winning laurels and eyed possible changes in the infield lineup:

> His experiments during spring training and the exhibition games point to the installation of Cecil Travis ... at third base. While some will doubt the wisdom of any move that would eliminate the veteran Ossie Bluege from infield scenery, Cronin has just about reached the conclusion that if Travis can take care of the traffic in a passable manner he can make himself more valuable than Bluege, because of the youngster's ability to belt the ball.[3]

Bluege was not quite ready to yield his job, though. One week later in a game against the minor league New Orleans Pelicans, Bluege collected three hits, including a triple, and demonstrated his trademark fielding acumen at third. Despite the obvious threat to his starting status, Bluege faced the competition professionally, and he was openly helpful to Travis and joined in Cronin's efforts to tutor the rookie in how to play the third base position.

When the club broke camp, Travis had made the opening-day roster, but Bluege was still slotted in the lineup as Washington's third baseman. It is likely — and understandable — that Cronin did not see the need to shake up the lineup that had gone to the World Series just six months earlier. Hopes ran high as the team won its first two games in Fenway Park, but the Red Sox rebounded to sweep a double header from the Senators, and Washington ended up losing five of its first eight games. Hoping to shake things up after the rough start, Cronin changed the team's lineup for its game against Boston on April 26. He inserted right fielder Dave Harris into the fifth spot; second baseman Bob Boken into the sixth spot; and Travis into the seventh spot, substituting for Bluege. The trio responded with consecutive hits in the first inning, when the team busted out for five runs. After Washington scored three more runs in the second, Boston clawed its way back into the game. The score stood 8–7 in the seventh inning when Travis hit a fly into left-center field. Boston's Carl Reynolds mistakenly started in on the ball, but it sailed over his head and Travis strode into second. A double by catcher Moe Berg scored Travis for an insurance run, and the team went on to win 10–7.

Travis finished the game two for four with two runs and two RBI. But it was a rough game defensively for the rookie. In the third inning, Travis bobbled a ground ball from pinch hitter Dusty Cooke, and the error sparked a five-run rally for the Sox. Later that inning, Bill Werber hit a double past Travis, and Nats starting pitcher Monte Weaver was sent to the showers. In the eighth inning, Joe Judge hit a single of Travis's glove, though Boston did not score in the inning.

Hoping that Travis would improve in the field while continuing to hit American League pitching, Cronin kept Travis in the starting lineup. Travis's presence in the lineup did give the Nats added punch. On April 30 against the Yankees, Travis stepped up to bat with two men on base to face the famed Charley "Red" Ruffing. Showing that one need not pull the ball to get extra base hits, Travis drilled a ball down the third base line for a two-run triple. (Ironically, in relating the strategy of Yankees pitchers in facing Travis, Ruffing would later reveal: "We pitched Travis fastballs so he'd only hit a single to left. If we pitched a changeup he'd hit a triple to right."[4]) Not to be outdone by Washington's rookie, Ruffing upstaged everybody by going to distance on the mound and, then, hitting a three-run home run in the ninth inning, winning the game for himself 7–4.

The 1934 Senators team struggled into May with a record of 6–6. Washington fans began to wonder what was happening to their beloved Nats. The *Post* started referring to the team as "The New Dealers" or "The New Deal Nats." The nickname seemed apt, as changes in the lineup seemed as warranted as the economic programs conceived by Washington's First Fan, Franklin Roosevelt. The moniker also underscored the unique nature of playing professional ball in the nation's capital. Looking back upon his career, Travis would say:

> To tell you the truth, I think Washington was a little better off than other cities during the Depression," It was a government town, and government workers had jobs. So they could come out and watch us play. On the other hand, most of them were from out of town, and they'd come root for their hometown team rather than us. Usually, more were rooting for the visitors than for us.[5]

Meanwhile, Travis became a central figure in the New Deal Nats and continued "to rip his way into the affections of Washington fans."[6] In early May, the *Post* noted the inevitability of "the Chattanooga kid" replacing Bluege, whom Travis had idolized as he learned the third-base position. In contrast to the "tiring" Bluege, who had started wearing eyeglasses on the field, Travis injected fresh new talent into the Senators lineup:

> Always a natural hitter, he has been quick to learn his hot-corner chores. He's still just a big boy with loose muscles, not yet dry behind the ears.
> He's one of those old-fashioned boys who always wanted to play ball, rare in these days of mad speed when baseball has become too slow for Young America in search of a thrill.
> "I wouldn't do anything else," he says quietly, a little surprised at the foolish question. "It's what my folks want me to do, too."[7]

One can imagine the alarm his parents would have felt had they been in Griffith Stadium on May 5, when Travis was struck on the head by a fastball from Thornton Lee, a rookie southpaw for the Cleveland Indians. The Senators were staging a fourth inning rally when Travis stepped into the box to face Lee. Travis worked the count to three and two. On the payoff pitch, Lee sent a high hard one "that didn't break a fraction of an inch as it collided with Travis' skull with the resounding whack of a shingle brought down upon a sounding board." Travis raised his hand to his head as he fell to the ground. The ball had struck him just under his right ear, at the base of his skull, knocking him unconscious. The 6,000 fans in Griffith Stadium sat in "shocked silence" as concerned players from both teams rushed to the plate. The club physician attended to Travis, and a group of teammates carried the injured player to the dugout. An ambulance took Travis to nearby Garfield Hospital.[8]

Once Travis was safely off the field, the game proceeded with "the grim spectre of tragedy overhanging the proceedings."[9] Anyone witnessing the incident would have thought back to the tragedy that struck Cleveland Indians shortstop Ray Chapman on August 16, 1920. Chapman was a popular player and had compiled a .278 career average through 1,050 games with the Indians. On that August day in the Polo Grounds, Yankees submarine pitcher Carl Mays threw a high, inside fastball to Chapman. The 29-year-old shortstop, who was famous for crowding the plate, froze as the pitch sailed at his head. The baseball fractured his skull and, the following day, Chapman was pronounced dead.

The Nats won the game 9–1, but the fans' minds were clearly on Travis's health. Unbeknownst to them, Travis came to in the clubhouse while awaiting transport to nearby Garfield Hospital. He said, "Ah don't

Players from both the Senators and Indians watch concerned as Travis (on ground) lies unconscious after being beaned by Cleveland's Thornton Lee on May 5, 1934. (Transcendental Graphics)

think there ah' any broken bones."[10] In the seventh inning, the public address system delivered an announcement that Travis was "resting and in favorable condition" at Garfield; the crowd issued "a collective and audible sigh."[11]

Early reports had Travis suffering a fractured skull (though strangely, an x-ray was not immediately taken). However, Travis's skull had remained intact. Apparently, the beaning, though ugly, was not as serious as it appeared. When Cronin went to the hospital after the game, the first thing Travis reportedly asked him was "Did we win the game?" Travis remained in the hospital as a precaution, but he reported no complaints—not even a headache. He expressed impatience at getting out of the hospital and back into the field. Cronin declared that he did not even worry about the beaning making Travis gunshy at the plate. "Shucks," Travis told Cronin, "I've been hit in the head before. It isn't worrying me any."[12] The *New York Times* ran a blurb saying, "Cecil Travis, Senators rookie, was said tonight at Garfield Hospital to be getting along nicely. Attendants said that Travis's skull was not fractured, contrary to early reports."[13]

Despite Travis's eagerness to return to the Nats lineup, he was kept out for a few games. On May 8, he sat in plain clothes and watched from the stands as Washington beat Chicago 7–6. Ossie Bluege temporarily filled in for Travis at third. Interestingly, Cronin had replaced Travis with Boken to finish the game on May 5, explaining: "Bluege got hit in the head and badly hurt by Vic Aldridge back in the 1925 world series, and so I did not think it would be good policy to put him in yesterday in place of any fellow who had been knocked out in the same manner." Bluege, noted Frank Young of the *Post*, "was probably the most worried of all of the Nats when Travis was injured yesterday.... He was one of the first to rush to Travis when he was hit, helped carry him off the field, and was in the locker room seeing if he could help the club physician when Boken was named as a pinch runner and play was resumed."[14]

Bluege remained a popular player with Washington fans and, especially, his teammates, but the team missed Travis's bat. In addition to Travis, both Al Simmons and Luke Sewell, who suffered a broken hand, had been sidelined with injuries. Washington's third baseman missed nearly two weeks recuperating from his beaning, and some wondered how the meek-mannered Travis would respond when he was back in the batters box.

As the fates would have it, not only was Cleveland the team's opponent in Travis's first game back, but Lee came in from the bullpen to face Travis. Travis had bore no ill will against Lee, refusing to be baited by speculation that the pitcher had thrown at him. "That Lee tried to bean me or even dust me is absurd," he said. "I never for a moment entertained such an idea. He simply lost control of the ball. I saw it coming toward me but couldn't duck in time."[15] But Travis still had to prove that he wasn't gunshy. In his first at bat against Lee, Travis stepped right up in the batters box, swung at Lee's first pitch and launched a ball the bounded deep into the left-center field gap. Travis pulled into third with a triple, effectively announcing he was back.

"I have heard of players being bat shy after they had been victims of a similar distressing episode, but I can honestly say that it didn't affect me in that way. I haven't any qualms about facing any pitcher," Travis said later.[16] Bucky Harris concurred, observing, "He's so plate-shy, he's crowding the plate."[17]

Although Travis did not display any problems getting back on the horse when it came to hitting, he had to shake off some rust in the field. In one inning of a contest with Cleveland on May 17, Travis managed the ignoble feat of committing two glaring errors and, more seriously, injured one teammate with his spikes and indirectly led to another teammate getting spiked.

Travis touched off the seventh inning when he muffed a ground ball by Indians outfielder Joe Vosmik. After second baseman Odell Hale tripled home Vosnik and first baseman Hal Trosky singled in Vosnik, catcher Frankie Pytlak attempted to bunt Trosky to second. Travis fielded the bunt and threw wide to second baseman Buddy Myer, who was covering first on the sacrifice attempt. As Myer attempted to catch the throw and keep his foot on the bag, Pytlak came down on the instep of Myer's foot.

The next batter, third baseman Willie Kamm, bounced a grounder between the mound and third base. Both Russell and Travis went for the ball, and Travis stepped on Russell's right ankle as the two converged. Travis's cleats left a four-inch cut in Russell's ankle, and the pitcher had to leave the game. With Russell in the clubhouse, the Indians' batters pounced on the Washington bullpen for eight more runs, and Cleveland won 14–6. The following day, the *Post* deemed the third baseman's defensive play as a "Travis'ty" and added "Travis ... as long as he had to spike a Washington pitcher today, might have chosen either Earl Whitehill or Alex McColl and done the Nats a service instead of incapacitating Russell, the only one of the three pitchers who was able to stop the Indians."[18]

After the game, team trainer Mike Martin announced that both players would miss at least three weeks because of their spike-related injuries. The disaster-plagued inning undoubtedly left a bad taste in the mouths of some of Travis's teammates. (Both players would return to the Washington roster, but Russell seemed to never recover fully, as he finished with a record of 5–10 and an ERA of 4.17.)

The following day, however, Travis did his best to make amends for the day before. Travis snagged two hard grounders, both potential extra base hits, and turned them into outs. First, he fielded a ball from Vosmik and threw him out at first. Later, he handled a chance from Pytlak's bat and threw out the lead runner at second. The *Post* declared, "Cecil Travis, who turned over a new leaf ... was a fielding fiend out there at third base, cutting down base hits like some ruthless wraith."[19] Travis further helped his cause with an RBI-hit that knocked in player-manager Cronin in the fourth inning.

While Travis would not ease doubts about his fielding overnight, no one doubted that he was a talented hitter. During the month of May, Travis reached base game after game. Though not demonstrating much power — he had not yet hit a home run that season — he proved a consistent ability to get base hits, and his hits often proved instrumental in Nats rallies.

On May 22, for example, Travis came to bat with Stone on base and the score tied 2–2. Travis singled to advance Stone, and both men scored when Detroit outfielder Gee Walker booted a single by catcher Eddie Phillips; the Senators won 5–2 behind a complete game performance from General Crowder. Travis quietly built a hitting streak that reached 19 until it was broken by Ted Lyons of the White Sox on May 28.

The baseball world began to take notice. In his column, "The Umpire," H. G. Salsinger wrote a profile on Travis, who was hitting .372 at the time, and his unlikely journey from a "base ball college" to the majors:

> Cecil Travis, Washington's new infielder, holds more interest for us than any other recruit whom we have seen this year.... Travis, the pupil, has the appearance of being quite a ball player. Prof. Elberfeld taught him third basing and ... also taught Travis something about batting and the pupil will outdo the master in this end of the business, unless all signs go wrong.[20]

Travis indeed was emerging as a consistent threat in the Senators lineup. During a 7–3 victory over the Philadelphia Athletics on June 7, he notched two singles that scored future Hall of Famers: Cronin in the second inning and Heinie Manush in the sixth inning. Against Chicago on June 18, Travis, Myer, and Cronin were "driving each other around the bases all day" in tallying 10 of Washington's 13 hits in an 8–7 win.[21] Travis collected four straight hits and knocked in three runs. In the ninth inning, after Cronin flew out with Myer standing on second base, but Travis picked up Cronin by slashing a single to left and scoring Myer with the game winner.

During a doubleheader with Detroit on June 23, Travis hit his first home run of the season. In game one, Travis stepped in against the Tigers' Vic Sorrell and unwound a deep drive into the Griffith Stadium right field stands, his first in the majors, and his only one of the season. The nature of the home run would be a rare one in the career of Travis, who specialized in line drives to the opposite field. His home run was also one of the lone highlights for the Nats that day, as they lost both ends of the doubleheader, 9–6 and 8–6.

The 1934 season was quickly becoming a lost one for the Senators, and the team seemed to be jinxed by injuries. Travis tripled in a key run in the team's 10–9 win over St. Louis on June 26, but Luke Sewell had to leave the game in the first inning when he was beaned by pitcher Bump Hadley. (Ironically, St. Louis catcher Frank Grube also had to leave the game in the first inning after he dislocated a finger on a pitch in the dirt.)

More seriously, Johnny Stone fractured his ankle on July 13 in Cleveland while sliding into second base, sidelining him for the remainder of the season.

Games with the Indians seemed to be bad luck for the Senators, but an encouraging omen was taken from that game. In the first inning, Indians manager Walter Johnson, the "Big Train" who had had a brilliant pitching career with the Senators from 1907 to 1927, attempted to avert a Washington rally by intentionally walking Travis; Fred Schulte then followed with a two–RBI single. That Johnson, a future Hall of Famer and one of the greatest pitchers of all time, gave Travis such respect seemed to confirm the rookie's status as one of the American League's most accomplished hitters. Indeed, while teammate Manush sat atop the American League in batting average in early July, Travis threatened to push the league leaders in this category with an average well above the .300 mark.

Major league play took a break for the second annual All-Star Game between the National and American leagues, played in New York City's Polo Grounds. Two of Travis's teammates, Manush and Cronin, made the starting squad for the American League. The American League won 9–7, with Cronin, batting eighth, went two for five with one run and two RBI; though Manush officially went zero for two, he and Charlie Gehringer pulled off the first double steal in All-Star competition in the first inning. But the performance of hometown hero Carl Hubbell has gone down as the game's most memorable performance; the knuckleballer made All-Star history by striking out five consecutive batters: Babe Ruth, Lou Gehrig, Jimmie Foxx, Al Simmons and Joe Cronin — all future Hall of Famers. Even with Hubbell's heroics, the pitching star of the day might actually have been Cleveland's Mel Harder, who took the mound in the fifth inning and proceeded to shut down the National League the rest of the way, yielding only one hit and one walk.

Later on that week, on July 14, Harder built off his All-Star performance by shutting out the Nats, 2–0. In the second inning of that game, back-to-back hits by Cronin and Travis went for naught when Cronin was thrown out at third by outfielder fellow All-Star Earl Averill, and Travis was picked off second base by Harder.

Three days later in Detroit, Travis dubiously distinguished himself in the field once again. In the sixth inning, Travis fielded a ground ball from Billy Rogell and, as the *Post* described, let loose "one of the prettiest wild throws committed on Mr. Navin's premises this season."[22] One runner scored from second, Rogell ended up on third, and Detroit mounted the eventual game-winning rally. To make matters worse, Travis came to bat with the bases loaded in the ninth inning and grounded into a game-ending double play. The next day, Travis ended another potential rally, this time in the first inning with two men on, striking out with "three whip-like cuts [that] created a vacuum throughout the park."[23]

"Travis needs a long rest," wrote the *Post*'s Povich.[24] "The 20-year-old third baseman has done well enough thus far, but the strain of his first season in the big show is beginning to tell on him."[25] Unfortunately, an extended rest was nowhere in sight. Clark Griffith observed: "Poor Cecil Travis need [*sic*] a rest out West, and what happened? Bluege goes down with the heat, and when he recovers we have to use him in the outfield." Travis was forced to endure the dog days of his rookie season.[26]

Likewise, the Senators were forced to play out a season mired in the second division while Detroit and New York were proving to be the league's elite. On August 7, Washington managed a split of a doubleheader against the Yankees at Griffith. In the second game, Washington pounded out 17 hits. Travis tallied an RBI double that was misplayed by center fielder Ben Chapman and bounced to the wall. An eighth inning Yankee rally was cut short when a 39-year-old Babe Ruth, appearing as a pinch hitter, popped up to Travis at third. Ruth, once a larger-than-life star in the sport, was taking a back seat to his teammate and rival Lou Gehrig. Gehrig, whom the Washington papers took to calling "Baggy Pants" because of his loose-fitting leggings, was embroiled in a race for the batting title with Washington's Manush. On August 8, Baggy Pants Gehrig went hitless while Manush went two for five and the Senators blasted Red Ruffing for six runs in the opening inning of a 9–2 win.

Series wins were few and far between for the Nats in '34, and Travis had more than his share of fielding woes, but it was clear that Washington had found a professional hitter. Lewis Atchison of the *Post* remarked on the fans' feelings of being robbed when rain denied Travis a crucial at bat in the team's game with the Philadelphia A's on August 12:

> The Nats came so close to winning a ball game yesterday it wasn't funny. It was anything but humorous when rain started falling in the eighth inning with Joe Cronin, representing the winning run, on second, Buddy Myer on first, and young Cecil Travis coming up to pinch hit for Fred Schulte.
> The pleasant picture of Travis slicing one into left field and Cronin sprinting home with that all-important run already had been born in the fans' minds when the rain came whirling down.... [27]

Indeed, the sweet-swinging Georgian was becoming enough of a story around the league that *Baseball Magazine* profiled him that month. Joe Cronin told Clifford Bloodgood:

I don't think I'm making any foolish claim when I predict that Travis is going to make a fine ballplayer.... He is one of the most natural hitters I ever saw come into the big leagues. As a rookie he has more poise and polish at the plate than many veterans of 10 years major league experience. No pitcher of reputation will disturb his calm, no delivery of a ball will disconcert him. He is a perfect picture at the plate. It makes no difference where the ball comes in, high or low, inside or out.

He is keenly interested in his career and quite willing to accept advice. Moreover if there is any problem of play that he can't quite fathom he won't be content to remain in ignorance.[28]

In late August, Travis missed some time with a charley horse. Bluege again took Travis's place at third, but Travis was forced back into action on September 3 when Cronin fractured the radius bone in his right arm during the first game of a doubleheader with Boston, and Bluege moved over to short. Travis hit third in the second game and went one for five and scored one run in a 4–4 tie.

Two days later, the Nats were mathematically eliminated from the playoffs. It was a disappointing season for the league champions of the previous season. For Travis, his rookie season had seen peaks and valleys. The rookie hit .319 over 392 at bats and compiled a fine .361 on-base percentage. Despite recording less than 400 at bats and often hitting toward the bottom of the order, he recorded 53 RBI thanks to clutch hitting. But in 99 games at third base, he committed 20 errors and notched an underwhelming .937 fielding percentage.

Still, Travis was recognized as one of the league's rising stars. In the off-season, the American League Service Bureau sent out a press release on Travis. In a society that was dependent upon the wire service in spreading news from city to city, the release told Travis's story to newspapers throughout the league for the first time: his growth on the sandlots of Georgia, his instruction under Kid Elberfeld, his signing by Chattanooga and seasoning in Newport before catching on with the Lookouts, his rise with the Senators. The author, Henry F. Edwards, observed:

Travis may never field as Bluege did in his prime but he will make more base hits. He never batted less than 300, either with Chattanooga or Washington, despite the fact he was a victim of injuries in '34, the most serious of which was being hit in the head with a pitched ball. His latest batting average is 319 for 109 games.[29]

Washington fans who had hoped for a repeat World Series appearance had to settle to radio broadcasts of the Detroit Tigers and St. Louis Cardinals facing off in a seven-game classic. The Tigers had won 101 games in the regular season, but the Cardinals were led by 30-game winner Dizzy Dean and his brother, Paul "Daffy" Dean, who went 19–11 that year. Detroit held a 3–2 lead in the Series but lost the final two games at home. The Dean Brothers pitched a combined 44 innings and registered all four wins for St. Louis. In the final game, won by St. Louis 11–0, left fielder Joe "Ducky" Medwick was pulled off the field for his own safety when the home fans began to pelt him with bottles and fruit. Meanwhile, frustrated Senators fans looked toward a return to excellence for their team in 1935.

4

The Hot Corner

As Travis prepared for his sophomore season, he and the Senators found out that they would have a new man at the helm in 1935. In October, Clark Griffith had traded the rights to their player-manager, Joe Cronin, to Boston for infielder Lyn Lary, along with the sum of $225,000. Griffith's reasons for trading the future Hall of Famer were purely financial; not only did the club receive monetary compensation, but it would avoid having to pay Cronin's yearly salary. Replacing Cronin as manager was Bucky Harris, who had managed the club from 1924 to 1928. But in comparison to the $100,000, three-year contract Harris had signed after the club's championship season in 1924, Harris reportedly signed for just $11,000 to manage in 1935.[1]

It was not the first time Griffith had made a managerial change based on money, nor was it the first time the team had replaced a sitting player-manager. After the 1928 season, Griffith had replaced Harris with Walter Johnson at a lower salary. Likewise, Griffith had replaced Johnson with Cronin in 1933.

For his part, Harris looked forward to his second go-round with Washington. "Last year," he mused, "along about June, I still thought Washington was going to win the pennant. The club looked as if it had everything. Then those injuries started to pop. Nobody could help that, of course, but you can't underestimate the power that the team still has."[2] Chicago White Sox shortstop Luke Appling voiced further endorsement for the potential of the 1935 Senators, singling out Cecil Travis as being due for a great season.[3] Appling, a rising star in the American League, was always good for a quote. "One player you couldn't escape talking to was Luke Appling," Travis later recounted. "Luke was always talking to you. He'd talk your ears off."[4]

Travis took the train from Atlanta down to Biloxi for the start of the Senators' training camp on March 8. The Biloxi weather did not cooperate, though, as it wasn't until March 11 that winds had sufficiently dried off a wind-soaked diamond and Harris was able to get his first look at his new infield: Travis at third, Lyn Lary at short, Myer at second and Kuhel at first. "There ought to be plenty of double plays in that outfit," said Harris as he watched Lary field a tough grounder and flip it to Myer.[5]

Harris and his new boss were equally high on Travis. Harris observed Travis's swing and claimed that he could be a home run hitter if he tried to pull the ball to right field. While Harris projected Johnny Stone as the team's cleanup hitter, Shirley Povich of the *Post* commented: "If Travis concentrated on pulling his hits into right field he would even exceed the distance of [Johnny] Stone's wallops, but with his effectiveness in slicing to left, Harris is not eager to have Travis change his style."[6] Griffith declared that his young third baseman would be worth $100,000 on the open market, and, he added, he would not let Travis go even if offered that amount of money in return.[7]

Griffith's statement was high praise indeed, given the owner's famously tight wallet. Washington was one of the few clubs that did not pay the team's laundry expenses during spring training. The team used to give each player $4 cash per day for meals on road trips, but when some players started eating at low-scale "joints" to save money, the team altered its policy: players were still allocated $4 per day at their hotel's dining room, but they had to sign in for meals. Griffith sprang for $3000 in railroad fare for a trip to play exhibition games on back-to-back days against the Cubs in Chicago. To Griffith's chagrin, the Interstates Commerce Commission code prevented baseball teams from getting special rates on railroad tickets.

Against the Cubs on March 19, Travis provided the critical blow with an RBI triple into Wrigley's left field. But the traveling may have been a bit much for the young Georgian. On March 27, Harris gave Travis permission to leave camp for a visit home to Riverdale after his third baseman reportedly came down with a "serious case of homesickness."[8] Travis rejoined the club in Birmingham later in the week. The following week, he belted a two–RBI double in a match against the Louisville minor league team. As the team looked ahead to the season, Povich announced: "Young Cecil Travis has a corner on it, if you'll pardon the pun.... Cece is going to be this club's third baseman for at least 10 years.[9]

On April 9, Washington played a final tune up with the National League's Brooklyn Dodgers, which Brooklyn won 7–4. Both members of the right side of Harris's infield, Travis and Lary, aided the Dodgers by committing errors. But praise continued for Travis's bat. His former manager, Joe Cronin, was on hand to watch the game. "He's another fellow who can hit in his sleep," Cronin said. "There's one way to pitch to him — pitch — and duck."[10]

On April 17, President Roosevelt continued a tradition by throwing out the first pitch of the Nationals' season opener against the Philadelphia A's. FDR rolled into Griffith Stadium at the head of a presidential procession of six White House automobiles. After taking his seat over the home team dugout, the president threw a ball high into a group of waiting players, who awaited it like the toss of a wedding bouquet. The six-foot-two Bobby Burke came away with the prize; Joe Kuhel was knocked to the ground and a number of other players were trampled in the playful scene.

Travis appeared in the lineup at the five position on defense and, fittingly, wearing uniform number five for the first time. (He would keep this number throughout most of his career.) He surprised the home fans when his glove proved to be instrumental in the victory. In the sixth inning, Travis snagged a hard-hit grounder by Eric McNair with the bases loaded. Two innings later, Travis halted a two-run rally when he snared another hard-hit ball, this one from the bat of Dib Williams, and started a double play. Despite a home run by Philadelphia's Jimme Foxx, Washington won the game 4–2.

The Nats then faced their old manager and his new team when the Red Sox came to town. In watching the preseason matchup between the Senators and Dodgers, Cronin had noticed that Brooklyn's left fielder had shaded Travis toward center field, playing him to pull. "They don't know how to play this Travis," Cronin had commented.[11] Cronin used his knowledge of Travis's swing to rob his former pupil of a hit on April 19. Playing in the hole toward third baseman Bill Werber, Cronin made a diving catch of a wicked Travis liner headed past Werber and into left field. Cronin also had the last laugh in the win column as Boston swept all three games in the series. In the third game, Travis made the last out when he popped out to Werber with the tying and winning runs on bases.

After taking two of three from the A's at Shibe Park, though, Washington visited Fenway and swept three games from Cronin's Sox. The series sweep gave Washington seven wins in its first 11 games. Harris had begun to rest Travis, Stone, and Kuhel against some southpaw pitchers, in favor of right-handed batters Bluege, Schulte and Kress, respectively. But Travis remained firmly in the team's plans.

Branded a "lucky" hitter after his five opposite-field hits in his 1933 debut, Travis unquestionably benefited from luck in a game against St. Louis in early May. Browns pitchers Bob Weiland sent a high, hard one at Travis. Most likely, Travis had a split-second replay of his scary beaning from the previous season. Travis ducked for cover, and in the process he inadvertently struck the ball with his bat. The ball ricocheted and went for a single that scored Buddy Myer from second base. The fortuitous RBI single turned out to be crucial in the team's 10–9 win.

The team struggled in May. An 8–2 loss at home to the Browns left Washington under the .500 mark at 13–14 and in sixth place in the American League. Shirley Povich observed:

> Some of the older members of the Nats will never understand why Joe Cronin last year broke up the ball team that won the pennant for him in 1933 ... against all baseball precedent, he traded Goose Goslin to Detroit and replaced Ossie Bluege with Cecil Travis, despite the fact that neither veteran manifested any signs he was slipping.[12]

At the same time, Travis continued to justify his presence in the Washington lineup. At mid–May, he held a .305 batting average, second on the team to Stone's mark of .316.

The young third baseman got an up-close look at one of the best hitters of all time during a three-game series with the Browns at Griffith Stadium. Rogers Hornsby, the St. Louis player-manager, was years past his prime in 1935, but fans still remembered his incredible feats. "The Rajah" was perhaps the greatest right-handed hitter in history, having notched three .400 seasons, including a .424 mark in 1924. He was also a two-time MVP, a Triple Crown winner in 1925, and player-manager for the St. Louis Cardinals first-ever World Series winner in 1926. Hornsby was more of a manager than a player in 1935, but on May 22 he inserted himself in the lineup at third base. The game mirrored Travis's own debut from the previous season. Joe Kuhel tested Hornsby with a bunt down the third base line and was subsequently thrown out by four feet. Travis also attempted a bunt toward Hornsby's way, and the future Hall of Famer threw out Travis as well. The Nats then stopped bunting Hornsby's way, and they won the game 5–2.[13]

On May 27, Washington won the second of two games against Cleveland, and Travis contributed an RBI double. The win raised the team into fourth place, only 3½ games out of first. But the two-game mini-streak turned out to be a mirage. Washington lost its next eight games. Nats bats accounted for only 23 runs during that stretch — just under three runs a game. Povich observed:

> Only two of the lads have been hitting with men on bases when hits mean runs. I speak, of course, of Jake Powell and Buddy Myer. The others — Heinie Manush, Joe Kuhel, Johnny Stone, Cecil Travis, Lyn Lary, and Cliff Bolton — have been getting their hits when they did the least good.[14]

On June 1, a desperate Bucky Harris tried benching Manush, Kuhel, Stone and Travis against A's left-hander Vernon Wilshire, but the team still lost 5–0.

The team spent most of the month of June in sixth place in the American League. Not only was the team having trouble scoring runs, but the pitching staff was grumbling about catchers Cliff Bolton and Sammy Holbrook. (The team had traded its popular catcher, Luke Sewell, to the Browns in the offseason for pitcher Bump Hadley.) The Senators sank to 11 games out on June 24 despite the tireless efforts of Earl Whitehill, who pitched a 14-inning complete game against Detroit in Tiger Stadium. The game was tied 5–5 after nine innings. Travis dropped a pop fly from Bill Rogell in the tenth, but Whitehill got out of the inning. In the thirteenth, Travis singled in two runs in a three-run rally, but the Tigers answered in the bottom of the inning with an RBI single by Hank Greenberg and a two–RBI double by ex–Senator Goose Goslin. Tiger relief pitcher Elden Auker shut down Washington in the fourteenth and then won the game for himself with a sacrifice fly.

Years later, Auker authored *Sleeping Cars and Flannel Uniforms* (2001), a fond memory of baseball from days gone by. Auker remembered the long train trips in the days before air travel:

> Click, click, click, click, click, click, click. Nothing quite like the sound a train makes purring through the night, eating miles peacefully, swiftly, reliably. You hear that soothing sound and there's no mistaking it for any other. An automobile's horn makes you jump. A jet's roar makes you flinch. But a train's click makes you relax. Taking the train was the only way to go. It's a far more comfortable way to get from city to city than the airplane.[15]

Auker would get to know Senators pitcher General Crowder when the two were teammates in Detroit. Crowder, who'd won 50 games over the 1932 and 1933 seasons for the Senators, was also a threat with a deck of cards. Auker recalls:

> Card playing was in Crowder's blood. He was weaned on it. He had an interesting background and grew up in a hurry. He was a professional gambler as a kid. He worked in a gambling house and a "house of ill repute" as a youngster in North Carolina. He was a runner for the girls and the gamblers. If they needed drinks, he got them drinks. He ran himself ragged doing errands for the men in the gambling room and the women in the, ahem, bedroom. Whatever they needed, he did it for them. In return, he said they looked after him, made sure no harm came to him. He never engaged in any sort of sexual relationship with them, or if he did he never shared that with us.[16]

Travis would keep a less romantic picture of the long road trips to Washington and New York and St. Louis. Decades later, he would chuckle over the "hardships" faced by modern-day players:

> I'd like to see some of those players now, they gripe about flying three to four hours, four to five hours, on a plane, oh, have to leave at midnight. I'd like to see some of them get on some of those trains w/o any air conditioning after the ball game and leave and travel all day, all night and get in the next day and play a ball game ... it was ridiculous ... but they gripe now.[17]

The long road trips to the Midwest could be especially draining. Travis and his teammates played cards to kill the time. One day, Nick Altrock, who was now employed as a member of the Senators coaching staff, showed outfielder Jake Powell a new card trick. He had Powell draw three cards from a full deck and then had Powell put them back into the deck.

"Now, how do you want me to give 'em to you, one by one, or all at once?" Altrock asked Powell.

"All at once," Powell said.

Altrock then flung all 52 cards into Powell's face.[18]

All clowning aside, these long road trips also must have intensified the day-to-day conflicts that are common among players on most teams. Travis himself became the object of griping from some members of the pitching staff, who complained to management about his defensive play. It did not help that the man Travis had replaced at third, Ossie Bluege, was in the midst of a fine comeback season in which he hit .262 while flashing his glove at shortstop and third, and even playing some at second base and in left-field. But when a rival newspaper targeted Travis's defensive shortcomings during the team's early season slump, suggesting that Travis might be best converted into an outfielder or first baseman, the *Post*'s Shirley Povich penned a lengthy piece in defense of Travis. Povich reported that Harris was "elated" with Travis's play at third and that Griffith regarded him as the league's premier third baseman. It was acknowledged that Travis still had difficulties in charging slow rollers, but Povich wrote that Travis was "a cat" in going to both his left and his right to snare hard-hit balls, and that his throwing arm was "sure death to base runners." The sportswriter also noted:

> They don't have the nerve to find fault with Travis' hitting. Its greatness is too obvious. He came to the Nats at the end of the 1933 season touted as a great natural hitter. His better than .300 average of last season, his first full year in the majors, didn't do much to disturb that opinion. And at this writing, the kid is powdering that old apple for an average of .306,

which is not only highly respectable, but just about the best average of any third baseman in the league by more than 10 points.[19]

Povich also revealed that Griffith had turned down the an offer of $40,000 from the Cleveland Indians for Travis the previous spring, and that no team could hope to purchase Travis's services for less than $100,000. "The defense rests," Povich concluded.

Proving himself even-handed, Povich noted two days later: "Against left-handed pitching, Harris has decided to promote Jake Powell to the clean-up role, a position in which Johnny Stone, Buddy Myer, Joe Kuhel, Heinie Manush, Cecil Travis and Fred Schulte have been tried this season — and found guilty, for the most part."[20]

Surprisingly, the modest, soft-spoken Travis— the same player who had left spring training with a case of homesickness— did not let criticism of his play deter him. Instead, he continued to emerge as one of the best hitters in the league. On July 10 against Detroit, he went three for five, scored two runs, and knocked in two more as Washington scored seven first-inning runs and held on for a 12–11 win. Three days later against the Browns, the Senators scored its first doubleheader sweep. Travis knocked in three runs in the first game with a single, double and triple; interestingly, both extra-base hit were "pull" jobs: a double down the right field line and a triple off the right field wall. He struck another hard ball toward the right side in the second game, a double that ricocheted off the glove of ex–Senator Lyn Lary (whom Washington had traded to St. Louis in June).

Washington continued to slide. On July 16, it lost to the lowly Browns, and Travis committed a glaring error in judgment. The Nats were protecting a 4–3 lead in the eighth inning when St. Louis loaded the bases. It seemed Washington had a chance to keep its lead when Travis fielded a grounder for a possible double play. Travis went to step on third, but then he changed his mind and decided to throw home. His split-second delay allowed the tying run to score. Moments later, the Browns pushed the go-ahead run across the plate. Adding insult to injury, Travis came to bat in the ninth representing the tying run, but he was retired by ex–Senator Dick Coffman.

Washington tried to reach back into its past glory when the Indians visited on July 22. The Senators held Walter Johnson Day in celebration of the Cleveland manager. The event helped fans remember happier times, including the team's only World Series title in 1924. But these memories proved fleeting as the Nats lost 6–4. Two days later, Washington lost a doubleheader to Cleveland and dropped 16 games below .500.

Travis suffered a charley horse in the final week of July and missed the team's series with the Yankees, but he returned with a bang on July 31 against Cronin's Red Sox. Travis went four for four with three singles and a triple, figuring in each of the team's runs in a 6–4 victory. Talk around Washington focused on what to do with the Senators' rising young hitter. He clearly could hit big league pitching better than most players, and at the 21-year-old was bound to get even better. But his own teammates questioned his abilities as an infielder. Clark Griffith remained a fan of Travis, but reports had Harris, the man who filled out the team's lineup card, growing dissatisfied with Travis's play at the hot corner. The *Post* reported:

> Bucky Harris and Clark Griffith are distinctly at odds in their estimations of Cecil Travis as a third baseman.... Griffith maintains that Travis is a fixture in the job with the Nats ... but it may be significant that for the past week Harris has sent Travis to the outfield for outfielding practice under his special supervision ... with the sensational Buddy Lewis coming up from Chattanooga next year, Travis' hitting power may be utilized in the outfield while Lewis gets a trial at third base.... [21]

Days later, Griffith perhaps sounded like his political brethren in Washington when he responded to the article. The Senators owner and president noted that Travis had indeed shown some sub-par play and maintained that the recent summer "hot spell" had drained the lanky, young player. But Griffith maintained, "Bucky Harris and I are not at odds on the subject. Harris is not dissatisfied with Travis' play at third base," He asked, "Who is there that we have who is a more valuable third baseman than Travis?" He also noted that even the great Ossie Bluege had recently had a two-error game and "could have been charged with two more." At the same time, though, Griffith acknowledged that moving Travis to the outfield at some point was not out of the question.[22]

In fact, Harris began to tutor Travis in the outfield, and a move to left field seemed imminent. Washington pitcher Earl Whitehill was quite vocal in his criticism of Travis, who seemed to commit most of his errors when Whitehill was on the mound. The pitcher was riding Travis throughout the season, so much so that Harris practically encouraged the softspoken Travis to punch Whitehill in the nose. (Joe Engel had reportedly given Travis similar advice in Chattanooga.)[23]

Another pitcher was critical of Travis having replaced Bluege at third base. Years later, General Crowder related that he had been in a "violent dispute" with management for benching Bluege in favor of Travis.[24] Perhaps not coincidentally, Crowder would be waived by Washington on August 4, having slumped badly and compiled a 4–10 record with a 6.79

ERA for the team in 1934. (Detroit claimed Crowder, and he rebounded to win five of six decisions down the stretch.)

Criticisms of Travis's defensive abilities aside, it was nothing new for a younger player to be snubbed by veterans, especially when the younger player threatened the job of a popular veteran. "The old players, they all sorta stuck together. It was sorta tough for young players to get in there," Travis remembered during one interview.[25] Travis persevered, and later in his career, he would remember the hurdles he had faced as a young player in the culture of a major league team. George Case, the speedy outfielder who came up to the Senators in 1937 and went on to an 11-year career, stated that Travis was "just about the only player who took him under his wing."[26]

The team floundered in seventh place throughout August. Travis showed flashes of brilliance on August 14 in Tiger Stadium, fielding five tough grounders at third. And he remained a consistent threat with the bat. His average stood at .310 after the team's 7–4 win in Comiskey Park on August 22. In the contest, Travis singled twice and tallied an RBI with a sacrifice fly in the ninth. He also turned a nice double play on a sacrifice attempt by Luke Appling. The following day, Travis doubled twice and scored once in a 2–0 shutout behind Bump Hadley.

On the first of September, Washington's Bobo Newsom faced off against Boston's Lefty Grove. Grove, in the midst of a comeback season in which he would go 20–12, would lose the game 2–1— his fourth loss in five decisions facing the luckless Senators in 1935. Grove did well to hold Washington to two runs as he yielded 12 hits; Newsom, Powell and Travis combined for 11 of the 12. The win temporarily moved Washington from seventh to sixth in the standings.

Travis seemed to be turning a corner. But in September 6 double-header loss to the St. Louis Browns, he collided with catcher Cliff Bolton as the two pursued a pop-up in foul territory off the bat of Lyn Lary. Lary then reached on an error by Red Kress and went on to score the winning run for St. Louis in game one.

Harris had apparently seen enough. On September 10, Travis made his debut in the Washington outfield. He had just one fly ball hit to him, and he caught it despite the glare of the Comiskey Park sun. Travis remained in the outfield for the rest of the season. Travis handled his banishment to the outfield with good spirits, and he certainly did not let it affect him at the plate. He ended the season hitting so well that Harris moved him to the cleanup spot, despite the fact that he had not (and would not) hit a home run all season long. Travis finished well with a season mark of .318. Although he tallied only 35 extra-base hits and 61 RBI, he recorded an on-base percentage of .377 and scored 85 runs. He also led the league in getting hit by pitches nine times.

As a team, Washington led the league in hits in 1935, with five regulars hitting .300 or better. Buddy Myer, who was in contention for the batting title throughout the second half of the season, finished with an average of .349 and an even 100 RBI. Myer would finish fourth in the American League MVP vote, which was won by Detroit's Hank Greenberg. But Washington finished in sixth place with a 67–85 record, thanks largely to a staff ERA of 5.25.

The club announced that Harris would remain at the helm for the 1936 season, reportedly at a salary of $12,000. It also announced that Travis would remain in the outfield and that the third base spot would be filled by one of two promising prospects in Washington's minor league system: Buddy Lewis from Chattanooga or Roberto Estalella from Harrisburg. Harris declared that Travis "can't miss being a good outfielder," and indeed, Travis's "long, loping strides" and his strong arm seemed well suited for the outfield position. Harris also looked forward to more productivity from Travis at the plate: "And he'll be a still better batter next year.... He's learning to "pull" the ball now instead of hitting all of his drives into left field."[27] Travis's season at the plate gained him further attention throughout the league. On October 13, the *Los Angeles Times* ran the following notice: "Cecil Travis has been shifted to the outfield and Washington will list him as an outfielder next season. Travis is a pretty good batter."[28] Later that month, Travis was named as one of 24 players on the MVP "honor list."[29]

The most interesting statistic to come from the league office after the season, though, was Travis's fielding percentage. The second-year player who had essentially lost his job at third due to criticism over his fielding finished with a mark of .963 — second in the American League only to the Yankees Red Rolfe, who narrowly edged out Travis with a percentage of .964. Povich parlayed the data into a journalistic "I told you so":

> Unless figures do, indeed, lie, these sensitive nostrils recognize a more than faint odor of raw-dealism in the case of Cecil Travis.... His power with the bat was acknowledged, but from the outset of the season, Harris held no high regard for Travis' defensive play. The squawks of Pitcher Earl Whitehill, a notorious squawker, contributed nothing to Harris' esteem for Travis' defensive ability, apparently. It was Travis' misfortune to commit his most previous errors when Whitehill was on the mound, and the temperamental southpaw minced no words in his criticism of the young third baseman.

Povich admitted that Travis's lack of range was not reflected in his fielding averages, and that such "errors of omission" were behind Harris's banishing Travis to the outfield. Still, Povich suggested that "any man who played third base for Washington last season had the hardest third-base job in the league because of the atrocious Washington pitching," which made Travis's nearly leading the league in fielding even more impressive.[30]

For his part, Griffith — who had a reputation for making personnel decisions behind the scenes — had given in to Harris's decision, and he was now touting Travis's potential as a member of the Senators outfield. Indeed, the team stood firm in its plans to covert Travis into a left fielder. In addition to complaints by Whitehill et al., the future of Chattanooga third baseman Buddy Lewis looked increasingly bright. Chattanooga manager Clyde Milan told the parent club that Lewis would be a better third baseman than Travis ever could be. The move of Travis to left also made sense given the team's plans to dangle Heinie Manush as trade bait in the offseason.

The Senators, who finished first in hits as a team but in a distant sixth in the standings, desperately needed pitching and felt it could sacrifice a bat toward that end. In fact, the team had offered Johnny Stone to the Yankees in the 1935 season, but New York was scared off after Stone had struck out six times in a row against in a series with the Yankees. (Stone, it should be noted, had been under the weather and had even fainted in the team's clubhouse.) After the Stone deal fell through, Washington looked to trade Manush, who had reportedly lost interest in playing for the Nats when Cronin was sold to Boston. Manush had been playing in a barnstorming game in Vancouver at the time, and when he learned of the trade, he ripped the *W* from his Washington uniform, declaring his team's chances "shot," and voiced his desire to be traded to Boston, as well.[31]

Manush would have to play one more season with the Senators, but on December 17, 1935, Washington did trade him to Boston. The move made sense, as the team was now overloaded in the outfield, and the disgruntled Manush — who hit only .273 for the Senators in 1935 — was the team's highest paid player with a salary of $12,000.[32] Strangely, Griffith sent him to the Red Sox in exchange for two outfielders: Roy Johnson and Carl Reynolds. But Washington then sent Johnson, a left-handed hitter, to the Yankees, who needed a lefty to compensate for the declining Babe Ruth, in exchange for right-handed hitting outfielder Jesse Hill. Harris planned to install Hill in left field, hoping that an added righty in the lineup would make the Senators less vulnerable to left-handers. While Hill would push Travis out of the left field spot, Griffith had formulated a new plan; he would turn Travis, whom many felt could not cut it as a third baseman, into a *shortstop*.

In mid–January, Griffith spoke to the *Post* about his plans for Travis, admitting that he had not discussed the move with Travis yet, though he planned to when they met to discuss Travis's contract for the upcoming season. Griffith said that he would not force Travis to try shortstop if the Georgian were unwilling, but the owner planned to offer Travis a raise in salary if he could play shortstop for Washington. Griffith remained high on Travis's future with the team. After describing Boston infielder Bill Werber as a "$100,000 ball player" at the end of the previous season, Griffith now claimed that he would not trade Travis for Werber even up; furthermore, he predicted Travis would improve into a .320 hitter.[33]

It seemed Travis would have little choice. With Hill named the team's new left fielder and third base reserved for the promising young Buddy Lewis, Travis had to make it at the new position or else end up "just a good third baseman and a good outfielder without a job on the team."[34] Povich, having some fun with the team's game of musical chairs, comically tried his hand at foretelling the future, predicting that Travis would be named the team's shortstop in mid–March, then returned to third base, and then back to the outfield, all within the same week.[35] Though offered as humor, the columnist's piece was a rather insightful indictment on the team's pattern of indecisive and often contradictory statements with regard to Travis. But the amiable Travis, who played shortstop for his intramural team in high school, agreed to try his hand at shortstop for Washington. Bucky Harris ordered him to come to training camp in Orlando—the team's new preseason home—10 days early so that he could get a head start on practice. Harris, himself an ex-infielder, planned to oversee Travis's training personally and to tutor him in the art of turning double plays. He told the *Post*:

> I think I can help him. I played alongside of Roger Peckinpaugh for six years, you know, and there was never a better shortstop than Peck.... They may have to take me out there in a wheel chair after the second day when my legs start creaking, but I'll be out there alongside of Travis in those early days at camp. But I think I can get myself in shape.[36]

Harris added: "Think of the break that would be for us if Travis can hold down the shortstop job.... Why, if he makes good there we'll probably have the hardest hitting shortstop in the league, to say nothing of solving our present weakness."[37] Promising rookie Buddy Lewis, along with outfielder Dee Miles and Roberto Estalella (whom Harris now planned to convert into an outfielder), were asked to report early to Orlando.

Travis's willingness to accept yet another position change must have endeared the player to Griffith. Furthermore, the meek-mannered Travis probably was not one of the most difficult players with whom Griffith had to deal at the bargaining table, especially at that point in the player's career. Although Griffith had twice declared Travis a $100,000 man, in reality Travis reportedly had made little more than half of Heinie Manush's $12,000 salary in 1935.[38] Washington was traditionally tight-lipped in financial matters, but in early February team secretary Edward Eynon announced that Travis had signed and returned his contract, which included a pay increase. At the same time, a young star from the Pacific Coast League, Joe DiMaggio, returned a contract unsigned to the New York Yankees; speculation had DiMaggio seeking $8,000 for his first season with New York.[39]

One hour after Travis's arrival in Orlando on February 25, Harris rushed his new shortstop onto the freshly groomed field at Orlando's Tinker Field, and two hundred fans watched the beginning of the infield experiment with Lewis at third, Travis at short, and Kuhel at first. Harris, walking the infield for the first time since 1929, was "wheezing like an old ferryboat" as he led the infield practice. His early assessment: Travis and Lewis would be fine at shortstop and third. Travis liked his own chances at adjusting to the new position. "Ah always did play shortstop befo' ah played third base," he told Povich. "Ah reckon ah can do it again. Fact is, ah like to play shorstop."[40]

The next day, Harris declared: "If Travis isn't a swell shortstop, I'm a Chinaman." Povich added:

> As Harris' Welsh lineage is well known, it appears that Travis is to the Nats' regular shortstop for 1936. But Travis himself gives the impression in his talk that Harris has no right to be surprised at his shortstop play. "Why, Ah always was a shortstop until one day they needed a third baseman at Chattanooga," drawled Travis. "To tell the truth, Ah never did cotton to third base."[41]

As Lewis prepared to take supplant Travis as the team's third baseman, the club's other third base candidate, Roberto Estalella, didn't help his case by arriving late to camp. When Harris chastised him upon his arrival, the Cuban smiled and explained that he had not received his transportation money from Washington on time, and then he'd had trouble finding a boat from Havana to Jacksonville. "Ho-kay now," Estallella explained. "Me fine. Attaboy. Good pep tomorrow."[42] Harris informed him that the team planned to make him an outfielder, and Estallella appeared unconcerned. It may have been possible that he didn't understand what Harris said. The next day, there was an awkward moment on the practice field when the Cuban player motioned for the 19-year-old Lewis to move over so that Estalella could take some practice at third.

On the last day of February, baseball commissioner Judge Kenesaw Mountain Landis got an up-close look at the new Washington infield when he visited the Nats camp. The March 1 edition of *The Washington Post* featured a picture from the Nats camp of Cecil Travis along with Clark Griffith and league commissioner. Landis would have seen promising signs in Travis, who demonstrated a good arm for the position and also an ability to go deep to both his left and right.

When Washington began its exhibition season, Harris envisioned the following lineup:

1. Jesse Hill, left field
2. Buddy Lewis, third base
3. Buddy Myer, second base
4. Jake Powell, center field
5. Cecil Travis, shortstop
6. Carl Reynolds, right field
7. Joe Kuhel, first base
8. Cliff Bolton, catcher.

There was speculation that Travis, who had never hit less than .300 in any level of professional baseball, could replace Powell as cleanup hitter if need be. Travis continued trying to throw the full weight of his swing into inside pitches so that he could drive balls to right. (This might have explained his league-leading number of HBPs the previous season.)[43]

At the beginning of April, the Associated Press reported that a poll of 97 baseball writers picked the Senators to finish seventh in the American League in 1936. Griffith was incensed: "Bosh ... I have never seen such nonsense. Why, we'll make this thing look silly. What can those people be thinking about?" He added:

> We're going to be the surprise team of this league, I tell you. Some people just can't believe that Buddy Lewis already is a great third baseman and that Cecil Travis is a swell shortstop. They think we're just experimenting. But we're done with that kind of business. Our ball team is all set, and it's a good ball team.'"[44]

The *Los Angeles Times* agreed, at least, with Griffith's assessment of Travis as a shortstop. The *Times* noted:

The Washington Senators are willing to wager they have the ablest key-stone combination in the junior loop. They point out that if Buddy Myer was good enough to participate in a record number of double plays last season, while performing alongside five different shortstops at various times, certainly he should go even better with the surprising Cecil Travis, converted third baseman.[45]

Travis continued to show his talents as a bright hitter. On April 10 against Philadelphia, Travis led an 11–3 onslaught with four hits in five at bats.

For the team's regular season opener against the Yankees, Washington's Buck Newsom faced off against Lefty Gomez. Against Gomez, Harris used the same lineup he used for the start of exhibition play save for Lewis, whom Harris rested in favor of the veteran Bluege; Bluege added a right-handed bat against Gomez, and Harris wanted to save the 19-year-old rookie from possible stage fright in front of the president of the United States and 31,000 other fans in Griffith Stadium.[46]

Travis, perhaps feeling some stage fright of his own in his debut at shortstop, committed two errors, but neither led to a run. In the second inning, he led off with a line drive into center field but was thrown out trying to stretch a double into a triple. In the fifth inning, Ossie Bluege inadvertently hit Newsom in the head with a throw to first base. But Newsom shook off the beaning, and the two teams brought a scoreless tie into the bottom of the ninth inning. Travis made fans forget his previous errors when he started off the ninth by pulling a Gomez delivery into right field for a single. Carl Reynolds stepped up to the plate and fouled off a bunt attempt. The home crowd groaned. Harris took the bunt sign off, and Reynolds rewarded him by lining a double into center field, scoring Travis with the winning run.

The Senators won the next day, 6–5. After Travis collected two hits and an RBI, Yankees manager Joe McCarthy issued him an intentional walk in the eighth inning, loading the bases. Reynolds then came to the plate, and relief pitcher Johnny Murphy walked him to force in the winning run.

Travis starred in a 3–2 victory in Shibe Park on April 17, going three for five against the A's. After another one-run win the following day, Washington was in first place with a record of 4–1. The *Post* raved:

At shortstop, Travis has been proving a daily delight to Manager Harris with his steady, often spectacular play. This noble experiment of Harris' is apparently a huge success what with Travis supporting his steady play in the field with a brand of hitting that may even lift him to recognition as the league's outstanding shortstop.[47]

But the team quickly fell back into its losing ways of the previous two seasons, losing five of its next six games. On April 20, a Travis throwing error helped end a shutout bid by Washington pitcher Pete Appleton against Boston. Travis committed two more errors in Appleton's next start, an April 25 contest with Philadelphia at Griffith Stadium, but he also started two double plays that stopped A's rallies, and Washington ended a four-game losing streak with a 10–3 win.

On April 29, Tiger slugger Hank Greenberg suffered a broken wrist in a collision with Washington's Jake Powell and was lost for the season. Washington won the series, then swept a two-game series from the Browns, raising its record to 11–8. But the team's bats had a power shortage. Buddy Myer, the team's best hitter in 1935, had a .216 through May 9.[48] Then Travis fell into a slump, going four for 25 in mid–May. On May 20, Harris announced that he was going to move Travis back into the outfield — not because of his fielding, he said, but because he felt the move would help Travis's hitting. Harris explained:

> I regard Travis as a great hitter, but the responsibilities of an infield job is affecting his batting.... There's a lot to think about there at shortstop, and Travis is only a kid of 22 after all. In the outfield, he should strike his true batting stride and be a great help to the team.[49]

Harris noted that he wasn't unhappy with Travis's play at short, but that he wanted to see Travis grow into a power hitter. Harris said he would start by platooning Travis with Reynolds in right field, and when Travis accustomed himself to right field, he would play the position full time. Clark Griffith still saw Travis as the team's shortstop of the future, but Harris felt the move would help jumpstart Travis's bat. The move would also allow Harris to insert Red Kress into the Washington lineup as shortstop. The reserve outfielder had provided an unexpected bright spot, getting eight hits in his first 13 at bats.

As chance would have it, Harris changed his mind once again. On May 24 in Fenway Park, he wrote Travis into the lineup as the team's *left fielder*. Not surprisingly, the *Post* reported that Travis "fielded uncertainly" in the position, but he did record an assist when he threw out Rick Ferrell, who was attempting to go from first to third on a single.[50] Still, Harris removed Travis for a defensive replacement, Jesse Hill, in the later innings of the contest.

While Harris's ever-changing plans for Travis must have been disconcerting to the 22-year-old, he benefited from a stabilizing influence in the presence of rookie Buddy Lewis, who was Travis's roommate. The mild-mannered

Travis found a kindred spirit of sorts in Lewis, whom Newsom said "looks like Cecil Travis' baby brother." Povich added:

> The resemblance is, indeed, marked. Like Travis, Buddy Lewis is tall, apparently frail, a bit knock-kneed and truly boyish looking. Travis is a dead ringer for an immature college freshman, but Lewis looks for all the world as if he had just escaped from some prep school."[51]

Lewis carried a .365 average into late May while playing well defensively at third, and he was being mentioned in conversations with another American League rookie named Joe DiMaggio.

John "Buddy" Lewis had first been scouted by the New York Giants at the age of 16 when he was playing sandlot baseball in Gastonia, North Carolina. He out for the Giants in Central Park but felt snubbed by manager Bill Terry, so he went back home and soon after attended Wake Forest for four years on a football scholarship. He returned to Gastonia, and in 1934, while Lewis was playing American Legion ball, a friend of Joe Engel recommended that he give Lewis a tryout. The Chattanooga Lookouts signed him in August, and he became a fixture in the organization. In 1935, the Chicago Cubs offered Joe Engel $35,000 for his contract, then raised their offer to $50,000, before Engel told them that Lewis was being groomed as a future third baseman for the parent club.

The "tall, pink-cheeked" Lewis would team with Travis to become a formidable hitting duo for Washington.[52] The two roommates combined for six hits against Philadelphia on May 26. Lewis hit a single, double and triple, and Travis tallied a triple and two singles in the 8–2 victory that moved the club back over the .500 mark. Washington hovered around .500 throughout May. At the end of the month, Harris praised Travis's play in the outfield. "Cecil Travis is now a fixture in the outfield for the Nats whenever the Washington club faces right-handed pitching," the *Post* announced.[53] Because Travis still had limited experience in the outfield, Harris announced that he planned to alternate Travis between left and right field, depending upon the ballpark in which the team was playing and which field was the "short" field. Travis returned to third base for a short time in June when Lewis suffered a torn fingernail, but he switched back to the outfield upon Lewis's recovery.

Travis's single was Washington's only hit off Cleveland's George Blaeholder through eight innings on June 10. Then, Travis knocked in his team's only two runs when he homered with Lewis on base in the ninth. Though the team lost the game, Washington put together a good month of June and climbed into third place in the American League. And by the end of the month, Travis had become the team's permanent right fielder.

The Washington outfield now consisted of John Stone in left, former Yankee Ben Chapman in center, and Travis in right. The three players combined for the best trio of outfield arms in the league. Travis had an even stronger arm than Stone, and neither player had as strong an arm as Chapman, who went to his fourth All-Star game that July.[54]

The Nats won eight of 12 in early July, moving seven games over .500. On July 19, the team split a doubleheader against Cleveland in which a 17-year-old fireballer named Bob Feller made his Major League debut. In the second game, Feller came in to relieve after Chapman doubled and Stone, Travis, Myer and Bolton followed with successive singles. Feller walked the first two batters he faced but retired the next three batters. Washington won the game 9–6, ending Cleveland's nine-game winning streak.

Washington and Travis both slumped at the end of July. As the team lost seven games in a row, Travis struggled in right field. "Out in right field, it is always a question whether Travis will catch a fly ball or suffer brain concussion in the attempt," the *Post* quipped. Meanwhile, his average fell under .300 for the first time in his career.[55] He was declared the goat of a 6–5 loss on July 29 when he threw to second instead of home in the seventh inning, allowing the winning run to score.

In early August, Travis was moved once again, this time back to shortstop. With Myer injured and Kress cooling off from his early-season hot streak, Harris announced that he would move Bluege (who had been filling in at short) over to second, leaving shortstop free for Travis. But the position would not stay his alone, as Kress and Bluege still saw time at short. On August 11, Harris even started Travis at second base; batting third, he went just one for four but scored two runs, helping Washington beat the Yankees 7–3. In an August 16 doubleheader with Boston, Travis played second in the first game, batting sixth, and shortstop in the nightcap, batting seventh. The Nats swept the twin bill; Travis delivered a bases-clearing double in the first game and went two for four in the second. The sensational hitter without a home went on a tear at the plate. He moved his average back over .300, and when he was pressed into service at shortstop in a series at Philadelphia, he played the position "sensationally."[56] Once again, Harris anointed Travis the team's shortstop.

This time, Travis finished out the season as the team's shortstop. Washington finished strong, winning 16 games in September to go 82–71 on the year, good enough for third place. Travis, who bounced from position to position and lineup spot to lineup spot, finished with an average of .317. He had also improved his power number in 1936, recording 34 doubles, 10 triples, 2 home runs, and — most surprisingly — 92 RBI. It became clear that the club needed to keep in the lineup, one way or another.

5

"The Unknown Slugger"

During the 1936 season, Travis had been the model of a team player in good-naturedly agreeing to play wherever Bucky Harris wrote him into the Washington lineup. For the 1937 season, he wanted a contract to reward his efforts. In January, he returned his contract to Griffith unsigned — a common practice of players in negotiations at the time. "Griffith has always been good to me," Travis told the *Post*; continuing,

> "I was shifted around from my regular third base position to shortstop, batted .317 and received a nice bonus. Griffith told me I had played well and that he was counting on me at shortstop this year.
> "I don't want to be called a holdout," Travis said, "I sent my contract back and wrote Griffith I thought I should have more money."[1]

Griffith expressed willingness to renegotiate with Travis but wrote his player to tell him that he wanted to see the 23-year-old show some more edge in his play. Said Travis to the *Post*:

> Yes, Clark Griffith wrote me that I lacked aggressiveness.... He said that if I expected the raise I asked for I'd have to punch some guy in the nose. Well, I'm not in the habit of going around jabbing folks in the kisser, but if that's what it takes I think I can handle my own — but we'll have to make financial arrangements for the fines. Now if Griffith wants some punching done and will pay the fines, that will be okeh [*sic*] with me.[2]

Travis exhibited "a neat bit of jabbing with his left and a cross with the right" in sparring with one of the farmhands on his family's estate. Striking the pose of a bare-fisted fighter for the camera, he commented: "This whole thing is going to create quite a bit of fun this summer." But he added:

> I don't believe, though, I'll have to bust anybody in the eye to get the increase I'm asking. Griffith has always been good to me.... We won't have

any trouble getting together. I expect to hear from him in a few days now and I don't think he'll hold to his nose-punching ultimatum before coming across.[3]

In addition to a raise in salary, Travis also looked forward (with hope) to sticking at one position for the Senators. "Griffith told me I had played well and that he was counting on me at shortstop this year," he said.[4] After Travis reported to camp in Orlando on March 2 — with a signed contract that included an undisclosed increase upon his $6500 salary the previous season — Harris echoed Griffith's hopes in spring training. "There will be no more experimenting," Harris declared. "I've told Travis the shortstop job is his without fear of competition and he won't have that to worry about. That was his big handicap last season."[5] Washington staged a two-hour workout for the benefit of photographers, with Travis and second baseman Buddy Myer performing slick double-play drills.

The Senators' spring training was disrupted slightly that week by the arrival of 12-year-old Jimmy Brady. The "chubby, black-haired" youth had been the object of a police search after his disappearance from the Brady household earlier that week. Jimmy had purchased a train ticket to Jacksonville and then another to Orlando to see his beloved Senators. After he had been apprehended by the Orlando police, he was placed in the charge of an Orlando couple, Mr. and Mrs. Howard Rowton, who were family friends of the Bradys. After some local sight-seeing, Jimmy demanded that the Rowtons take him to the Palatka ballpark facility where the Nats trained. Later, Jimmy exclaimed, "Lookit that right field fence, will ya? Gee, my pal Cecil Travis would bust everything they pitched to him right over that fence. He'd hit a million home runs in this park." Jimmy's parents and sister soon arrived to retrieve their wayward son. "You run away from home and get the whole family in the papers with your escapades. Young man, you will hear from this," Mr. Brady told him.[6]

Travis did not go on a home run tear that spring, but he did collect hits in bunches. He tallied three hits in a split-squad game on March 13 and notched another three-hit game on March 21 against the Phillies. He also managed the dubious accomplishment of lining into a triple play not once but twice that spring, once against the Giants and again in a game with the Tigers. In the latter game, though, he drove a triple into left-center field with the bases loaded, winning the preseason contest for the Senators.

During a practice session on March 26, Travis was fielding a throw at second base from catcher Shanty Hogan when a coach, who was hitting flies to the outfielders, looped one close to Travis. The coach yelled "Heads up!" and as Travis looked up, Hogan's throw to hit him in the middle of his forehead.[7] He wasn't seriously hurt, though, and did not let the accident affect him and his fine preseason play. He continued to hit, and, even more tellingly, Travis flashed the leather that spring. In a game with the National League's Cardinals, he demonstrated excellent range in going to both his left and right to field grounders, and he also showed off his arm on strong throws to first. St. Louis manager Frankie Frisch tipped his cap to Travis on back-to-back defensive gems. Travis also doubled twice and singled once in the same game. "You lucky stiff," Frisch told Harris after the game. "That kid will be tops among the American League shortstops, or I don't know a ball player when I see one."[8]

"Travis has been positively sensational at his new shortstop post," Povich declared toward the end of the exhibition season.[9] "Cecil Travis has developed into a good shortstop, a great shortstop, and it has made our infield. There is no reason why, in time, he should not take his place alongside the really great shortstops of our national pastime."[10] Travis would find his way into the record books in 1937, but for a peculiar reason: The double play combination of Travis and Myer along with third baseman Buddy Lewis and first baseman Joe Kuhel would form the only infield in baseball history comprised exclusively of left-handed hitting starters.[11]

The left-heavy Nats left Orlando in early April on their trip north to Washington. The team stopped off for an exhibition matchup against the Chattanooga farm club on April 10, and Travis struck a single and double against his old team in a 5–2 win. But he was struck down when he was spiked by the Giants' Joe Martin in the team's final preseason exhibition, just one day before its annual season opener before President Roosevelt and 32,000 fans. The spiking left an "ugly, swastika-like" two-inch wound just above his left knee and sent Travis limping off the field. "Travis is lucky in that no tendon was severed," said the team's trainer. "It is a deep gash, and he is unable to take a step without pain. There's only a chance that he will be in the opening-game line-up. He may not be back in the game before a week."[12] Trips to the trainer were becoming regular occurrences for Travis, who would earn the nickname Kid Bandage.

Travis missed the season opener, but Washington fans were treated to the Senators debut of Al Simmons, whom the team had acquired from Detroit for $15,000 earlier in the month. The future Hall of Famer enjoyed the pomp of circumstance surrounding the national pastime in the nation's capital; an amateur movie buff, he managed to shoot some film of Roosevelt before the game. The fun was spoiled for the home crowd when the Philadelphia A's won the game in the tenth inning. Travis returned to the lineup for the team's third game, but the Nats lost again, 7–1, and the shortstop committed a throwing error.

Travis injured himself once again on April 28. After going two for five in a home game against the Yankees—the second consecutive game in which he'd done so—he wrenched his right knee while sliding into third base. He was taken to Georgetown University Hospital, where it was discovered that he had torn a knee ligament and would be out for two weeks. The team, which had won only one of its first six games, struggled into mid–May with a record of 6–12.

Travis was released from Georgetown Hospital to attend the Fathers and Sons Banquet benefit at the Mayflower Hotel. He joined such Washington baseball dignitaries as Clark Griffith, Bucky Harris, Walter Johnson, Buddy Myer, Buddy Lewis, and Al Simmons, along with Lou Gehrig, Jake Powell and Joe DiMaggio from the New York Yankees, who were in town. The team physician then ordered Travis back to the hospital for another week. He would not play until May 18, a day after the team had sunk into last place in the American League. Travis singled as a pinch hitting appearance in a 7–6 defeat of the St. Louis Browns, and the win raised the team back out of the cellar.

By the end of the week, the team had actually climbed into fifth place. After Whitehill pitched Washington to a 7–5 win over Cleveland, Travis went one for two and scored a run in a 4–1 victory. The win moved Washington to within one game of the .500 mark at 13–14.

That would be the closest that the team would get to .500 for the rest of the season. It would be another long year for Travis and the Nats. Travis continued to struggle with both fielding and injuries. *The Post* dubbed him the "losing pitcher" of a 3–1 loss to Detroit on May 24 after his throwing error allowed two runs to score; he also popped up with the bases loaded.[13] The following day, Travis took a ground ball in the face during the pregame warm-up and was forced to leave the field.

As a team, the Senators would have little success in 1937. But Washington fans had something to cheer for whenever Travis stepped to the plate. Although Harris was now batting him sixth or seventh to bolster the lower end of the lineup, Travis raised his hitting to the next level. He smacked two doubles and knocked in two runs against Boston on May 30. The next day, he rapped a triple and a sacrifice fly. A six for nine performance in a Sunday doubleheader with the White Sox on June 13 boosted his average well over .350. Travis's early-season average had gone largely unnoticed, as the time he had missed due to injuries left him under the minimum number of at bats. But on June 18, his 101st at bat rendered him eligible for the batting race, and the next day the Associated Press announced his entry into baseball's "Big Six" with a .366 average. The mark left him second in the American League behind Lou Gehrig, who was batting a lusty .394.[14]

Washington enjoyed a brief five-game winning streak in late June. The Nats exploded for 14 runs against the Indians on June 23, and Travis provided the game's highlight when he stepped to plate with one on in the fourth inning. Washington's shortstop drove a line drive into the deepest reaches of Griffith's Stadium's center field and circled the bases for an inside-the-park home run. He was the hitting hero again on June 30 against Boston when he banged a two-run triple in the second inning and then started the team's game-winning rally in the eighth inning with another triple. The next day, he started another winning rally against the Red Sox with a double in a 3–2 triumph.

Travis's average dipped slightly to .351 in early July, but he then put together a torrid week that that raised his average to .368, just nine points behind Gehrig's league-leading mark. The pages of the *Post* said proclaimed that Travis could "hit in the dark" and that he had "reduced to pure guesswork all efforts to shade his hitting territory." Bucky Harris liked Travis's chances at winning the batting title:

> He's worth a bet.... Anybody who meets the ball the way he does can keep up with any hitter in the league. Good pitching won't stop him, either. And left-handers don't bother Cece. He's a slap hitter, doesn't go for bad balls and he makes those guys pitch to him.... Travis has a good chance to win that $500 bucks they give to the leading hitter.[15]

On July 31, Travis was the toast of the nation's capital. His four-for-five performance of the previous day raised his average eight points to .375, lifting him past both Gehrig and DiMaggio. The *Post* announced: "The name that leads all the rest this morning in the American League batting averages is that of shy, modest Cecil Travis, Washington shortstop."[16] All four of his hits— two singles, a bases-loaded triple, and a home run to deep center field —came off left-handers in the 13–2 rout of Cleveland. Later that night, Travis joined Buddy Lewis, Walter Johnson, and radio commentator Arch McDonald on a midnight cruise held by the U.S. Government League on the S.S. *Potomac.*

Gehrig temporarily took over the lead when Travis went zero for four on July 31, but Travis hit at a .500 clip (14 for 28) in the first week of August to regain the lead. Travis brought a remarkable .388 average into an August 6 Ladies Day contest with Detroit. Washington was never in the game and lost 10–3, but the home crowd stayed to the end to root for Travis. Travis managed only one hit in his first four appearances, but in his fifth at bat he rapped a single to right field, preserving his league-leading mark at .388. The *Los Angeles Times* ran a picture of Travis with the caption "The Unknown Slugger."[17]

Meanwhile, in the National League, Joe "Ducky" Medwick was hitting at an unconscious pace of .402. (Bill Terry had been the last player to finish the season above the .400 mark, posting a .401 average in 1930.) Ironically, Travis had more space between himself and second-place Gehrig than Medwick did between himself and the Cub's Gabby Hartnet, who was running second in the National League.[18]

Washington hosted Detroit for a Saturday doubleheader on August 7, and Travis went zero for three in the first game but salvaged his average by going two for two in the nightcap. He had to leave the second game after suffering a collision when Chet Laabs attempted to steal second base. Laabs knocked Travis over and stepped on his hand, giving Travis two nasty cuts from his spikes. Travis stayed in the game but two innings later, Al Simmons noticed that Travis was still suffering dizzy spells from the collision, and Harris replaced Travis with Bluege. Travis was okay the next day and even raised his average slightly by going one for two.

On August 11, Travis was a spiking-collision victim once again, this time with roommate Buddy Lewis. The two went to field a ground ball and Lewis stepped on Travis's ankle, and Travis had to leave the game. His average stood at .386. Harris kept him out of the starting lineup the next day, but then Travis limped up to bat as a pinch hitter late in the game and rapped a double off the Griffith Stadium right field wall. But despite the successful pinch hitting appearance, Travis seemed to be feeling the effects of Lewis's spiking. In mid- to late August he fell into his worst slump of the season, going seven for 33 and dropping his average 17 points. In the third week of August, Detroit's Gehringer raised his average from .364 to .378 and soared past Travis, Gehrig and DiMaggio into the American League lead. Aside from occasional flashes of brilliance — including a two–RBI triple on August 21 that was lost to the ages when a Fenway Park rainstorm ended the game before it had become official — Travis did not break out of his batting slump until August 25, when he rapped three hits in a 7–6 victory over the Browns at Sportsman's Park.

In the second game of an August 29 doubleheader in Cleveland, Travis and the Senators faced off against Bob Feller, who was now a starting pitcher for the Tribe. Travis's two–RBI double was the crucial hit in the Senators' sixth-inning rally that hung the loss on Feller. In the bottom of the inning, Travis snared a line drive by Bruce Campbell and doubled off Moose Solters at second.

Travis's slump had dropped him well off the pace in the American

League batting race. But on September 21, he went two for four against the Indians to raise his average back to .352, well behind Gehringer's mark of .383. In the National League, Medwick had fallen off to .376 but still led the Senior Circuit by 15 points over teammate Johnny Mize.

Washington finished the season by splitting a doubleheader in Shibe Park on October 3. Batting third in the order, Travis celebrated his best major league season to date by going a combined four for six and raised his final average to .344. The mark was good for fifth in the league behind Gehringer (.371), Gehrig (.351), DiMaggio (.346), and Chicago's Zeke Bonura (.345). Senators teammate Johnny Stone finished just out of the top 10 with an average of .330. Travis had seen a slight drop-off in his power numbers (37 extra-base hits compared to 46 the previous season) but did log career highs in hits (181) and on-base percentage (.395). Despite the plate heroics of Travis and Stone, Washington finished in sixth place with a record of 73–80.

The Yankees, meanwhile, rode the seasons of DiMaggio and Gehrig to a 102–52 record and the American League pennant. For the second consecutive year, New York beat the Giants in a five-game subway series. In November, Major League Baseball revealed its MVP voting. Gehringer narrowly edged out DiMaggio, 78 points to 74. Travis finished eleventh with 12 points.[19]

The 1937 season had been a breakout one for Travis, but questions about his future with the Washington Senators still remained. Although Travis had played an entire season at one position, Harris still had concerns about his shortstop's range. Furthermore, Travis committed a number of throwing errors during the course of the season.

Although no one could question his penchant for the base hit, the possibility that his 1937 season had been a flash in the pan lingered. In an example of poor fortune telling, Shirley Povich (who would be inducted into the sportswriters and broadcasters wing of the Hall of Fame in 1975) commented: "On the part of Travis and DiMaggio, their lofty averages may have been a temporary flash. But Gehringer, along with Gehrig, were the solid men in the race — guys who were not hitting over their heads and whose capture of the titles would occasion no amazement."[20] And even if Travis continued his penchant for the base hit in 1938 and beyond, some questioned the productivity of his hits. Even though he had recorded 181 hits in 1937, he scored only 72 runs and knocked in only 66. Povich hypothesized:

> If Manager Bucky Harris were asked point blank who his two most valuable players of 1937 were he'd haul off without hesitation and name Third

Baseman Buddy Lewis and Outfielder Johnny Stone. Travis had a sensational season but, day in and day out, Lewis and Stone were carrying a heavier load. Travis' record as a producer of runs was rather dismal despite his lofty batting average.[21]

Indeed, both Lewis (who had hit second) and Stone had more RBI than Travis did in 1937.

Over the winter, Travis kept in shape by performing farm work and hunting. The *Los Angeles Times* photographed him chopping wood on the family farm. The photo ran with a caption that described him as the "slugging shortstop of the Washington Senators," noting that he had finished among the top five hitters of the American League.[22]

In January, Travis traveled to Washington with Lewis, his in-season roommate, to see the frugal Clark Griffith, from whom they sought raises in their salaries. Griffith rewarded them both; reportedly, Travis was signed for $7500, Lewis for $7000. "Ball players of today are getting smart," he said. "They know very well that they do better on their contracts when they come to see me in person. They always pry a bit more out of me."

"But don't print that," Griffith added with a laugh, noting that he did want his ball players to think that "all they have to do is pay me a personal visit to get those outlandish salaries some of 'em think they ought to have."[23] Travis received another reward in early February when the Touchdown Club held its annual banquet in the main ballroom of the Willard Hotel, where he and more than 500 guests were treated to a six-course dinner. Touchdown Club named Travis his team's most valuable performer in 1937 and awarded the Senators' star slugger with a gold watch. Travis posed for the press with Marshall Goldberg, All-American halfback for the University of Pittsburgh.[24]

The good mood seemed to carry over into spring training in 1938. The Senators had something to celebrate in the acquisition of first baseman Zeke Bonura, for whom Washington had traded Joe Kuhel to the White Sox. The addition of Bonura, who had hit .345 with 19 home runs and 100 RBI in 1937 for the Chicago White Sox, added another bat to the top of the Washington lineup. In early April, the *Post* noted that even "Silent Cecil Travis" was heard to have uttered an "Attaboy!" during one of the team's offensive bursts.[25]

The newfound optimism was soon tempered, though. On April 2 against the Minneapolis Millers of the American Association, staff ace Wes Ferrell got hit hard, giving up hits to the first five batters of the game. The Senators led 12–7 after four sloppy innings, and one fan yelled, "Which is the married men's team?" But the Nats' bats, with Travis batting cleanup and going two for six, rapped out 18 hits and 18 runs to beat the minor leaguers.[26]

The Senators staff was lackluster in the spring, as were the team's batters. Lewis and Travis were especially slow in getting out of the gate. "That's what has lost us ball games more than anything else.... When you have two fellows batting second and third in your lineup and failing to get their hits, that makes it pretty tough on a ball club," Harris said. "But in one way I'm glad its [sic] Travis and Lewis who have been keeping us down. If it were something else, I'd be a lot more disturbed, because I know that Travis and Lewis will hit."[27] Indeed, on April 13 against the Boston Braves, Travis appeared ready for the regular season when he rapped a game-tying, bases-loaded triple in the ninth inning and then won the game with a sacrifice fly in the tenth. (His triple might otherwise have been an inside-the-park home run if not for the temporary ground rules that called any ball hit into the sign painters' platform in center field a triple.)[28]

Travis struck three base hits on April 14 and then, with the painters gone, got his inside-the-parker on April 16. The Washington infield — Lewis, Travis, Myer and Bonura — gave the team and its fans hope for the upcoming season. John Kiernan of the *New York Times* said: "The Washington Senators have what might be called a smashing infield: Zeke Bonura, Buddy Myer, Cecil Travis and Buddy Lewis."[29] Both Harris and the *Post* predicted the Senators would finish in the top half of the American League.

The team came out of the gate fast. Washington opened the regular season by hosting a three-game series with Philadelphia. In the opener, the Nats won a slugfest 12–8. (The *Post* headline noted: "President Hurls Day's Best Pitch.") Although Travis committed an error on a relay throw early in the game, he tallied two hits in the slugfest.[30] The following day, the Washington lineup stayed alive as the team won 9–2; Travis doubled and scored in three at bats. In the series finale, Dutch Leonard tossed a 3–0 shutout to give Washington a series sweep.

The Senators quickly cooled off in a three-game series at Yankee Stadium, losing two of three. The team won two of three from the Red Sox, lost two of three in Shibe Park, and lost two of three to the Yankees back at Griffith. In the one win, Travis knocked in a run with an infield hit and also shone in the field with "fancy plays on a half-dozen hard-hit balls."[31]

Beginning with a pitcher's duel on May 4, in which the Griffith Stadium crowd saw Dutch Leonard outduel Bob Feller 1–0, Washington went on a tear, winning seven in a row. After two wins against the Tribe, the Senators swept a two-game series from Chicago, 4–3 and 5–4. In the second game, Travis came to bat in the tenth inning and sent rookie reliever

Bill Cox's first pitch into center field for the game-winning RBI. The next day, Washington welcomed St. Louis to town, and Travis continued his heroic hitting by knocking in five runs with three hits in four at bats, including a three-run inside-the-park homer, carrying his team to a 9–7 victory.

Leonard followed with another gem in the second game of the series, which Washington won 7–1. "Cecil Travis has finally learned how to play shortstop and they have been getting pitching from Dutch Leonard, which is well-nigh matchless," read the *Post*.[32] The win moved Washington into first place. The next day, the Nats beat the Browns 8–6, raising its early-season record to 15–7.

The Detroit Tigers came into town for a two-game series on May 11. Travis snuffed a rally by gloving a smash off the bat of right fielder Pete Fox in the first inning with two men on, and it looked as if the Senators would continue their winning ways. But the team managed only seven hits off the Tigers' Vern Kennedy and lost 4–1. The winning streak was over.

Washington lost the final game of its homestand, 7–6, then left for a 12-game road trip beginning at Fenway Park. The Red Sox greeted them rudely, bombing Washington 10–0. In the second game of the series, Boston bats stayed hot against Dutch Leonard and the Red Sox won 10–9. The loss dropped Washington into second place. A 4–3 Red Sox victory the following day moved the Senators down to third in the tight American League. The Senators then lost their first game in Detroit 13–7 and fell into fourth place.

The team had gone 3–9 on its road trip. Interestingly, a number of Senators hit well during the stretch. Al Simmons hit .369; Lewis, .339; Stone, .309; Bluege, .388. Travis had been respectable but not stellar, hitting .286.[33] It seemed that the team had trouble winning if Travis did not stay above .300, as had been his wont throughout his entire career.

Travis and teammates were relieved to return to Griffith for 12 games beginning on June 1. Against Chicago, Travis celebrated his team's homecoming with an RBI triple that broke a scoreless tie. The following inning, though, Travis failed to glove a ground ball hit by ex–Senator Luke Sewell, and a fan yelled out, "He's a bum!" But in the very next inning, Travis made a back–handed stop of Gee Walker's smash, turned and gunned out Walker at first; the same fan yelled, "Whoopee!"[34] It would not be Travis's last experience with the fickleness of baseball fans.

Fate also seemed fickle for the Senators. The team won four straight in late May and then put together three consecutive wins to begin June. On June 2 against Chicago, Travis doubled twice and played a strong defense behind Dutch Leonard, who was emerging as Washington's only consistent starter. The following day, he checked two Chicago rallies with fine defensive plays and also reached base three of four times. In that game, which Washington won 5–1, brothers Rick and Wes Ferrell each doubled in runs for the Nats. The Senators sat in third place, seven games over .500 at 25–18.

During the team's rebound, Travis's bat caught fire. After Washington defeated St. Louis 6–4 on June 9, both Travis (at .347) and Myer (at .342) ranked among the league's top five hitters.[35] On June 14, Travis went wall-banging against the Indians, going three for five and scoring an inside-the-park homer on a drive off Griffith Stadium's left field wall.

At the same time, the Senators began to cool off again. Washington strung together series losses to the Indians, Browns, Tigers (a sweep), and Indians again. The team sank once again in the standings, but Travis received good news at the end of the month when he and his roommate and friend, Buddy Lewis, as well as Senators catcher Rick Ferrell, were named to the American League All-Star team for the first time.

The team was announced from coast to coast on June 27. The American League roster also included Bill Dickey, Red Ruffing, Lefty Gomez, Lou Gehrig, and Joe DiMaggio from New York; Lefty Grove, Jimmie Foxx, Joe Cronin, and Roger "Doc" Cramer from Boston; Vern Kennedy, Rudy York, and Hank Greenberg from Detroit; Johnny Allen, Bob Feller, and Earl Averill from Cleveland; Buck Newsom from St. Louis; Bob Johnson from Philadelphia; and Michael Kreevich from Chicago. On a roster that included several future Hall of Famers, the *New York Times* cited Travis as one of the league's top stars: "The junior circuit stars will have plenty of power.... Averill was leading the league last week with a .384 average, and Travis, Foxx and Gehringer all were among the league's first 10 batsmen."[36]

Three days before the All-Star Game, which was played on July 6 at Cincinnati's Crosley Field, Travis displayed All-Star form in knocking in six runs in the victorious nightcap of a split doubleheader at Shibe Park.

After a loss and a rare tie in a home doubleheader with the Yankees on July 4, All-Stars from New York and Washington caught a train for Cincinnati. One reporter who had been covering the National League for most of the season motioned to Travis and Lewis and asked a colleague, "Who are those two young fellows over there? They're not ball players, are they?"[37]

American League manager Joe McCarthy named Lewis the starting third baseman. Despite conjecture that Travis and Ferrell would see playing time in the later innings of the game, neither did. The senior circuit could have used Travis's offense; the National League won 4–1 behind pitchers Johnny Vander Meer and Bill Lee, who combined for six scoreless innings.

Fresh off his experience as an All-Star reserve, Travis rejoined the team for its July 8 game against the A's at Griffith. He sparked an 11–0 rout of Philadelphia by going four for four and two RBI. Unfortunately, Travis would once again experience a spike-related injury less than a week later. On July 13, in an attempted steal of third base, Cleveland outfielder Roy "Stormy" Weatherly spiked Travis's right knee. Travis suffered a "small but deep gash" and left the game to be taken to Georgetown Hospital.[38] Initially, trainer Mike Martin did not think the injury was serious, but Travis's knee was slow to heal. Travis wanted to get back into the lineup on July 19, but the doctor told him to give it one more day's rest. The prognosis was changed once again, and Travis stayed out until the team's doubleheader with St. Louis on July 24. The teams split the twin bill, and Travis collected two hits in the first game.

On July 27 in Detroit, Travis collected three hits but took second stage to the Tigers' Hank Greenberg. The 27-year-old slugger blasted two home runs in the first two innings of the game, leading the Tigers to a 9–4 win and, perhaps more interestingly, giving him a 33 on the season. Back in 1927, when Babe Ruth had set the single-season home run record with 60, he had also stood at 33 on July 27. Ruth, though, had hit his thirty-third home run in his ninety-first game; Greenberg had reached the same mark in only 88 games, and baseball pundits wondered if the famous Jewish slugger would challenge Ruth's record.

As the 1938 season entered the dog days of summer, Travis pursued his own mark of excellence. He, Cleveland's Averill, and Boston's Foxx jockeyed for position in the American League batting race. Foxx held the league in early August, but Travis temporarily pulled back in front on August 11. Ironically, his one-for-five performance that day moved him ahead of Foxx, who'd gone hitless. When the Senators returned to Griffith Stadium for a series with Foxx's Red Sox, Travis led Foxx by one point, .349 to .348.[39] Their league-leading marks represented a significant falloff from the same time in the previous year, when Travis was leading with a .388 mark, DiMaggio and Gehrig were in the .370s, and Gehringer, the eventual champion, was hitting .363. Bob "X-Ray" Ray of the *Los Angeles Times* speculated: "when you note so many good batters have fallen off, you can't tell the old X-Ray that they haven't removed a lot of base hits out of the big league baseballs."[40]

Foxx and the Sox came to Griffith for a weekend series on August 12, and the home team swept all three games. The *Post*'s Arch McDonald praised Travis's Saturday performance for playing "a sparkling game at shortstop all afternoon."[41] On one play, Travis made a crucial defensive stop when he went far into the hole to glove a grounder from former manager Joe Cronin and wheeled to force out a baserunner at second.

Travis had established himself as a star in D.C., one of those rare players who brought players to the stadium and kept them interested until game's end. When Harris rested Travis on August 21, columnist Jack Munhall complained: "Wonder why Bucky Harris benched Cecil Travis, who is only the league's leading hitter, Saturday and kept the exhausted Buddy Lewis in the line-up?"[42]

On August 25, Travis singled, doubled and tripled in Washington's 8–2 defeat of Detroit. Four days later he provided key plays on each side of the ball in a "ladies' day" matchup with Cleveland. Travis's bunt single following a Lewis walk started a two-run rally in the fifth inning. Later in the game, the Indians' Averill stood on second base when Hal Trosky stepped to the plate and blooped a lazy fly over Travis into left field. Travis raced back and, "with the official scorer already putting it down as a hit," the shortstop made a "miraculous" over-the-shoulder catch on the ball. Travis then doubled off Averill, who was already rounding third when Travis had made the grab.[43] McDonald credited the catch with a "turning the tide of battle" in the 6–4 Washington victory.[44] On September 6, his mark stood at .349, the same average he had 364 days before. Travis seemed to be cementing himself as the team's shortstop, but his hold on the American League lead in hitting proved as fleeting as it had the year before. He suffered a week-long slump in early September that plummeted him from first to ninth in the league. He broke out of the slump with a remarkable six-for-seven performance in a September 17 doubleheader against the Browns. Travis rung up four singles, a double, a home run, and six RBI.

Bouncing up and down in the lineup — sometimes hitting third, sometimes seventh — Travis closed out yet another fine season at the plate. Having established himself as the team's everyday shortstop, he logged a career-high in plate appearances (567) and recorded personal bests in hits (190), walks (58), runs (96) and even home runs (five). His .335 season average was his sixth in six seasons in the majors (counting his brief term with the club in 1933) and his eighth in eight seasons as a professional player. And his 1938 on-base mark was a sparkling .401. He would finish ninth in MVP voting, with Boston slugger Jimmie Foxx taking home the honors after a monster year in which he hit .349 with 50 home runs and 175 RBI. Finishing second, fourth, and sixth in the voting were Bill Dickey (.313, 27 HR, 115 RBI), Red Ruffing (21–7, 3.31 ERA) and Joe DiMaggio (.324, 32 HR, 140 RBI), all members of the New York Yankees. The Yankees won the American League and then swept the Chicago Cubs in the World Series.

The Senators, meanwhile, had finished one game below the .500 mark, in fifth place, despite once again leading the league in hits. The pitching staff was Washington's downfall once more, recording an ERA of 4.94. The *Post* reported that Travis might be used as trade bait in Griffith's hopes to get not one but *two* good pitchers in return, such was Travis's perceived value.[45] The day before Halloween, the *Post* reported that Detroit had inquired about Travis. Even though Griffith effectively killed the deal by demanding Rudy York (a 30-homer, 120–RBI man in 1938) in return, trade rumors would haunt Travis's growing contingent of fans throughout most of his remaining career.[46]

6

Trade Winds and
the Florida Flu

The April 1939 issue of *Scholastic Coach* magazine profiled Travis along with Lou Gehrig, Mel Ott, and Paul Waner to illustrate how different major league players achieved success with different grips and batting stances. The article's author analyzed the stance, hitting position, step, swing, and follow-though. "Travis," the article noted, "is employing a choke grip opposite the plate with the feet only slightly apart."[1] Although the *Scholastic Coach* article provided few startling revelations, it did illustrate how respected a hitter Travis had become.

Back in January, Travis and his roommate and partner on the left side of the Senators infield paid Clark Griffith a visit to discuss their contracts for the upcoming season. Both Travis, the team leader in average, and Lewis, the team leader in runs scored, emerged smiling, having received pay increases from the team president. Griffith was able to fund both increases due in part to two off-season moves. In December, he had sold Al Simmons to the Boston Braves for $3000 and traded Zeke Bonura — who had come off a remarkable statistical season in which he'd registered 22 home runs and 114 RBI while also leading American League first sackers in fielding percentage — to the New York Giants for Jim Carlin, Tom Baker and $20,000 in cash. Despite the impressive numbers, Bonura had frustrated team management with his lack of range, and the prevailing opinion was that his .993 defensive average was inflated by his unwillingness to pursue difficult chances in the field.

That off-season, Detroit and Washington discussed a possible trade involving Travis. Reportedly, Griffith was eyeing the Tigers' Rudy York, who could provide the power numbers that Travis had not produced. (In the event of a trade, Washington had recently acquired the rights to shortstop Charley Gelbert from the Toledo Mudhens in the offseason.) Detroit was not eager to part with York and trade talks cooled, but Shirley Povich predicted: "The Detroit Tigers are expected to make another bid for Cecil Travis when they realize, in spring training, the extent to which Shortstop Billy Rogell has slowed up."[2] (Rogell had hit only .259 in 1938, his twelfth season in the bigs.) The possible trade of Travis to the Tigers had interesting potential for both Detroit and Travis; the addition of Travis's bat to a perennial first-division would increase both his and Detroit's chances at seeing postseason play.

But Travis remained a favorite of Griffith, and the owner made it clear that he was not eager to part with his shortstop. Responding to a report in March that the Cleveland Indians also had expressed interest in Travis, Griffith retorted: "Somebody's crazy. Cleveland has never made me an offer for Travis. I wouldn't trade him anyway." He also discounted a possible trade to the Tigers, saying, "I wouldn't accept the Detroit offer [in the winter], and they've never made me another. My price on Travis is too high for any club in the league."[3] Griffith's words must have been reassured Travis's growing fan base in Washington and the surrounding areas. At the time, the Senators were the southernmost major league team on the east coast, and the Georgian native was perhaps closest thing that the team had to a homegrown star. Meanwhile, another Travis, Cecil's niece Dot, was emerging as a star of the Capital District–area Blair High School basketball team.

Another story taking shape in Orlando that spring was that of Mickey Vernon, a rookie first baseman from Greenville, South Carolina. Vernon, who had hit .329 in the Southern Association, threatened to unseat Jimmy Wasdell at first. Vernon would be part of stellar rookie class in 1939 that would also include Charlie Keller, Dizzy Trout, Early Wynn, Hal Newhouser, and a cocky young hitter from San Diego named Ted Williams.

Whether Vernon or Wasdell would win the first baseman's job, the 1939 Senators lineup would be heavy with left-handed hitters, including the entire infield of Lewis, Travis, Myer, and Wasdell/Vernon. Some commentators felt the team would be vulnerable to left-handed pitching. Characteristically, Griffith acknowledged the problem but provided a positive spin, noting that his team would face mostly right-handers and that the Senators lineup was still good enough to beat most left-handers:

> You can add up the star southpaw pitchers in this league on the fingers of one hand. I'll name them for you. There's Gomez and Grove. They're tops. [And] fellows like Fred Ostermuller and Thornton Lee have a knack of beating us.... I'm not worried about the other southpaws in the league. They aren't so hot.[4]

Travis, who had bounced around the bottom of the Washington lineup for much of his career, was penciled in at the fifth spot in the order. Harris was counting on the historically light-hitting Travis to knock in his share of runs and more. Interestingly, Travis singled in the winning run in the thirteenth inning of a March 19 exhibition game against his alleged suitors, the Tigers. Three days later, however, Travis was confined to his hotel room in Daytona Beach with what was described as a "mild attack of influenza."[5] His absence was noted by Rogers Hornsby, who displayed characteristic bluntness when he asked, "Where's the power on this club? I see Buddy Myer and Buddy Lewis, and I know Cecil Travis is around somewhere, but who else is going to drive in your runs?" Hornsby was also critical of the team's penchant for signing Cuban players, such as pitcher Alex Carrasquel and outfielder Bobby Estalella, slated as the team's cleanup hitter. "Those Cubans don't have it here," Horsnby said, tapping his heart. "At least most of 'em don't…. As a class the Cubans choke up. I'll take American boys for my ball players." The Rajah also criticized the play of Washington's incumbent. Voicing a complaint that would have made future batting coaches Charlie Lau and Walt Hriniak shudder, Hornsby said: "I've seen that Wasdell. He'll never hit in the big leagues until he starts swinging his bat with two hands. These kind of guys who follow through with a one-handed swing don't have any power or any balance."[6]

Hornsby also commented upon the apparent decline of the New York Yankees' "Iron Horse," Lou Gehrig. When asked why Gehrig was looking so "tired" that spring, Hornsby noted: "Sure it's the legs…. They are the first to go. They got me, too. Gehrig's legs were overdue to crack. He's a big man. Put a lot of strain on them for 15 years."[7]

The previous season, the first baseman had continued his major league record for consecutive games played but had hit only .295, the only time he had finished below the .300 mark since his rookie season in 1925.

Post writer Harry Ferguson surmised that Travis might one day become a first baseman himself. "Bucky Harris at Washington not only has a wobbly pitching staff but is uncertain about his infield. If Jim Wasdell does not develop at first bas[e] this season, you may see Cecil Travis shifted over there from shortstop."[8] Indeed, as Travis had proved himself a superior hitter but had yet to quiet all critiques of his fielding ability, first base seemed a logical destination for him at some point in his career.

Meanwhile, it was unclear when Travis would return to any position for the Nats. After spending five days in the hospital with flu-like symptoms, Travis was taken to Orange General Hospital in Orlando. He had been slow to recover, and doctors ordered the move when he suffered a relapse on March 26, when his temperature rose to 103.[9] Fluoroscope exams showed that Travis was suffering from a "slight bronchial ailment," and doctors reported that his condition was not serious, though Travis was to remain at the hospital for two or three more days.[10]

Travis was back on the field on April 9 for a preseason game against the Boston Braves, and he even contributed seventh-inning RBI single in the team's 12–7 win. The *Washington Post* reported that "Cecil Travis showed little effects of his recent one-man flu epidemic," but this report of his return overlooked the fact that Travis had lost considerable weight during his long illness.[11] Travis played the last three innings of the following day's game as well, demonstrating that he would be ready for the opening day lineup.

Washington was shut out by George Caster in its season opener at Shibe Park; neither Travis, Lewis, Estalella nor Wasdell hit the ball out of the infield. The team then returned to Griffith Stadium for its home opener with New York the following day. Lefty Gomez, one of the lefties that Harris feared, beat Washington 6–3. The Senators won the next day behind Dutch Leonard, 3–1. After losing the final game of the series, the Nats went to Fenway for a two-game series. In the first game, Travis tripled in a run in the fifth inning, singled in another run in the seventh inning, and was responsible for another run when pitcher Elden Auker failed to field his drive back to the box in the eighth. In the bottom of the eighth, Travis saved at least two runs in the eighth when he snagged a grounder from Jimmie Foxx behind second base and flipped the ball from his glove hand to Buddy Myer for an inning-ending force play. Washington won the game 10–9.

In the last weekend of April, Travis and the Senators played a two-game series at Yankee Stadium. In the first game, New York center fielder Joe DiMaggio tore muscles in his right foot while fielding a line drive. The Senators won 3–1, and DiMaggio missed the next 35 games. The following day, the Nats won again, this time 3–2. First baseman Lou Gehrig went zero for four, dropping his early-season average to .143. It would be the last game that the "Iron Horse" would ever play. Two days later, he voluntarily benched himself, ending his consecutive games record at 2,130.

After sweeping the Yankees, Washington swept another two-game series from the Browns, bringing their record to 7–4. First baseman Johnny Wasdell tied a major league record by committing four errors in the series finale, but he made amends by knocking in the winning run his club's 11–10 triumph. The win gave Washington five wins in a row and moved the Senators into third place. But then the team immediately followed its winning streak with six consecutive losses.

Meanwhile, Travis was off his normal hitting pace in the early stages of 1939. In an uncomfortable parallel with Gehrig's mysterious health problems, the effects of Travis's preseason illness seemed to linger. He broke out temporarily for a more typically Travislike day on May 6 in Comiskey Park. In a 14–12 slugfest won by the White Sox, Travis went four for four with two singles, a triple and a two-run home run. His round-tripper was the club's first of the year. But something was wrong. Two innings before hitting his home run, he told teammate Sammy West, "I'm sick as blazes.... I don't know if I can make it for the rest of the game."[12]

After the game, Travis was hospitalized, again with a fever of 103. He was diagnosed with grippe, which teammate Charley Gelbert had also recently contracted. (Sammy West, Dutch Leonard and Harry Kelley would also fall victims to the epidemic on the west-

Travis at spring training in Orlando, Florida, in 1939. Travis looked poised for another All-Star campaign with the Senators that year, but a lingering case of the flu slowed him for much of the early season. (National Baseball Hall of Fame Library, Cooperstown, N.Y.)

ern road swing.) Travis and Gelbert remained in Chicago while the team went to Cleveland for two games, but Travis rejoined the team for its next series in Detroit. (Gelbert skipped the Detroit series and went directly home to Washington.) On May 11, he helped the team end its losing streak with a single in the middle of its game-winning rally in the ninth. Six days later, Travis singled in two of Washington's four runs in a win over Detroit at Griffith.

Still, Travis struggled both at the plate and in the field. He had missed a good amount of playing time as the result of his two bouts with illness, and he had also lost a good amount of weight — around 20 to 30 pounds, depending on various accounts — which undoubtedly sapped his strength. On May 21, the home crowd voiced its displeasure when Travis lost a pop fly in the sun; one fan observed that Travis was met with a "loud chorus of boos" in his last two at bats.[13] Povich, long a supporter of the gentlemanly

Travis, wrote, "The folks who booed Travis that day are the sort who would slap their grandmother for misplacing her glasses." The columnist suspected that Travis, who looked "leg-heavy and slow," had still not completely recovered from the flu he had contracted in Florida. Povich also reminded his readers of the fact that this was the same "courageous" player who had tallied nine total bases while playing with a high fever that hospitalized him not a week before. "That's the guy they booed Sunday for missing pop fly he wasn't supposed to catch."[14]

A week later, one *Post* reader who had been at the game responded with a letter to the editor. He said that "Cecil had a bad day in the field" and that "the booers seemed to be trying to outdo the cheering, but the handclappers about held their own." Fearing that the young infielder's confidence would be damaged by further booing, the fan (who signed his letter "One Who Clapped") wrote, "I hope that the Washington fans give him a hearty hand the next time he plays on the home grounds."[15]

Travis, spared the smell-the-blood style of today's reporters, shrugged off the incident and continued to take his swings. Still ailing on May 24, he slammed the second of his five home runs that year, an inside-the-park line drive that found its way to the center field corner of Griffith Stadium. Travis, probably exhausted from his circling of the bases, left the game soon after as the Nats coasted to a 16–6 rout of the Browns.

After the Red Sox swept a three-game series with the Senators at Fenway, Washington lost two of three at home to the Philadelphia A's. Reviewing the team's 14–22 start, the *Post* singled out the 1939 version of the Senators infield as perhaps the worst in the league. At first, Johnny Wasdell had been little better than the "lumbering" Zeke Bonura. (Reportedly, Griffith had described Bonura as "the worst ballplayer he ever saw.") Buddy Myer was no longer considered one of the league's top second basemen, and Lewis was proving less than advertised at third. Meanwhile, Travis, playing at less than 100 percent, was "not a good shortstop":

> There is a clamor for the conversion of Travis into a first baseman, but that may not be the solution of the Nats' infield troubles. Travis has not been in extreme good health since the start of the season. When the hits start to rattle from his bat with their accustomed frequency, his short-stopping deficiencies could be overlooked. There isn't any evidence that Travis would be a better first baseman than he is a shortstop.[16]

As yet another season looked lost, Griffith began to search more earnestly for answers. With Wasdell providing negligible power at first as predicted by Hornsby — he would fail to homer in 1939 — and the team unsure about the youngster Vernon's abilities to handle first on a daily basis, Griffith expressed interest in trading for the Detroit's Rudy York. York, an All-Star catcher the previous season, had slugged 33 homers and knocked in 127 runs for the 1938 Tigers. In 1939, Detroit was converting York to first base to make room for Birdie Tebbets, a better defensive catcher. (Meanwhile, the team planned to move its star first baseman, Hank Greenberg, into left field.) Povich wrote that "York would look very important on first base for the Nats," and Griffith was giving "serious thought" to trading not only Travis but also catcher Rick Ferrell.[17]

Travis heard more boos from the home crowd that spring. Griffith called Travis into his office for a friendly talk, and the owner told his struggling shortstop to not worry about the fans and to just play at the level of which he was capable, which would be good enough for Griffith. It's unknown whether they discussed the trade rumors involving Travis, but it became a non-issue, at least for the time being, when it was reported on June 6 that Detroit had turned down a York-for-Travis deal. A Washington official said, "The Tigers told us, 'Nothing doing.' They said they won't part with York."[18]

Meanwhile, Travis was regaining his stroke at the plate, and he came alive during the team's 10-game road trip in June. He tripled in two runs in the ninth inning of a 13–9 victory in Cleveland on June 7, rapped out a single and two doubles against the Indians on June 8, and knocked in a run in the series finale. Travis and the Senators then went to Detroit for three games, and Griffith resumed trade talks with Detroit. On June 11, the *Post* announced Detroit had turned down a trade offer of Travis and Ferrel for York and outfielder Roy Cullenbine. That same day, Travis demonstrated his hitting prowess by blasting out a home run and a double, though he looked bad in an ill-advised attempt to stretch his double into a triple.

After the game, Travis traveled by train from Detroit to upstate New York. The village of Cooperstown, founded on the southern shores of Otsego Lake in the late eighteenth century by the father of author James Fenimore Cooper, was to be the home of the National Baseball Hall of Fame and Museum. On June 12, Major League Baseball took a one-day hiatus as the game celebrated its mythological centennial with the official dedication of this new museum. Following the ribbon-cutting ceremony and the inaugural inductions of Hall of Famers, Travis was to play in an exhibition of all-stars from both leagues.

On the train trip, Travis met fellow Georgian Ty Cobb, who had been named in the first Hall of Fame class back in 1936. (Baseball had named inductees in the three years that preceded the opening of the museum in Cooperstown.) "I remember that he gave me one bit of advice," Travis said later. Cobb, who also was successful in business ventures, told Travis: "Save your money."[19]

After Cobb and the other 25 inducters were honored, Travis and the other current stars on hand played a seven-inning exhibition on Doubleday Field — the first major leaguers to play there. Newly named Hall of Famer Eddie Collins managed Travis and his fellow American League stars against a National League squad managed by original inductee Honus Wagner. The game, in which "The Wagners" beat "The Collins" 4–2, also featured an honorary appearance by Babe Ruth, who had retired from the game in 1935. The exhibition would stand as the antecedent of the annual "Hall of Fame Game" between rotating major league teams, a tradition that began in 1940.

Following the itinerary in Cooperstown, Travis traveled back to Washington to rejoin the Senators for the team's homestand. Trade talks between the Senators and Tigers remained dead, but with 20 minutes remaining before the June 15 trading deadline, the Cleveland Indians entered the picture. Cleveland attempted to land Travis, but they withdrew their interest when Griffith wanted their star first baseman, Hal Trosky, in return.[20]

Travis would, in fact, remain a fixture at shortstop and (for the most part) in the fifth spot in the order for the Senators for the rest of the season. Meanwhile, the baseball world discovered that one player who had been a permanent fixture in his team's lineup had seen his last action that season. The Mayo clinic had discovered that Gehrig's dramatic decline was due not simply to tired legs, as Hornsby had guessed in the spring, but to amyotrophic lateral sclerosis (ALS), an insurable disease of the motor neuron cells in the brain and spinal column. On June 21, the Yankees announced that Gehirg had retired as a player and that he would remain with the team as their captain.

The club scheduled a "Lou Gehrig Appreciation Day" ceremony between the two games of its scheduled game with the Senators on July 4. Although Travis and his teammates could not have known that they were witnessing history during Gehrig's last game on April 30, there was no doubt as to the history involved in honoring the great first baseman and respected Yankee captain. After the Senators won the opener, 3–2, before 61,808 fans and a gathering of past Yankee greats, Gehrig accepted a number of gifts from his club, including an engraved silver trophy. Gehrig then stepped to a microphone and furthered his legacy by uttering a speech that still stands as one of the sport's most memorable moments:

> Fans, for the past two weeks you have been reading about a bad break I got. Yet today, I consider myself the luckiest man on the face of the earth.

I have been in ballparks for 17 years and I have never received anything but kindness and encouragement from you fans.

Look at these grand men. Which of you wouldn't consider it the highlight of his career just to associate with them for even one day?

Sure I'm lucky. Who wouldn't have considered it an honor to have known Jacob Ruppert? Also, the builder of baseball's greatest empire, Ed Barrows? To have spent six years with that wonderful little fellow, Miller Huggins? Then to have spent the next nine years with that outstanding leader, that smart student of psychology, the best manager in baseball today, Joe McCarthy? Sure, I'm lucky.

When the New York Giants, a team you would give your right arm to beat and vice versa, sends you a gift, that's something. When everybody down to the groundskeeper and those boys in white coats remember you with trophies, that's something. When you have a father and mother work all their lives so that you can have an education and build your body, it's a blessing. When you have a wife who has been a tower of strength and shown more courage than you dreamed existed, that's the finest I know.

So I close in saying that I might have had a bad break, but I have an awful lot to live for.

The following day, *The New York Times* would call it "as amazing a valedictory as ever came from a ball player."[21]

After Gehrig's speech, Babe Ruth paid tribute to his former teammate and sometime rival. The history of the moment was perhaps overpowering to the Senators. New York won the nightcap 11–1.

While New York held onto first place despite Gehrig's tragic diagnosis, Washington languished in sixth place for the entire second half of the season. Buddy Lewis, once scene as the team's third baseman of the future, was struggling badly at the hot corner. His manager mused:

This is the first time I've ever seen a young ball player slip as a fielder.... The natural thing is for them to improve, but Lewis has actually gone back. The situation is beyond me. I'd have bet, three years ago, that by this time Lewis would be one of the great third baseman of baseball.[22]

At bat, though, Lewis remained impressive. He hit .341 through the first three months of the season while displaying occasional power. Like his roommate and fellow All-Star of 1938, Lewis was gaining the reputation of an excellent hitter in search of his true position.

The Senators closed out the first half of the season with a rare five-game series in Philadelphia's Shibe Park. The team got its first taste of a new phenomenon with which the American League was experimenting:

night baseball. The A's had already begun playing night games, and the first game of their series with Washington was played under the "soft, yellow-ish brilliance of 780 flood lamps beaming down upon the playing field from eight 150-foot towers."[23] Travis singled in his first nighttime at bat and later scored on Buddy Myer's triple, but the Senators didn't fare any better at night than they had in the daytime, losing 9–3.

The team rebounded to win three of the next four from Philadel-phia but still lost eight of 15 on the road trip. After winning only two of its first five games back in the friendly confines of Griffith Stadium, Washington found a groove and won nine in a row. The Senators infield was starting to gel. Chicago came to town on the first Friday in August, and Mike Kreevich tied a Major League record by grounding into four successive double plays. The *Post* remarked: "The play of both Cecil Travis and Charley Gelbert at shortstop has bordered on the remarkable side, and Mickey Vernon is providing the best first-base job the Nats have received all season."[24] Chicago manager Jimmy Dykes was especially impressed with Travis, and it was reported that he would make a trade offer for Travis, whom Dykes hoped to have at third base for the White Sox in 1940.[25]

Dykes and the Sox left town without Travis, and the first-place Yan-kees came in to face the suddenly hot Senators on August 8. Behind start-ing pitcher Joe Krakauskas, who was having some mid-summer success in an otherwise unspectacular season (11–17, 4.60 ERA), the Senators took the opener, 7–4. The next day, New York ended Washington's winning streak with 15 hits—including a Joe DiMaggio home run that soared deeper into Griffith Stadium's left field bleachers than any ball had that season.[26] In the final game of the home stand, though, the Senators rebounded as Dutch Leonard beat Yankees starter Monte Pearson. The team had won 9 of 10 games but its record was still 11 games under .500 at 47–58.

Washington then dropped five of a brief six-game trip to Boston and New York, and it lost its first two games back at home before splitting a doubleheader with Boston on August 19. But Clark Griffith was in a good mood. He announced the signing of shortstop James Pofahl, whose con-tract Griffith had purchased from the Minneapolis Millers for $40,000. The 22-year-old Pofahl had been leading the American Association in hitting before a sprained wrist slowed him, and he still maintained a .303 aver-age at the time his rights were purchased.

Naturally, the purchase of Pofahl led to speculation once again about the future of Travis with Washington. With the team already owning the service of two shortstops, Travis and Gelbert, Griffith suggested that Travis might even be converted into a third baseman. And the possibilities of a future trade with Chicago—or even Detroit, who still needed a short-stop—remained.[27]

The Senators headed to Detroit for a series in the last weekend of August, and if Detroit was harboring any notions of trading for Travis, his performance in the series scared them away. As long-time Travis supporter Povich reported, Washington's shortstop "played the worst ball he has been guilty of all season" in the late–August series:

> What the Tigers saw last week when they saw Travis was a bungling, but-ter-fingered fielder whose throwing wasn't so good, either. He muffed an easy double-play chance and paved the way for the Tigers to win the game that day. He exhibited an obvious uncertainty on ground balls....[28]

And at the plate, Travis managed only one single in the series. When the Senators said goodbye to Tiger Stadium, the once-intriguing trade appeared dead.

Ironically, Travis returned to his All-Star form in the following series in St. Louis. In a doubleheader, he drew gasps from the press box and the Browns faithful in the stands with one fine play after another, turning all 13 chances into outs:

> He roamed to the right and the left with equal facility and deadly effect. Virtually all of the 13 chances he accepted were tough. Some of them loomed impossible until he converted them into putouts. He went behind second base on two occasions for bare-handed stops and flipped the ball behind his back to Buddy Myer for force plays. Oldest inhabitants of the St. Louis press box were of a single mind that no shortstop had ever turned in such a scintillating afternoon."[29]

To add to his fielding, Travis launched a homer that bounced atop the center field roof of Sportsman's Park in the final game of the series.

It wasn't long after that the trade rumors resurfaced. Bob Ray of *The Los Angeles Times* reported that Hank Greenberg might be donning a Senators uniform in 1940. According to Ray, the Tigers were now viewing York as their first baseman of the future, and Travis might still be used as bait for Greenberg. Interestingly, although Greenberg himself had challenged Babe Ruth's home run record only years before, Ray noted that many felt the "big Indian" York might break Ruth's record if he played everyday.[30]

In fact, Travis would remain with Washington, and the Senators would remain in sixth place in 1939, finished with a record of 65–88. The team's lone seasonal highlight came when ace Dutch Leonard won his twen-tieth game in the final week of the regular season. Leonard was the only starter to claim a winning record for Washington in 1939. Fellow staff members Ken Chase, Joe Krakauskas and Joe Haynes combined for a record of 29–48. Travis finished with a .292 average (his lowest in professional ball) and only a .342 on-base percentage with five homers (second on the team to Lewis's 10) and 63 RBI (third behind Taffy Wright's 93 and Lewis's 75)— tepid numbers compared to his established standards.

Povich made Travis's case that:

> In the year when his batting slumped — he is under .300 for the first time in six years in the big leagues— he has magically acquired a field touch of which he was never deemed capable. There never were any complaints about his throwing arm, but there was always the suspicion that he could not get the jump on a ground ball. He has been getting that jump.[31]

Considering how much the *Post* columnist clearly liked the gentlemanly Travis, though, one might read some strained optimism in between such lines. And indeed, it would not be long before Travis— who had played the past three seasons as Washington's everyday shortstop and had even made the 1938 All-Star roster at that position — would face yet another position change. Meanwhile, he would seek to regain his All-Star hitting stroke as the Senators team sought a return to respectability.

As the New York Yankees closed out a successful defense of the American League pennant in 1939, a far more forbidding force was building in Europe. German forces, under the direction of Chancellor Adolf Hitler, launched a *blitzkrieg* on Poland on September 1. Britain and France, allies of Poland, delivered an ultimatum for Germany's withdrawal. After Hitler had failed to respond, Britain's Prime Minister Neville Chamberlain declared on September 3 that his country was now in a state of war with Germany.

World War II had effectively begun, and the Third Reich and its rising war machine sent currents of fear across the Atlantic.

7

Back in the Box

The more things changed, the more they remained the same. In the break between the 1939 and 1940 seasons, Travis faced two possibilities: getting traded to another team, most probably Detroit, or remaining with Washington as the team's third baseman.

Given Travis's performance at shortstop in 1939 — the ill-fated series in Detroit notwithstanding — it seems remarkable that the club would once again ask Travis to change positions. But Griffith was enamored of young Jimmy Pofahl, whose natural position was shortstop, and it became clear that Travis would have to vacate the position once again. With Buddy Lewis's ongoing struggles at the hot corner and his likely reassignment to the Washington outfield, Travis was headed back to third.

First, though, it remained to be seen if Travis had a longer-distance move in store. In November, *The Los Angeles Times* quoted Tigers general manager Jack Zeller regarding a Washington offer of Travis to Detroit for slugger Hank Greenberg, which Detroit had turned down. Interestingly, Zellar said of Greenberg: "Personally I don't know of any club that would swap for him except Washington and Clark Griffith would have trouble in satisfying his salary demands."[1] Zellar's sentiment toward the slugger, who had hit 131 home runs over the past three seasons for Detroit, are surprising indeed. But Greenberg had fallen out of favor in the Tigers organization during the 1939 season, and especially with team owner Walter Briggs. One source close to the team told the *Post*: "Briggs believes that Greenberg did not give his best efforts to the Tigers last year.... Briggs paid Hank $30,000 for the season and, businessman that he is, he expected Hank to hit 50 home runs for that kind of pay. There was a time when Briggs and Greenberg were chums, but that is no longer the case."[2]

Clark Griffith and Bucky Harris went to Cincinnati in early December for Major League Baseball's winter trade talks, and the Associated Press reported in December that a Travis-for-Greenberg deal might be done within the week. According to Povich, though, Griffith and Harris were dangling Travis in a possible deal for York, and such a deal seemed imminent until it was dealt a two-fold blow: the Cubs entering trade talks for shortstop Billy Rogell and Boston's sudden interest in acquiring the Tigers' York.

As trade talks with Detroit cooled, Harris contemplated the switch of Travis to third base. Harris praised Travis's "great defensive performance" as a shortstop in 1939 and argued that a shortstop as good as Travis would make a "great third baseman." Harris also noted that Travis was a better defensive player than he had been before Buddy Lewis came to the team two years earlier, when Travis had last played third:

> He's smarter, he gets a better break on the ball, and there never was any complaint with his throwing arm.
>   If what we hear about Pofahl's ability to play shortstop is true, that would make Travis available for third base, and with Travis around there would be no point in keeping Lewis on third. We need Lewis' batting punch in the outfield and I'll stake my reputation on Buddy's ability to hold down an outfield job.[3]

Ultimately, Detroit would complete a trade with the Cubs, sending Rogell to Chicago in exchange for Dick Bartell, an again veteran coming off his worst season, when he had hit .238 while continually fighting leg injuries. What would prove significant, however, was that the Tigers lost neither of their star first basemen in the deal, and Greenberg was slated as an outfielder for Detroit in 1940. Povich surmised: "Bartell ... scarcely filled [Detroit's] shortstop needs.... Washington's bosses are reasoning that when the Tigers are in the South and come to the full realization that Bartell may be no improvement over Bill Rogell, they will renew their efforts to acquire Travis."[4]

Travis's friend and roommate, Lewis, paid a visit to Griffith's office in mid–January. It was an annual pilgrimage that Lewis usually made with Travis, but Travis had written Lewis and told him that he couldn't get away from the farm to make the trip. The 23-year-old Lewis made the trip alone. When he arrived at his Griffith's, his boss said, "Every time I see you in the winter it costs me money.... Why don't you talk contract with me by mail like the other players do?"

"Well," Lewis answered, "I always get more dough when I see you personally."

Griffith told him: "That's what I thought.... As long as you're here, I guess I've got to talk to you. But hereafter no more of the personal visits, understand?"

Afterwards, Lewis told the *Post*, "I did all right... He isn't so tough to do business with. I'm tickled with my new contract. I'd say Mr. Griffith is a great fellow." Travis's re-signing sounded likely, as well, according to Lewis, who said, "He told me he liked the contract Mr. Griffith sent him."[5] But two weeks later, when Travis met with Griffith for contract talks in Charlotte, North Carolina, the two could not agree on terms. Griffith reported: "We're only $500 apart. We'll get together."[6] Travis had made $12,000 the previous season, but — in keeping with an era when players were judged year-by-year on their performance — Griffith was asking his infielder to take a pay cut after his comparatively poor 1939 campaign.

A number of players were slow to sign in 1940, including Rick Ferrell, Buddy Myer, rookie Pofahl, and 20-game-winner Dutch Leonard. Griffith had given Leonard a $1000 bonus for his excellent 1939 season and offered an increase in $3,750 for his 1940 salary, but Leonard sought more money from the frugal Washington owner. Of Travis and Myer, Griffith pointed out: "I never have any trouble coming to terms with them.... They'll sign before they report here."[7]

Griffith, though, was especially irked by Leonard's and Pofahl's holdouts. On February 27, he said, "Unless Leonard reports here by Friday and accepts the final offer I sent him last week, he'll be subject to both a suspension and a fine.... I've been very liberal with him and have made my last offer." Of Pofahl, Griffith added, "He should be grateful for the chance to break into the big leagues." He said, "I will have no trouble in signing Travis, but Leonard and Pofahl are exhausting my patience."[8]

Eventually, Ferrell, Leonard, and Pofahl would all agree to contracts with the club, as would Travis. A day after the *New York Times* reported that Griffith was *still* offering Travis to Detroit for either Greenberg or York, Travis reported to camp in Orlando on February 28. He was still not under contract, but Travis and Griffith took care of that the same day when the two split the aforementioned $500 difference. Travis reportedly agreed to $11,000 for the 1940 season.[9]

In the midst of the contract negotiations, it seemed that no one had officially informed Travis of plans to move him back to third base. Povich highlighted Travis's Georgian drawl in his "This Morning with Shirley Povich" column of February 29:

> Ah heard repo'ts that ah was gonna play third base next season, but ah don't know if it's some kind of a rumor of a real repo't.... Ah kinda wish somebody would tell me if ah'm a shortstop or a third baseman. Ah guess though, it don't matter much.... Ah always figured anybody who could play shortstop could play third base.... They tell me this Jimmy Pofahl

who's coming from Minneapolis is a bearcat around shortstop and maybe he'll play a piece of third base for me.

Travis also spoke on the record about his disappointing 1939 season. Having since returned to his normal weight, Travis refused to blame the early season illness that had taken approximately 20 pounds off his already lanky frame the previous spring. Instead, he pointed to his attempt to provide more power for Washington:

> Ah was pulling the ball to right field last year, like they told me to, but ah know ah hit best to left.... Ah don't know if ah'm gonna trifle with that pulling business next season. That was the first time ah never hit .300 in mah life. Ah think ah'm gonna keep hitting the only way ah know how. Nobody ever booed a base hit.[10]

As camp began, people said to be close to the Detroit Tigers organization predicted that Detroit would accept Griffith's standing offer of Travis for York once Greenberg showed that he was not an everyday outfielder. "Then the Tigers will get panicky and make the trade with Washington," an anonymous observer said.[11]

Travis struggled at third early in the exhibition season, but Harris shrugged it off, saying, "I wish I was as sure of every position on the club as I am of Travis at third."[12] Harris theorized that Travis's arm could be better utilized at the hot corner. Whereas a shortstop often played in the hole and, thus, had to cleanly field all chances to have time to throw out the batter, at third Travis wouldn't necessarily "have to field a ball cleanly to get the batter out. He can knock down a ground ball, pick it up, and still throw out most runners in this league by plenty with that whip of his."[13]

Harris also planned to further utilize Travis's exceptional arm on cutoff plays from the left side of the outfield — a role usually performed by the shortstop. Pofahl, instead, would Pofahl would cover Travis's vacated post at third base on such plays. Harris said, "With Travis, Pofahl, [Jimmy] Bloodworth and Wasdell we'll have a tight infield that can be brilliant. Our outfield isn't a great one, but it will be fast."[14]

But after the club's poor performance on the mound in 1939, it remained to be seen if the staff would be any better in 1940. An exhibition game with the Kansas City Blues minor league squad on March 19 provided anything but hope; Washington pitchers gave up 23 hits in a humiliating 22–5 loss to the Blues. Kansas City's Jack Saltzgaver struck for three triples and five RBI against Senators pitching.

It seemed that Travis was indeed one of the few things that Harris did not have to worry about, and this was especially true of his new third baseman's hitting stroke. Travis, unlike the rest of the team (which experienced a collective batting slump that spring), tore up "grapefruit league" pitching and even hit for the cycle on March 20 against Cleveland. He collected three-hit games that spring, doing so on March 27 against the team that had almost owned his services, Detroit; again on March 29, when he tallied three of his team's seven hits; and again on August 5 against the Atlanta Crackers. Through 15 spring-training games, he carried a blistering .446 average and appeared poised for a big season.[15] He also was pulling more of his hits to the right side of the field. Staying true to his earlier stance that he would not change his swing, Travis explained:

> Bucky Harris and Mr. Griffith have been trying to get me to pull my hits for three or four years, but I don't bat that way naturally. This year, though, I feel stronger. I'm going to try to bat to right. I'm going to try to pull everything into right field until I get two strikes against me. Then I guess I'll take my hits anywhere I can get them.[16]

The way the 1940 season started for the Senators, the club was happy to take whatever hits Travis rapped out. In the annual season opener at Griffith, the Senators faced off against Boston's 40-year-old ace, Lefty Grove. The game had started on an ominous (though comical) note: As President Roosevelt delivered his traditional first pitch before the game, he cocked, fired, and threw wildly, unintentionally striking the camera of photographer Irving Schlossenberg, Who was attempting to capture the presidential moment for posterity. After the incident, Boston's Grove held the home team hitless through seven innings. In the eighth, Travis broke through with a single off the knee of third baseman Jim Tabor. After yielding another scratch hit to Jimmy Bloodworth, Grove shut down the Washington bats and won a 1–0 decision over Dutch Leonard. Later, Grove would admit, "I was just fogging 'em in there and didn't notice the hits and walks until what's-his-name (Cecil Travis) got that hit off Tabor's knee. [Then] Jimmy said something about it being the first hit."[17] When a teammate asked him if he was disappointed that he lost his no-hitter in the eighth inning, Grove replied: "No ... no-hitters are bad luck."[18] In addition to breaking up Grove's no-hitter, Travis also made a stellar play on Doc Cramer's hard grounder in the seventh inning, which Arch McDonald of the *Post* called "the outstanding fielding performance of the game."[19]

The Senators' bats were equally inept the following day behind newly acquired started Sid Hudson. The Red Sox won its second consecutive shutout, 7–0, behind starter Jim Bagby. Washington scored a total of five runs in its first four games but finally broke out their bats in its April 24 contest in Fenway Park, which Grove started. Travis started things off in the fifth inning with a double of the center field wall, and Jimmy Bloodworth followed with a home run. The Senators scored nine runs in all and notched their first win of the new decade.

Washington returned to sweep two games from the Athletics and then won the first of a three-game series with the Yankees to even its record at 4–4. Travis, continuing his hot hitting from the spring, had jumped out to a torrid pace of .429.[20] By the first weekend of May, he had cooled off only slightly and was hitting .375.[21]

Travis was playing excellent defense in the early season as well, making a number of plays that earned him praise in the Washington dailies. In a game on May 12, he displayed quickness and agility in charging a bunt from Philadelphia second baseman Benny McCoy, bare-handing it and firing to first for the out. The display of quickness and range might have sparked something in the mind of his manager, as Harris started Travis at shortstop the following day. The team had lost 13 of its first 22, and Pofahl, the former American Association hitting star, was slumping against major League pitching. Harris sought to inject some life by shifting Travis, bringing Lewis back to third, shifting George Case to right field and sending Johnny Welaj out to center field; thus, Harris was essentially replacing Pofahl with Welaj, who would hit third in the lineup.

Welaj played immediate dividends, figuring in three of the Nats' runs in Washington's 4–2 victory in Tiger Stadium on May 14. Both Shirley Povich and Arch McDonald praised Travis's play at shortstop; the former said he was "positively sensational in his fielding" and the latter concurred, awarding Travis three points in his "Man of the Month" feature. The next week, Povich suggested that Walter Briggs was "berating himself" for turning down the now-famous York-for-Travis trade.[22] Indeed, while Travis had regained his pre–1939 stroke, Dick Bartell — the shortstop for whom the Tigers *had* traded — would hit .233 for Detroit in 1940. (To be fair, though, York would hit .316 with 33 home runs and 134 that season.)

If Povich, for one, seemed to be quick to tout Travis's talents, he also was fair-handed in citing Travis's errors — often in a humorous manner. On May 20, Travis led off the ninth against Chicago reliever Clint Brown with a single and later stood on third representing the tying run. But Travis missed the sign for the squeeze play, and when George Case laid down a would-be perfect squeeze, Travis remained on third and was ultimately stranded there at game's end. Povich wrote: "Sh-hh! Not so loud. You might arouse Cecil Travis from his deep slumber. When last seen Travis was dozing placidly on third base."[23]

Largely, though, Travis was having a fine season. He rapped out two doubles on May 22 to help Washington triumph in St. Louis, 9–2, and he went two for five the next day in a wild, 12-inning contest with the Browns. In the top of the twelfth, Jimmy Bloodworth put the Senators ahead with a two-run homer, but the Browns struck back against emergency reliever Sid Hudson for three runs in the bottom of the inning to win the game 8–7. Although Travis's average dipped somewhat in May, he still was hitting .350 in the month's final week.[24] And he was still playing out of position. Harris noted:

> I know that Cecil Travis is a better third baseman than Buddy Lewis, and that Travis is out of position at shortstop. But we have to keep Lewis in there on account of his batting. We've been getting more runs in the last two weeks than any Washington club I've had in the last six years. I'm not going to disturb that batting order. It looks too good to me.[25]

As if on cue, Welaj — the player whose presence in the lineup was made possible by Travis's move to short — homered in the tenth inning to beat Philadelphia and complete a two-game series sweep.

Harris would have to change his lineup soon, though, as Travis was hospitalized after suffering yet another spiking in a May 26 game with Philadelphia. This time, the spike injury occurred while Travis covered second on a steal attempt. Travis made a nice play to scoop the throw from catcher Rick Ferrell and held onto the ball as Wally Moses slid into second, spikes first. Travis held onto the ball to retire Moses but received an ugly gash on his left shinbone. He was taken to Georgetown Hospital for treatment. Harris was forced to put Pofahl, hitting just .234, back into the lineup as Travis missed the next 13 games.

Travis returned on June 7 and promptly injected some much-needed offense into the Washington lineup. With the Senators and White Sox tied 1–1 in the seventh, Travis tripled and scored the go-ahead run, and the Nats won 3–2.

Travis cooled off slightly, his average dropping to .329 in mid–June. Meanwhile, the Senators sank into last place after dropping a doubleheader in Tiger Stadium on Jun 15. The following week, Harris shook up the lineup; he moved Lewis back to the outfield, Travis to third, and Charley Gelbert and Buddy Myer at shortstop and second base, respectively. The *Post*, understandably, ran a criticism of Harris:

> Harris has Cecil Travis, a third baseman, playing shortstop.... That's what is the trouble with the Nats— Guys playing out of position — especially after the ball is hit. Harris has only one very flimsy excuse for butchering his infield the way he is doing and it follows: He has no first baseman, no

second baseman, and no third baseman. The only big league infielder on the team is Travis.[26]

But back to third Travis would go, and he would remain there for the remainder of the season.

The team's struggles continued and Washington was in last place at the All-Star break, but Travis's move back to third was fortuitous for the lanky hit specialist. On Saturday before the break, American League president Will Harridge announced that Travis had been named to replace Yankees third baseman Red Rolfe on the All-Star team. Rolfe had been suffering from poor health and was forced to miss the game. In fact, American League manager Joe Cronin surprised many by announcing that Travis would start the game. While the decision was undoubtedly surprising to some, it did make sense considering the other third baseman on the American League roster, Cleveland's Ken Keltner, was hitting just .229 at the break while Travis was hitting a shiny .346 and had hit safely in his last 14 games.[27]

It turned out that Travis would not only start the game but lead off for the American League as well. The leadoff spot was unfamiliar territory for Travis, but this move made some sense, too, as Travis was reaching base even more frequently than he ever had in his career. (He would log a .455 on-base percentage in 1940, a career-best at that point for Travis.) The starting lineups for the All-Star batting order read:

SS Arky Vaughan, Pittsburgh	3B Cecil Travis, Washington
2B Billy Herman, Chicago	LF Ted Williams, Boston
RF Max West, Boston	RF Charlie Keller, New York
1B Johnny Mize, St. Louis	CF Joe DiMaggio, New York
C Ernie Lombardi, Cincinnati	1B Jimmie Foxx, Boston
LF Joe Medwick, Brooklyn	SS Luke Appling, Chicago
3B Cookie Lavagetto, Brooklyn	C Bill Dickey, New York
CF Terry Moore, St. Louis	2B Joe Gordon, New York
P Paul Derringer, Cincinnati	P Red Ruffing, New York

Come game time, Travis and the rest of the AL roster would give fans in St. Louis little to cheer about. Before American League starter Red Ruffing had recorded even one out, the National League went ahead on Max West's three-run homer. National League pitchers Derringer, Bucky Walters, Whit Wyatt, Larry French and Carl Hubbell limited the American League to just three hits—two by Appling and one by pitcher Buck Newsom. Travis went zero for three but had, nevertheless, seen his first at bats in the annual summer classic.

Travis returned to his regular day job in Washington and faced off against the Tigers, who held a slim lead atop the standings in the American League. Although hitless in his first All-Star appearance, Travis extended his regular season hitting streak in by singling to left in his third time up. The Senators won 7–3, temporarily dropping Detroit into second place for a day behind Cleveland. Detroit quickly struck back to sweep a doubleheader the next day. Travis extended his streak to 17 with a two–RBI double in the first game and two hits in the second game.

A groin injury sidelined Travis for the next four games, and Bloodworth filled in at third. Travis was deemed ready to play in the July 18 game against Chicago, but Harris, reportedly "in no mood to break up a winning combination," kept Travis on the bench.[28] But Harris sent Travis to the plate as a pinch hitter for Bloodworth in the eighth inning with a runner on first and Washington trailing Chicago 4–3. Travis roped a single past ex-teammate Joe Kuhel, extending his streak to 18 games. He later scored the eventual winning run on a bases-loaded walk, and Washington extended its season-long winning streak to five games.

Washington promptly lost its next three games, though, and Harris looked to shake things up once again by moving Travis into the cleanup spot for Washington. The decision was ironic, considering the criticism that had dogged Travis throughout much of his career: that he was a fine slap hitter but not a run producer, that he didn't hit in the clutch. Travis responded to the challenge, collecting extra-base hits and leading the team in run production on its road trip while maintaining an average well above .300. He doubled twice in a doubleheader split in Cleveland on July 28; set the tone of a 14-hit attack with a 2-RBI double in the first inning of Washington's 13–5 victory in St. Louis on July 31; tripled in two runs with two outs in the ninth on August 3 in Chicago; and went three for seven in a doubleheader sweep of the White Sox the following day, including a double that scored the winning run in the tenth inning of the first game. Clark Griffith sounded like a proud father in commenting on Travis's performance in the cleanup spot:

> I told that boy three years ago that I'd give him a raise in salary if he'd hit to right field instead of punching the ball to left.... But he didn't seem interested. Now he's beginning to understand that he can hit as well to right and that his long hits are doing the club more good.[29]

At the same time, Travis continued to establish himself as more than capable as a third baseman. During the recent Comiskey Park doubleheader, Travis had "elicited gasp after gasp" from the Chicago crowd with his "spectacular play around third base."[30] The August 6 *Post* observed:

In every city in the West, players and fans were aghast at Travis' clever fielding around third base. He was giving the Nats the best protection at the bag since Ossie Bluege gave up the job five years ago, and his throwing arm has been so spectacular that brilliant throws were commonplace with him."[31]

Later that day, with Washington rookie Sid Hudson was working on a no-hitter in the sixth inning, Travis turned in the play of the day on a one-hand pickup of a grounder by Wally Moses. Hudson ended up with a one-hitter and an 11–0 shutout, one of the rookie's 17 wins that year. Hudson won his next start on August 11, and Travis singled in a key run in the 2–1 decision.

Washington was not a pennant contender in the remainder of the season. The Senators would finish in seventh place with a disappointing record of 64–90. But Travis used the last month and a half of the season to further establish himself as a pull-hitter with some "pop" in his bat. In the team's final game of 1940, he racked up two hits, including a triple, to finish at an excellent mark of .322, eighth-best in the league. More significantly, though, Travis finished with career highs in doubles (37), triples (11), RBI (76), and slugging percentage (.445), while maintaining a very good on-base mark of .381.

No one had better power number, though, than Hank Greenberg — ironically, the player that Briggs had viewed as practically untradeable only months before. Greenberg hit a blistering .340 while pacing the American League with 41 home runs, 150 RBI, and a .670 slugging percentage. More importantly, he led the Tigers in unseating the Yankees for the American League crown. Detroit faced Cincinnati, who repeated as National League champs, in a seven-game classic. Greenberg, nearly a world beater, led his team with a .357 World Series average and tied Reds third baseman Bill Werber with a Series-best 10 hits. But doubles by Mike McCormick and Jimmy Ripple produced a two-run rally in the seventh inning of Game Seven that gave the Reds a one-run win. The city of Cincinnati — home to the first-ever professional baseball team back in 1869 — had its first World Series title.

As the baseball world enjoyed the end of the 1940 season, a greater concern loomed on the world horizon. Germany waged war on Britain from July through October, and the United States inched closer to war by providing aid to its shell-shocked ally. On September 27, Germany, Japan and Italy signed their Tripartite Agreement, unifying as Axis powers. Days later, President Roosevelt ordered all Americans out of the Far East. In his "fireside chat" of December 29, FDR told the nation:

I have the profound conviction that the American people are now determined to put forth a mightier effort than they have ever yet made to increase our production of all the implements of defense, to meet the threat to our democratic faith.

As President of the United States I call for that national effort. I call for it in the name of this nation which we love and honor and which we are privileged and proud to serve. I call upon our people with absolute confidence that our common cause will greatly succeed.

On September 16, Congress had passed the Burke-Wadsworth Selective Service Act. While pundits discussed the effects that a military draft would have on American life, baseball fans wondered how it would affect the rosters of their favorite teams. As the *Post* noted in November, "Sid Hudson, Cecil Travis, Buddy Lewis, Rick Ferrell and dozens of other major league ball players from the South will not be affected by the military draft during the 1941 season ... because voluntary enlistments in most Southern states will exceed the draft quotas."

For Travis, Lewis, and legions of other professional ballplayers, the reality of political events would soon eclipse their baseball lives. But as Travis and his fellow major leaguers followed events from the far corners of the globe, they could not have foreseen the historic season that would play itself out in 1941.

8

First in Hits

The year 1941 would produce a baseball season that fans would talk about for decades. It also saw the unfolding of events across the globe that would forever affect world history. In preparation for possible military action in Europe, the U.S. government had instituted the Selective Service draft in the autumn of 1940. It was the first in the history of peacetime, and all men aged 21 to 35 were required to register for the draft. The draft would enlist 1.4 million Americans for military service. In March, Philadelphia Phillies pitcher Hugh Mulcahy became the first major leaguer drafted. It remained to be seen how many others were destined for military service.

As Washington, D.C., prepared for the possibilities of war, it also prepared for the more enjoyable idea of baseball in the 1941 season. The Washington Senators faced an uphill battle; oddsmakers set their chances at 75:1. What's more, the team seemed especially vulnerable to the draft, which gave single men higher "priority." Three-fourths of the team's projected starting infield — shortstop Cecil Travis, third baseman Buddy Lewis, and second baseman Jimmy Bloodworth — was single, as was Sid Hudson, the team's promising young pitcher. Complicating matters further were rumors that neither Lewis nor Travis was happy with the latest round of musical chairs in the Washington infield. "Mr. Griffith wrote me a letter saying the new plans for 1941 included putting me back on third base, but I don't want to play in the infield," Lewis told the *Post*. "And I won't play third unless I'm forced to." He added: "Cecil wrote me that he doesn't want to play shortstop. He wants to play third base where he says he is happier." Meanwhile, neither player had been offered a raise in salary for the upcoming season despite having been the only Senators regulars to hit over .300 in 1940.[1]

Lewis, who asked for more money as incentive for moving back to third, must have received it. Griffith announced in late February that he and Lewis had agreed upon terms, and that Lewis had telegraphed that he'd be "glad to play anywhere — except on the bench."[2] Two days later, Travis also accepted terms for the upcoming season, ending six weeks of negotiation. It was reported that Griffith had offered him a raise of "at least" $1000 on his 1940 salary of $13,000, making him the team's highest-paid player.[3] Travis arrived in Orlando on the night of February 28 and promptly signed his new contract.

Implicit within the raise that Griffith had granted Travis was his desire that his All-Star infielder would demonstrate more power at the plate. Zeke Bonura had been the team's only 100–RBI man in the previous four seasons, and the team still lacked a true power hitter. Griffith and Bucky Harris wanted to see more run production from Travis's hits.

Both men, then, must have been delighted at what they saw out of Travis in that spring. Travis seemed to get right back into the "swing" of things, collecting three hits in the team's first exhibition game on March 9, a 6–5 victory over the National League's Reds. Travis struck three more hits against the Giants two days later, including — prophetically — a line-drive home run over the Tinker Field fence in right. On March 14, he lined another round-tripper in St. Petersburg against the Cardinals.

In late March, Washington took five straight exhibition games from the defending league champion Detroit Tigers. Travis was instrumental in this pre-season surge. At the Tigers' Lakeland facility on March 23, Travis drilled a line-drive grand slam into right-center. He homered again on April 3, off Detroit's Bob Uhl, blasting what the *Post* described as "the longest home run in the history of Tinker Field's right field history."[4] The shot gave Travis four home runs in the preseason — interestingly, all drives that he had pulled to the right side. The *Post*'s Shirley Povich named the sudden transformation of Travis from "poke hitter into left field to a long distance power hitter into right," as being the "strangest development" of the preseason.[5] Such was Travis's slugging that Harris even began to consider his shortstop for the team's cleanup spot in the lineup.

The sudden show of power was almost shocking considering the source — four preseason round-trippers from a player who had never hit more than five in an entire major league season. His increased hitting muscle was a lesson in physics attributable to three things: a new stance, a new grip, and a new bat. That spring, Travis had moved farther back in the batter's box, giving him a split-second more time to get the bat head out in front of the ball and enabling him to extend his swing farther. "I was more of a late-swing hitter and I waited to hit the ball," Travis would say when reflecting back on his career. "[But] I had to change things around with my swing at times. They start to pitch you different ways after a while.

When they start that, you've got to change around, too."[6] Travis began to stand so far back in the box that some opponents complained that his left foot was out of the batter's box.

With more of an extended swing, Travis also moved his hands down the handle of the bat. He had choked through most of his career to increase his bat control, but in swinging from the knob of the bat, he was able to get more leverage — and thus more power — from his swing. (In keeping with his strategy of staying one step ahead of the league's pitchers, however, he occasionally choked up and went with outside pitches to left field.)

One day during spring training, Travis had picked up teammate Ben Chapman's bat. Chapman used a bat that was 36 inches long and, at 36 ounces, the heaviest in the league. As Travis took some swings with Chapman's model, he decided he liked the feel of it, and the strong-armed infielder was able to swing it with control through the strike zone. (Ironically, at the beginning of his career, management had encouraged Travis to use a lighter bat, apparently theorizing that he was an opposite-field hitter because his bat was too heavy.) He started using the heavier bat in games, and its greater mass of the combined with Travis's greater extension to produce even more force upon impact with the pitch.

Travis and the Senators came home to Griffith Stadium on April 11 to host the Baltimore Orioles in a final preseason game. Only 2,000 fans showed up for the contest. (Up north, nearly 19,000 fans turned out at Ebbets Field to see the Dodgers host the Yankees in an interleague exhibition.) Undaunted by the thousands of empty seats, the Nats routed the Orioles 11–4. Two days later, the *Post* previewed the upcoming season. "These Are the Lads That Will Carry Washington's Hopes Into Another Pennant Race" was the headline of the photo essay that introduced the Nats' starters: right fielder George Case, who Povich had noted "is curbing his habit of starting with the crack of the bat — in the wrong direction"; center fielder Roger Cramer, "perhaps the best bunter in the league" and, known for his handsome looks, "a sure shot to be a ladies day favorite"; left fielder Ben Chapman; third baseman Buddy Lewis, the team's heaviest hitter; shortstop Cecil Travis, "the best hitter on the Washington club.... Shy about everything except going to the plate with a bat in his hand"; second baseman Jimmy Bloodworth, dubbed "the only man on the club who can ride the ball out of any park in the league" yet coming off a lackluster .245 average in 1940; first baseman George Archie, MVP of the Pacific Coast League in '40; veteran catcher Rick Ferrell; and pitcher Dutch Leonard, the team's ace, who had gone 14–19 with a 3.49 ERA the previous season.[7]

Bucky Harris was cautiously optimistic as he looked ahead to the season. "This is a Washington team that I believe I will be proud of. To me it is already transparent that we are improved in every department over last season," he told the *Post*.

"I might be worried about the hitting of this team if it were not for the fact that I have confidence in our pitching. We won't need as many runs to win as other clubs in the league."[8] In addition to Leonard (14–19, 3.49 ERA in '40), the Nats' rotation included Sid Hudson (17–16 4.57), lefty Ken Chase (15–17 3.23), and newcomer Steve Sundra. Washington had acquired Sundra from the Yankees in the off-season. The right-hander had gone 21–11 during four seasons with the Yankees, but he had become unhappy in New York when he was relegated to the bullpen for the 1940 season.

Harris predicted, "I will not be even mildly surprised if we finish in the first division." But in a prophetic juxtaposition, Bloodworth's profile noted: "Off the field, he's a clown. He picks the Nats to win the pennant and he's serious."[9]

Despite the optimism that abounded that early April in the Nats camp, not all bode well for the team. Buddy Lewis, the team's only proven power threat going into the season, had been informed by the North Carolina draft board that he was slated to be inducted into the Army on May 10. When hearing the news, Bucky Harris said: "'Now isn't that just fine. It ought to fix this team up just great. Holy catfish!'"[10] Povich summed up the situation: "On a team that boasted little slug, Lewis was the only guy who fitted the role of cleanup hitter.... The job will flatter whoever gets it when Lewis leaves."[11]

Nevertheless, Povich suggested, "Harris would not be exactly heartbroken if Lewis were suddenly called up for Army duty as he may be. Harris would like to see Lewis' bat in the lineup, but bluntly speaking, he would rather see somebody else playing third base for his ball team."[12] Lewis, a born designated hitter three decades before his time, was an experiment at any position he played. He had had a rough time in the outfield, where he played 112 games, in the 1940 season. Harris' plan to start speedsters Chapman, Cramer and Case in Griffith Stadium's vast outfield would stabilize the Washington outfield dramatically, while moving Lewis to third would at least keep his bat in the lineup until he was drafted. In the case of Lewis' induction, it was speculated that Harris would try a third-base platoon of Bloodworth, who'd seen some action at third the previous season, and Jimmy Pofahl, a promising rookie infielder.

On April 14, some 33,000 fans showed up at Griffith Stadium to see the Yankees and Senators officially open the 1941 major league season. Vice president Henry Wallace and Senators owner Clark Griffith led a parade to center field for the raising of the American flag. Then Nats rookie Arnold Anderson caught the ceremonial first pitch from President Franklin Delano Roosevelt. Roosevelt joked, "I'll probably kill somebody," remembering the previous year's opener, when his ceremonial toss proved errant and smashed the camera of a *Post* photographer.[13] No harm was done that day, however, except to the Senators' pride. New York's Marius Russo tossed a three-hit shutout, and Washington went down 3–0. In fact, the only excitement generated in the nation's capital that day seemed to be the buzz surrounding the upcoming title fight between Joe Louis and Buddy Baer, scheduled to take place at Griffith Stadium on May 23 or 24.

The Nats were slow out of the gate in the early season. On April 17, Washington blew a 7–4 lead against Boston in the ninth inning, dropping their record to 0–3. More discouraging, though, was the news that Travis also appeared to be headed for military service. When he arrived at Griffith Stadium on April 15, he found a postcard from his draft board in Fayetteville, Georgia, informing him of his Class 1-A draft status. Travis was slated for induction in early May.

"Ah'm going," Travis told the *Post*. "Ah don't want to be deferred," he said, alluding to a new Selective Service ruling that allowed for 60-day extensions to men who were labeled Class 1-A and "available for immediate service" but who need time to "straighten out their affairs."[14] It was felt that both Lewis and Travis, who made approximately $1,000 a month and helped support their parents, would be eligible for 60-day extensions to give them the chance to earn the extra two months' salary. Travis was reported to be the highest-paid player on his team, due to make $14,500 for the 1941 season. He gave portions of his baseball income, along with that generated by the farm he owned in Riverdale, Georgia, to help support his father and his mother, who were 80 and 70, respectively. Still, Travis's initial reaction was to ready himself to military service.

Facing the loss of his two best hitters, Bucky Harris commented: "It looks like the United States has declared war on the Washington team.... I wish he'd tell me what I'm going to do about an infield."[15] The *Post* highlighted the growing conflict that was growing in the nation's capital between want for home team pride and the call of a higher duty:

> There isn't another fellow in it who can get runs across the plate or who deserves to hit fourth or fifth on a big league team. The Nats will be a puny outfit when the blow falls. The Devil himself could have conceived

no more diabolical a thrust at the Nats than the selective service draw that turned up the numbers of Lewis and Travis. [16]

Bucky Harris huddled with Clark Griffith to discuss their options in case the team lost Lewis, Travis, or both. In early April the team had been in trade talks with the Yankees regarding Frankie Crosetti. Shirley Povich surmised that Harris and Griffith would revisit talks with the Yankees for the 30-year-old shortstop. Crosetti had been a sparkplug for the Yankees, scoring 486 runs from 1936 to 1939. But in 1940 he had hit only .194 in 546 at bats, and in 1941 he lost the starting job to rookie Phil Rizzuto.

In the meantime, Washington got a glimpse of what life would be like should they lose Travis to the Army. In a game against the Yankees on April 18, Rizzuto spiked Travis as he slid into second base, delivering an ugly gash to Travis's left knee. He was forced to leave the game, with Jimmy Pofahl subbing in. The team announced that the injury was expected to keep Travis out of Washington's lineup for "at least a week."[17] However, Travis missed only two games and was back in action against Boston on April 20, when he collected four straight hits through seven innings against pitcher Jack Wilson. In Travis's fifth at bat, in the ninth inning, only a great play by outfielder Lou Finney kept Travis off the bases. Finney raced into the right-center field gap and made a nice catch to rob Travis of an extra base hit.

Travis jumped out to a rabid pace at the plate that spring. He carried a league-leading .586 average in New York on April 24. The only thing hotter than his bat turned out to be his temperature when he was struck with a case of ptomaine later that evening. After dinner, Travis told Lewis, his roommate, that he wasn't feeling well, and Lewis summoned team trainer Mike Martin. When Martin took Travis's temperature and found it to be 104, he had Travis placed in a doctor's care.[18]

Memories of Travis's illness-plagued 1939 season were still fresh in the minds of the team's management and fans. The Senators lost six of their first nine games and needed Travis to return quickly — and he did. His body still covered by a "bright red rash," Travis returned to the lineup three days later against the Yankees. Remarkably, in his first three at bats, he collected a triple and two doubles, temporarily raising his average to .630. After making outs in his next two at bats, his average fell to a still-remarkable .588. Manager Bucky Harris told Shirley Povich: "Now if that guy would only contract typhoid fever with a bit of triple pneumonia thrown in, he might do us a lot of good yet."[19]

While Travis had been slowed by illness in 1939, in 1941 he quickly shook

off his early-season sickness and continued hitting American League pitching at a feverish pace. On May 1, he was the offensive star in a 7–0 shutout of the White Sox behind winning pitcher Dutch Leonard. In the first
inning, he doubled and then scored the Nats' first run. In his second at
bat, he hit his first home run of the year — a drive into the upper deck in right-
center field. In his third at bat, Travis knocked in Washington's third run of
the game with a sacrifice fly. In the eighth inning, Travis doubled in
the team's fourth run. Povich beamed: "The lanky Georgia boy who is the
league's leading hitter at this point with a .571 average was kind of wonderful today."[20]

Despite his four home runs in Florida, Travis had gone into the season with a reputation as being a slap hitter who hit for average but
who had little power. But through the first month of the season, he had
demonstrated a new penchant for extra-base hits. Half of his hits through
May 2 were for extra bases. Travis told the *Post* that he was using a
bigger bat, and the traditionally lanky player noted he was playing at a
weight of 190 pounds. He also noted that although he had developed
painful blisters from his new grip at the bottom of the bat handle, the
added leverage in his swing was reaping great results as he reinvented himself from a slap hitter into a slugger. In his Georgian drawl, Travis said,
"Ah'm doin' all right thataway.... Ah just walk up there and don't fret
much."[21]

Travis had a knack for hitting any kind of pitch and never bothered
guessing whether a pitcher would throw him a fastball or changeup or curve.
Ossie Bluege, who was coaching third base for the team that season, told
the *Post* that he had alerted Travis a number of times that he could "tip him
off" to what pitches were coming, "but Cece always said 'never mind' — I
don't blame him. If I could hit like Travis, I wouldn't want the signs. They'd
only confuse him, and he's smart enough to know it." An anonymous
pitcher said: "There's no sense trying to outguess that guy, because he's just
a dead-pan up there who doesn't look as if he's thinking of anything. He's
no guess hitter.... If you pitch him inside, he'll pull the ball, and if you try
to pitch him outside, he loves to slap it to left. He hits all kinds of pitching." The same pitcher remembered when his manager once came up with
a plan to fool Travis with changeups: "We almost got killed. Travis banged
so many of those slow balls back through the box for hits that we were
taking our lives in our hands. We refused to throw him any more slow
stuff."[22]

Springtime in Griffith Stadium was quickly turning into the Cecil
Travis Show, starring the sweet-swinging hitter and his newfound power.
In the Nat's 9–7 defeat of the St. Louis Browns on May 3, he hit two home

runs and one double, raising his average to .538. The following day in a loss to the Indians, he slugged his fourth homer of the year, a 400-foot shot over the right field fence. He went two-for-five, which actually dropped his average to .526.

The looming war in Europe was taking its toll on teams throughout the league. The Detroit Tigers, who raised their 1940 American League pennant before their game with the Senators on May 7, took the field for the first time without their star slugger, Hank Greenberg. A day after hitting two homeruns in a 7–4 Tigers win over the Yankees, the 1940 A.L. MVP became Private Greenberg, U. S. Army, the second major leaguer — and the first legitimate star — taken by the draft. Without Greenberg, the Tigers lost to the Nats, 4–2, behind the pitching performance of Sid Hudson. The following day, Travis hit his fifth homer of the year, matching his roundtrip total from the entire 1940 season. The blast came in the fifth inning, when he took left-hander Archie McKain deep into the upper deck in right field. Not forgetting his opposite field stroke, Travis also tripled off the left field wall. The hometown paper lauded its leading star: "Poor Ailing Travis Only Gets Homer, Triple as Average Falls to Mere .459."[23] As the team returned home from a 17-day road trip and prepared to host the Philadelphia A's, Travis's newfound power created a stir around the league.

The Senators had sunk to fourth place by mid–May with a 12–15 record, seven games behind league-leading Cleveland, but one couldn't blame the team's shortstop for its losing record. Travis, who had carried a .322 career batting average into the season, was emerging as one of the premier players in the league. On May 16, the team belted out 18 hits against the Browns, but they trailed by one run when Travis stepped up to the plate in the ninth inning. Travis singled in rookie first baseman Jimmy Vernon to tie the game and later scored the winning run when pinch hitter Johnny Welaj singled him home. The following night, the Senators bashed out 13 more hits as Travis went two for five with two runs and two RBI, leading Washington to a 12–7 win.

Against first-place Cleveland on May 22, Travis clouted two triples and knocked in three runs to erase a 2–0 Indians lead. But Washington squandered the lead when starter Sid Hudson ran out of gas in the ninth, giving up two runs on four hits. Travis made a bid for a third extra-base hit when he led off the ninth and sent a drive into deep center field, but Cleveland's Roy Weatherly tracked down the ball at the base of the Griffith Stadium flagpole, and the Indians held on 4–3. Not even Travis's blistering bat could rescue the Nats from the long days that lie ahead.

Five days after Joe Louis defeated Buddy Baer at Griffith Stadium on a seventh-round disqualification, the era of night baseball came to Griffith Stadium on May 28. The Senators played the Yankees as Washington hosted its first night game ever. Griffith Stadium was equipped with eight light towers that held 740 bulbs, a system that cost $120,000. Pre-game festivities featured Walter "Big Train" Johnson, who threw the ceremonial first pitch. Johnson, the most famous player in club history, was asked to throw the first pitch when Commissioner Kenesaw Mountain Landis was unable to attend. The plan was to have Johnson throw a baseball through an electronic beam of light that was projected over home plate. When the ball broke the beam, it would trigger the stadium lighting. At 8:30, the Hall of Fame pitcher with 3,509 career strikeouts took the mound in the darkened stadium, wound up, threw the baseball — and missed the beam. He threw a second pitch, and again missed his target. Undaunted, the Big Train threw a third pitch and this time broke the beam of light, and the Griffith Stadium lights lit up the night.

In the game itself, the Yankees lit up Sid Hudson as the Nats pitcher again faltered in the late stages of a game. Hudson, who had one-hit the Browns the previous summer in a night game in St. Louis, carried a lead into the eighth inning. But the Yanks struck for five runs, highlighted by George Selkirk's grand slam, and New York won 6–5. It seemed not even the night could hide the Senators' sorry play.

On June 1 the team left D.C. with a 12-game losing streak, mired in seventh place in the American League standings. Team owner Griffith was at a loss of what to do to right his team, especially given the chance that any players he acquired to help the team could soon be drafted: "I'd be willing to borrow the money to buy pitchers and infielders, but I don't want to spend it for players who would only be with us a few weeks," he said. "There isn't any sign that this Army business is going to be for only a year." Griffith, who'd been involved in baseball for 53 years, said he's never seen anything like his team's recent play. Washington had won only one game since trading catcher Rick Ferrell to the Cardinals for pitcher Vern Kennedy on May 15, but Harris maintained the team's new catcher, Jake Early, was not to blame for the team's rough spell. He found the most fault in the Senators pitching staff, telling Shirley Povich:

> I'd have sworn we were going to get good pitching this season. That's what I liked best about this team in the South. But our pitching has been horrible. Dutch Leonard, Steve Sundra and Ken Chase have let us down.

The only man who looks like he might win a game for us soon is Sid Hudson. He's been getting beat because he's been making one bad pitch every game.

Povich observed: "The Nats' manager might have added, with some degree of truth, that there was more stuff on the ball when Early pitched it back to the mound than it had when it came plateward."[24]

The team found its new venue to be a fortunate one. Washington split a double header with the White Sox on June 1, winning the opener 3–2. Travis sparked a three-run rally in the second inning when he stole second, sliding in just ahead of Luke Appling's tag. Starved for good news, the next day's *Post* featured a large photo of Travis sliding into second ahead of Luke Appling's tag, under the headline "Travis' Theft of Second Helps—Nats Break That Awful Streak."[25]

It did not take long for Bucky Harris to abandon his experiment with Buddy Lewis at third base. Lewis missed a number of ground balls at third, as he insisted on stabbing at grounders from the side, rather than getting his body in front of them. Needing to keep Lewis' bat in the lineup while the Washington pitching woes continued, Harris moved Lewis back to right field. At first, Harris tried playing Bloodworth at third, but the infielder failed to produce at the plate and soon found himself benched. Harris then decided to switch Travis to third base, the position he played when he first joined the team back in 1933. Travis made a clean transition to third base, providing stability in the infield while continuing his torrid pace at the plate. Meanwhile, Pofahl was installed at shortstop, with Bloodworth and veteran Buddy Myer sharing time at second.

The retooled Senators lineup produced runs, but the pitching staff gave up more runs more often than not. On June 3, Washington pounded out 12 runs on 20 hits, but they still came out on the losing end of a 14–12 score. In that game, batting clean up, Travis went four for six and scored three runs, but he hit into a double play in the ninth inning when he represented the potential tying run.

The game proved a microcosm of Travis's season. Although his outstanding play could not lift the hapless Nats out of the second division, he was winning recognition throughout the league for his emerging career year. Povich noted that Travis looked to be "a cinch to be named as the third baseman of the American League All-Star team," to be played on July 8 in Detroit. Tigers manager Del Baker asked each of the American League managers to nominate 25 players to represent the junior circuit, the only provision being that they had to name at least one man from each team. (From 1935 to 1946, the manager of the defending league champions selected the entire squad.) Povich commented: "The only Washington player that Bucky Harris can conscientiously select will be Cecil Travis."[26]

On June 10, the Senators began a three-game series in Cleveland with the first-place Indians. Already in dire straits, the team was due to face Bob Feller, hot off a seven-game winning streak during which he had three shutouts. As if that wasn't bleak enough, Feller had pitched an 11-inning shutout against Washington in his last outing against the Nats. True to form, Feller pitched a gem against the Nats, limiting them to four hits and leading the Indians to a 4–1 victory.

In the next game, Lewis, Cramer and Travis went a combined eight for 12, including Cramer's four-for-four effort. Travis went two for three with two RBI, but the Indians won 6–4. Harris quickly became desperate in his search for a solution to the team's losing streak. He considered switching Lewis back to third base and Travis back to shortstop. Lewis' problems in the field had stayed with him as he switched to the outfield, where, the *Post* observed, "he is playing like a third baseman."[27]

Later that week, Lewis was notified by his North Carolina draft board that he had been granted a 60-day deferment until August 11. The Senators slugger said that he would join the Army on the eleventh, even though it was thought that subsequent rulings might entitle him to further deferments. Chicago White Sox pitcher John Rigney had recently made an appeal to President Roosevelt to get a deferment to play until the end of the season. (Rigney, ironically, would later throw out his arm during an exhibition game while in the service.) "[August 11 is] the date then, as far as I'm concerned. I appreciate the deferment I did get. It enabled me to get in most of my 1941 salary — I'll lose only about seven weeks — and they've been very decent to me. I'm not going to ask for anything more."[28]

Meanwhile, it was looking more and more that Travis would not get called before the end of the season. On June 13, the *Post* reported although Travis had been classified 1-A, he had drawn a high draft number and would not be one of the first names selected for service. There was also the possibility of his being eligible for a deferment, as well as new legislation under consideration in Congress that would exempt all men not called up before turning 28. (Travis would turn 28 in August.) Despite Travis's initially discounting a deferral, it was suspected that he might consider taking the 60-day option to help his club and earn the two months' salary for his family.[29]

Regardless of whether or when Lewis and Travis would be going into the Army, their immediate future in the Nats infield became clear when Jimmy Pofahl was suspended from the team. The 24-year-old had compiled a subpar .187 batting average on the season and had been demoted by Clark Griffith to the Chattanooga Lookouts farm team. Despite the fact that the owner claimed he told Pofahl that he would continue to draw the same salary while playing for Chattanooga, Pofahl refused the assignment and left the night of June 14 for his home in Fairbault, Minnesota. "He was doing us little good, and if he chooses to quit baseball, that's all right," said Griffith.[30]

Griffith had planned to send Pofahl to Chattanooga and call up Hillis Layne, who was second in the Southern Association with a .393 average. Unable to send the Lookouts a replacement for Layne, Griffith had to hold off on calling up Layne, so the team had to move Travis back to shortstop. Harris installed George Archie at third. Archie had been the team's first baseman until he had been unseated by Vernon.

Across the Atlantic, the winds of war kept blowing strong. After leading three unsuccessful assaults on the Mediterranean port city of Tobruk, Libya, between April 13 and May 4, Rommel finally scored a victory in mid–June at Halfaya Pass (known as the Battle of Hellfire Pass). Further north, on June 22, Hitler launched Operation Barbarossa against the Soviet Union.[31]

Fifty-four games into the season, Travis had a remarkable .361 average. But even this was well behind that of Boston's Ted Williams, who had jumped out to a mark of .410. In the month of May, Williams hit .436, the third-best calendar month of his career. From May 17 to June 17, Williams built the hottest 30-day string of his career, hitting .477 with 52 hits and 10 home runs.[32] On June 8, Williams' average was .431, and fans began to wonder if he would become the first person to compile a .400 season since Bill Terry hit .401 for the New York Giants in 1931.

As it turned out, though, not even Williams' assault on the .400 mark would be the biggest story of the summer. That distinction would go to Yankees center fielder Joe DiMaggio as he constructed his historic hitting streak. Coincidentally, both Williams and DiMaggio had launched hitting streaks on May 15, though Williams' streak lasted "only" 23 games, ending on June 8. DiMaggio's streak, however, was still going strong at 40 games as the Yankees showed up at Griffith Stadium on June 29 to play a doubleheader. Thirty-one thousand fans showed up to see DiMaggio challenge George Sisler's American League record of 41 games. Suddenly, Travis, playing in comparative obscurity on a losing team in Washington, was not even the most popular player in his home stadium wearing number 5.

In the first game, DiMaggio brought the crowd to its feet in the sixth inning. DiMaggio hit a line-drive double into the left-center field gap off Dutch Leonard, tying Sisler's mark. DiMaggio stood grinning on second base and tipped his hat to the fans, who cheered the new co-holder of the league record. In the second game, DiMaggio flirted early with a hit when he lined a Sid Hudson pitch to the opposite field, but the ball went straight to Cecil Travis at shortstop for an out. The Griffith Stadium crowd, normally in favor of a Nats putout, groaned when Travis retired his numbersake. Still hitless in the seventh inning, DiMaggio faced Anderson, who relieved Hudson. Anderson brushed DiMaggio back with his first pitch, a fast ball high and inside. On the next pitch, DiMaggio hit a low liner into left field to set a new American League record at 42 games. The crowd went wild and went home happy, not caring that the Senators were swept in the doubleheader, 9–4 and 7–5.

DiMaggio took over the headlines of sports pages in cities across the nation that summer. "Italian Star Runs Streak to 44 Games" read a headline in the *Washington Post* on July 2, one day after DiMaggio tied the Major League record with hits in both games of a doubleheader with Boston. (Baltimore Orioles outfielder "Wee" Willie Keller, whose well-known advice to hitters was "Hit 'em where they ain't," had set the record in 1897, when foul balls were not counted as strikes.) In the fifth inning of the first game, DiMaggio cued a bouncer down the third-base line. DiMaggio struggled to get out of the batter's box. Red Sox third baseman Jim Tabor charged the ball but pulled the first baseman off the bag with his throw. From the press box, official scorer Daniel M. Daniel held his forefinger to signal a hit, and the group of fans around him cheered wildly. The majority of the more than 52,000 fans present, however, viewed it as a questionable hit, and they withheld their loudest cheers until one inning later, when DiMaggio came to the plate again and hit a clean single to left field.[33]

In the second game, DiMaggio tied Keller's record with a hard single to right off Sox starter Jack Wilson. The game was delayed two or three minutes as the fans cheered wildly, hugged, and danced in the aisles. As it turned out, DiMaggio was lucky to get his hit early. The second game was called after five innings due to rain and darkness, and the Yankees won the abbreviated game 9–2.

The following night, DiMaggio broke the record in style. In his first at bat against Boston's Dick Newsome, he lined out to Stan Spencer in right-center field. In his second at bat, he hit a long foul drive into the third level of the left field stands, and then grounded out. Then, in the fifth inning, DiMaggio took a 2–1 pitch from Newsome and sent it over the left field wall. The Yankees, surging toward the top of the American League standings, won the game eight to four, and its star center fielder had a major leaguerecord 45-game hitting streak.

As Americans found an exciting diversion in following the Streak, the developing situation in Europe continued to worsen. Hitler's Army Group North, under Marshal Wilhelm Ritter von Leeb, stormed through Lithuania, Latvia, and Estonia, on its way toward a siege of Leningrad. By July 2, the *Luftwaffe* had defeated the Soviet Air Force and captured 150,000 soviet soldiers, 1200 tanks and 600 big guns had been captured. Hitler's forces, advancing into the Soviet territory at a rate of 25 to 30 miles per day, were now headed toward Moscow. [34]

The July 4 edition of the *Post* brought good news to Senators fans. They learned that their star infielder, who was third in the American League with a .364 average, had been granted a 60-day deferment by his draft board in Fayetteville, Georgia. The article reported that, contrary to earlier reports, Travis recently had been informed that his number would be called "within a very few days," and so he had applied for a 90-day deferment, which was "curtailed" to a 60-day deferment.

Travis, then, could turn his attention to the ninth annual All-Star game, scheduled for July 8 at Briggs Stadium, proceeds slated to go to the United Service Organizations. In the midst of a career year, it was no surprise that Del Baker, manager of the defending league champion Detroit Tigers, named Travis to the team. It was somewhat of a surprise, though, that Baker named Travis, who had played most of the season at shortstop, as the team's starting third baseman. But by designating Travis as a third baseman, Baker was able to name Lou Boudreau and Joe Cronin, both shortstops and future Hall of Famers, to the squad.

It was Travis's third All-Star game, his second as a starter. Teammates Sid Hudson and Dutch Leonard joined him on the squad. The starting lineups for the American League features, in order, Boston's Bobby Doerr at second, Travis at third, Joe DiMaggio in center, Ted Williams in left, Cleveland's Jeff Heath in right, Joe Cronin at short, Rudy York at first, catcher Bill Dickey, and starting pitcher Bob Feller. Travis, one of three American Leaguer players (along with DiMaggio and Williams) to play the entire game, performed well in the '41 summer classic. In the top of the third inning, he turned in a sparkling defensive play when he fielded a hard grounder from Bob Elliott's and threw him out at first base. In the bottom of the inning, he came to the plate against the Reds' Paul Derringer and showed off his trademark opposite field stroke by doubling to left center. He then scored the first run of the game when Williams doubled him home.

The National League led 5–3 going into the ninth inning. The Nats shortstop then played a pivotal role in an historic comeback launched by the junior in the bottom of the ninth. With one out, Keltner and Gordon had back-to-back singles. Travis ran the count full and then fouled off three pitches before drawing ball four. DiMaggio followed with a ground ball to shortstop Cookie Lavagetto that looked like a tailor-made double play. The Dodger shortstop fielded the grounder and threw to Herman at second for out number two, but Travis's hard slide into second made Herman step off line and throw wide to first base.

Travis's take-out slide set up one of the most dramatic conclusions in All-Star Game history. Williams stepped to the plate with two outs, men on first and third, and the American League trailing by one run. The National League players huddled on the mound with Chicago Cubs pitcher Claude Passaeu and debated their strategy for pitching to Williams. The previous inning, Passaeu had sent Williams back to the bench on a called third strike. This time, the Cubs right-hander fell behind Williams 2–1. On the next pitch, he delivered a chest-high fastball. Williams swung hard and connected with the fat part of his bat, sending a rocket high and deep into right field. It sailed well over the fence and caromed off the third deck of the Briggs Stadium stands for a three-run homer, winning the game for the American League.

The place erupted. "I've never been so happy," Williams remembered later. "Halfway down first, seeing that ball going out, I stopped running and started leaping and jumping and clapping my hands, and I was so happy I laughed out loud."[35] Columnist Gerry Moore later wrote, "Hardened veterans and more publicized stars like Joe DiMaggio, Bob Feller, Joe Cronin, and Jimmie Foxx were suddenly transformed into boyish hero worshippers while curly-headed Ted slowly trotted his triumphant form in familiar stoop-shouldered fashion, around the bases."[36] American League manager Del Harris surprised onlookers by planting a kiss on the face of Williams. Even the National League's Enos Slaughter was caught up in the moment; the Cardinals outfielder retrieved the home run ball, which had ricocheted back onto the field, and kept it as a souvenir. Years later, Collier's Kyle Crichton called it "a wallop which for altitude, violence, and timeliness has never been bettered by Babe Ruth, Lou Gehrig, Shoeless Joe Jackson, or anybody in the history of the world."[37] Ed Linn later wrote: "It isn't possible to conceive of the Golden Age of baseball without Ted Williams' home run."[38]

While Williams' deservedly went down as the game's hero, Travis's contributions were not lost. He received well-deserved lauds from his hometown paper, which declared him a hero and expressed pride in the "smashing game" played by the Senators' newest star.[39] The final box score for the timeless classic was as follows:

Nationals	AB	R	H	RBI		Americans	AB	R	H	RBI
3b Hack	2	0	1	0		2b Doerr	3	0	0	0
3b Lavagetto	1	0	0	0		2b Gordon	2	1	1	0
lf Moore	5	0	0	1		3b Travis	4	1	1	0
cf Reiser	4	0	0	0		cf J. DiMag	4	3	1	1
1b Mize	4	1	1	0		lf Williams	4	1	2	4
1b McCormick	0	0	0	0		rf Heath	2	0	0	0
rf Nicholson	1	0	0	0		rf D. DiMag	2	0	0	0
rf Elliot	1	0	0	0		ss Cronin	2	0	0	0
rf Slaughter	2	1	1	0		ss Boudreau	2	0	2	1
ss Vaughan	4	2	3	4		1b York	3	0	1	0
ss Miller	0	0	0	0		1b Foxx	1	0	0	0
2b Frey	1	0	1	0		c Dickey	3	0	1	0
2b Herman	3	0	2	0		c Hayes	1	0	0	0
c Owen	1	0	0	0		p Feller	0	0	0	0
c Lopez	1	0	0	0		ph Cullenbine	1	0	0	0
p Danning	0	0	0	0		p Lee	0	0	0	0
ph Ott	1	0	0	0		p Hudson	0	0	0	0
p Derringer	0	0	0	0		ph Keller	1	0	0	0
p Walters	1	1	1	0		p Smith	0	0	0	0
ph Medwick	1	0	0	0		ph Keltner	1	1	1	0
Totals	35	5	10	5		Totals	36	7	11	7

Nationals	IP	H	R	ER	BB	SO
Wyatt	2	0	0	0	1	0
Derringer	2	2	1	1	0	1
Walters	2	3	1	1	2	2
Passeau (L)	2⅔	6	5	5	1	3

Americans	IP	H	R	ER	BB	SO
Feller	3	1	0	0	0	4
Lee	3	4	1	1	0	0
Hudson	1	3	2	2	1	1
Smith (W)	2	2	2	2	0	2[40]

Fresh off their exciting All-Star appearances, Travis, Hudson and Leonard met up with their club in Chicago to face the White Sox on July 10. Washington began the second half of the season 21 games out of first place, with a record of 26–48, losers of their last seven. They extended the losing streak to eight with a 5–1 loss to John Rigney. The one consolation was that Travis, returning All-Star hero, went two for four. It was the nineteenth consecutive game in which Travis had hit safely, a feat obscured, not surprisingly, by DiMaggio's streak, which reached 49 that night when the center fielder singled in the first inning against the St. Louis Browns' John Niggeling.

The next day, DiMaggio again singled in the first inning, extending his streak to 50. He also followed with two more singles and a home run, leading New York to a 6–2 win over the Browns. With the home run, DiMaggio took over the AL lead in home runs (20), RBI (73), and hits (112). The win also extended the team's own winning streak to 11. Meanwhile in Chicago, Travis extended his hitting streak to 20 while the Nats stretched their losing streak to nine games. Travis hit safely in his first two at bats and knocked in the team's only run against White Sox left-hander Ed Smith in a 3–1 loss.

The Nats finally broke through the following night. Dutch Leonard locked up with the Chisox' Buck Ross in a pitcher's duel, which Washington eventually won 5–3. Travis doubled home two runs in his second at bat and later tallied an infield hit, bringing his own streak to 21 games. In St. Louis, DiMaggio doubled in the fourth off the Browns' Bob Muncrief, touching off a game-winning rally and sending his streak to 51 games.

On July 14, Travis went three for four to raise his average to .375 average, third in the league. Despite playing in shadow of DiMaggio's streak, the Nats shortstop was winning acclaim for his stellar season. Rogers Hornsby, the ex–Cardinals second baseman who would be elected to the Hall of Fame in 1942, raved about Travis:

> Now there's a guy who you can tell is a fine hitter by everything he does. He's relaxed and still tough. You gotta be relaxed up there or they make a sucker out of you. They'll run you out of the league if you can hit only a certain kind of pitching. This Travis is always getting a piece of the ball. I'm not surprised he has hit in 24 straight games.[41]

In his daily column, Povich recognized that not only was Travis reaching base with unprecedented consistency, he was also driving in runs like a true clean-up hitter; only Charley Keller, Joe DiMaggio, Rudy York and Ted Williams had more RBI at that point in the season.

While Travis did not yet have the high profile of a DiMaggio, Williams, or Bob Feller, he had earned an unparalleled respect among the league's umpiring crews. Travis carried his soft-spoken demeanor into the batter's box and would not argue questionable calls. So greatly did umpires appreciate the respectful Travis that, as Povich reported, during one recent game in Chicago, umpire Bill Summers *apologized* for calling a strike on Travis on a low ball. "I muffed that one, Cece," said Summers, "and you're the last guy in the league I'd want that to happen to."[42]

On July 17 in Detroit, Travis and the Nats faced a tough pitcher in Dizzy Trout. Trout struck out Travis in the first inning. In the third inning, Trout got Travis to fly out to center. In the fifth inning, Travis made a bid for a hit with a long drive to left field, but the Tigers' Rip Radcliff made an easy catch. In the eighth inning, Travis grounded into a force play at second base. An inning later, the game ended in a 7–1 decision for the Tigers. Travis's hitting streak had been stopped at 24.

Meanwhile in Cleveland, as fans speculated on whether Bob Feller would stop DiMaggio's streak when they would face off the following day, it was a veteran screwballer and a second-generation pitcher who stopped one day before that famed matchup. The Indians sent screwball specialist Al Smith against the Yankees. Against Smith, DiMaggio had one walk and two ground outs, each to third baseman Ken Keltner, who made outstanding plays to retire the Yankee Clipper. Then, in the ninth inning, DiMaggio faced reliever Jim Bagby, whose father starred on the 1920 league champion Indians. Bagby got DiMaggio to ground into a double play, and the Indians won the game 4–3. DiMaggio's historic streak came to an end at 56.

As the 1941 season moved into midsummer, Washington continued their surprising dominance over the defending champion Tigers, from whom they had taken eight of 12 games. The Nats opened up a three-game series against Detroit in Griffith Stadium on July 22. Hudson held the Tigers to eight hits and was aided by four double plays involving Travis. The lanky shortstop also went two for three at the plate, scoring a run and knocking in another.

The Nats won again the following night, this time behind a strong pitching performance by Dutch Leonard in a 6–1 victory. Looking for the series sweep on July 24, the Nats sent Bill Zuber against Detroit ace Hal Newhouser. The Tigers chased Zuber and carried a 5–2 lead into the ninth inning. Newhouser took the mound having allowed only four hits, two to Travis, but six bases on balls. He quickly brought the tying run to bat with walks number seven and eight to Bloodworth and Jake Early, respectively. He struck out pinch hitter Buddy Myer and got George Case to fly out. But Doc Cramer then singled home Bloodworth, and Lewis followed with a walk, bringing up Travis with the bases loaded. On Newhouser's first pitch, Travis hit a sharp single to center field. Both Early and Cramer scored, and when center fielder Tuck Stainback booted the ball, Lewis came all the way around from first with the winning run.

The rally gave the Nats a rare series sweep, and the team's eleventh win in 15 meetings with Detroit. And Travis, whose three hits made up half of the Washington's output off Newhouser, raised his average to .373. The Sunday edition of *The Post* featured a four-photo spread of Travis, under the headline "D.C.'s Favorite Ball Player, Travis, Who Is Maintaining a Lofty .373 Bat Average." Travis is shown kneeling on deck; at bat, hitting a "typical Travis hit — a line-drive single to left center"; toweling off in the locker room after the game; and looking through the refrigerator in his home on Nevada Avenue, where "like all ball players, Travis eats a hearty dinner and insists on [a] late snack."[43]

The 1941 season was featuring some historic individual performances. DiMaggio had shattered the records for hitting steaks in both leagues. Along the way, Williams had actually outhit DiMaggio during those 56 games — .412 to .408 — and at the end of July the "Splendid Splinter" was hitting a robust .410. Meanwhile, Washington's Travis was well on his way to becoming the only player in the majors to break the 200-hit mark that year.

In the first week of August, Travis and the Nats hosted DiMaggio and the Yankees for a two-game series. The teams split the series, with New York winning the first 7–5 and Washington winning the second 4–3. In the latter, Travis once again came to bat in the ninth inning with the chance to be hero. With two outs and the score 7–5 in favor of New York, the bases were filled with Senators as Travis stepped to the plate. But New York relief pitcher Johnny Murphy got Travis to ground out to first base for the game's final out.

On a Labor Day doubleheader in Boston, Travis faced off against the league's other leading MVP candidate, Boston's Ted Williams. Boston took both games, 13–9 and 10–2. Williams went 3 for 6 in the twin bill, raising his average back to .400. Travis went four for nine, lifting his mark to .360 and giving him a league-leading 183 hits on the season.

After the Senators left Fenway Park, the Yankees came to Boston looking to clinch the pennant. On September 4, they beat the Red Sox 6–3 and won their fifth American League title in six years. With the win, the Yanks (now 91–45) held a 20-game lead over second place Chicago, and 20½ games over Boston. It was the earliest in the season an American League team had ever clinched a pennant.

His team long out of the pennant race, Travis nevertheless kept his hit machine rolling. On September 6, he collected five more hits in a doubleheader with the Philadelphia A's. On September 8 his average stood at .363. The *Post* proclaimed: "He is the leaguer's best shortstop, and would probably be the league's best third baseman by an even wider margin."[44] A week later, Travis became the first (and only) player in the league to collect 200 hits in 1941. On September 15, Cecil Travis reached this milestone with a bases-loaded single off Hal Newhouser, and the Nats continued their peculiar mastery of Detroit, with Dutch Leonard recording his seventeenth victory of the year.

Boston's Ted Williams would not collect 200 hits that year because the selective hitter with the unparalleled eye drew 145 walks that season. (Travis walked 52 times in 1941.) But Williams was shooting for a more historic milestone. He had stayed healthily above the .400 mark all summer, but teams had taken to playing drastic defensive shifts against the deadly pull hitter. In the second game of a doubleheader at Griffith Stadium on September 24, Williams was able to just beat out a ground ball to second base as the Nats' Bloodworth was positioned in short right field. The home fans groaned when umpire Bill Grieve made the called Williams safe at first — in a stark contrast to the cheers DiMaggio had drawn during his assault on Sisler's hitting streak.

Williams went into the final day of the regular season on September 28 hitting .3995 — which, rounded up, would have gone down as a .400 average. Some thought Williams would sit out of the season-ending doubleheader against the A's to preserve his average. But Williams played, looking for the clean .400 season. In the first game, he singled, homered, singled, singled, and reached on an error. In the second game, Williams belted a single, ground-rule double, and a fly out to left field. His combined seven-for-nine performance gave him a season average of .406, the highest mark since Rogers Horsby hit .424 in 1924.

On the same day, Sid Hudson shut out the Yankees in New York, 5–0. The win capped a late-season mini-surge for the Senators and gave Washington a share of sixth place along with the St. Louis Browns, both teams finishing 70–84. In that final game, both Travis and DiMaggio went one for four, and Travis finished second in the American League with a sparkling .359 average, just ahead of DiMaggio's .357. Travis's on-base percentage was a lofty .410.

His final hit was his 218th for the season. No American League player would have that many hits in one season until Rod Carew knocked out 239 in 1977, 36 years later. Cleveland's Jeff Heath would finish second in 1941 with 199. (Heath also logged over 20 doubles, triples and home runs—a feat that no American Leaguer would match until George Brett in 1979.) Travis's mark of 218 hits in 152 games played meant that the Senators star had averaged a remarkable 1.43 hits per game. In addition, the player had sloughed off labels of being an unproductive singles hitter by achieving personal bests in doubles (39), triples (19), home runs (7), runs scored (106) and RBI (101) and slugging percentage (.520).

The American League Most Valuable Player voting for the season would go down as one of the most debated in baseball history. In an October poll, 55 percent of *Sporting News* readers said Williams deserved the MVP, with only 26 percent voting for DiMaggio.[45] But in the real vote, DiMaggio won. While Williams was arguably the better hitter, DiMaggio was widely regarded to be the better all-around player. Meanwhile, many baseball writers were all too happy to vote for the professionally enigmatic DiMaggio over Williams, whose cocksure and sometimes surly demeanor had earned him few friends around the league — even on his own team. Povich observed:

> Ted doesn't seem to have contributed any inspiration to the Red Sox in the same manner that DiMag fired up the Yankees. You'll notice they haven't given him any gifts. When DiMaggio was hurt and out of the lineup in Washington a couple of weeks ago, his Yankee pals tossed a party for him in their hotel and gave him something to remember them by, just out of pure goodness and affection for the quiet Italian.[46]

In the final voting, DiMaggio (.357 AVG, 30 HR, 125 RBI) finished first, just ahead of Williams (.406 37 120). Two pitchers, Bob Feller (25 wins, 13 losses, 3.15 ERA) and Chicago's Thornton Lee (22–11, 2.37), finished third and fourth, respectively. DiMaggio's teammate Charley Keller (.298 33 122) finished fifth. Travis, lacking high power numbers and having played on a losing team, finished a distant sixth. Nevertheless, *The Sporting News* recognized his fine season, naming him the best all-around shortstop in the game.

Over in the National League, the Brooklyn Dodgers reached the 100-victory mark but narrowly won the pennant by just 2½ games over the St. Louis Cardinals. The Dodgers' Dolph Camilli won the National League MVP after topping the league in home runs (34) and RBI (120), while teammate Pete Reiser led the league in batting (.343), runs scored (117), total bases (299), slugging percentage (.558) and triples (17). On the mound, All-Star starter Whit Wyatt and Kirby Higbe each won 22 games for Brooklyn, which won its first pennant in 21 years.

The Dodgers met the Yankees in the World Series for the first time in what would become a classic postseason rivalry. The Yanks took two of the first three games. Then, with Brooklyn one strike away from evening the series in Game four, Dodgers catcher Mickey Owen unwittingly became a part of World Series lore. The Yankees trailed 4–3 with two outs and the bases empty in the ninth inning, and Dodgers pitcher Hugh Casey struck out Tommy Henrich. But the pitch deflected off Owen's mit and bounced away as Heinrich reached first safely on the passed ball. The misplay opened the floodgates, as New York went on to score four two-out runs to win 7–4. "Sure, it was my fault," Owen admitted after the game, nearly in tears. "The ball was a low curve that broke down. It hit the edge of my glove and glanced off, but I should have had him out anyway."[47]

The next day, Ernie "Tiny" Bonham threw a four-hitter for the Yankees, and New York took the Series with a 3–1 win. It was the franchise's ninth world championship.

As the Yankees became the nation's top team, Uncle Sam continued to build his roster for the approaching war in Europe. On December 7, the Japanese bombed Pearl Harbor, and the United States declared war on Japan. Four days later, both Germany and Italy declared war on the United States. The nation was at war, and for Travis, hitting baseballs would not be a major concern for many years. Nor would his career ever be the same again.

9

America's Team

On January 7, 1942, Cecil Travis reported to Fort McPherson in Atlanta for his induction physical. *The New York Times* ran a feature on his reporting to camp, with a picture of him being examined by Lieutenant R. H. Gross. Three days later, the *Times* showed Travis, now sworn in as a private in the United States Army, with a wide grin on his face, holding a rifle in his hands, with the caption "Batting Star Trades His Bat For a Rifle."[1] Travis was assigned to the Fifteenth Battalion at Camp Wheeler in Georgia. The colonel on duty shook his hand and greeted him affably: "Well, son, you've finally caught on with a world's championship outfit."[2]

Travis was the latest major league star to leave the game for military service. Soon, with players such as Hank Greenberg going to the Army and Bob Feller going to the Navy, the military would boast a virtual all-star teams within its ranks. Will Harridge, the president of the American League, wrote:

> Looking ahead, I do not believe that the absence of those stars who have answered the call to colors will be in itself a damaging blow to baseball. It is true that fans will miss the performances of such players as Bob Feller, Cecil Travis and Henry Greenberg, to mention just three. But new players will come up, among them many of ability, and baseball fans always have enjoyed watching the progress of newcomers.[3]

Washington was hit especially hard. With Clark Griffith's loss of his two best players, Travis and Lewis, John Kiernan of the *Times* joked grimly, "Now Griff knows that war means suffering."[4] The minor leagues would also lose many players to the draft, and one of Washington's brightest pitching prospects, pitcher Dick Mulligan from the organization's Class B club in Trenton, enlisted in the Army Air Corps that January. As of January 24, the Associated Press reported that "approximately three dozen major leaguers and 300 minor leaguers" had traded baseball uniforms for military ones.[5] The Cubs were the only major league team that had not yet lost a player, while Washington had already lost seven.[6]

Baseball would go on, though for a time even that was up for debate. Some commentators suggested that baseball would be a frivolous concern during a time of war — especially when nationwide rationing would limit the use of raw materials for non-essential activities. On the other hand, a number of respected voices argued for the importance of baseball as a central activity in American life. World War I ace pilot Eddie Rickenbacker said, "When there is no more reason for self-reliance in this country, then and then alone will there be no more reason for baseball." New York mayor Fiorella LaGuardia said that he didn't mind "being rationed on sugar and shoes, but those men in Washington will have to leave our baseball alone." In Washington, Sen. Albert "Happy" Chandler declared: "I'm for winning the war, and for keeping baseball.... We can, and must, do both."[7]

On January 14, Landis wrote Roosevelt, asking him, "What do you want [baseball] to do?" Landis wrote, "If you believe we ought to close down for the duration of the war, we are ready to do so immediately. If you feel we ought to continue, we would be delighted to do so. We await your order."[8]

In what would become known as the "Green Light Letter," the president responded thusly:

January 15, 1942

My dear Judge:

Thank you for yours of January fourteenth. As you will, of course, realize the final decision about the baseball season must rest with you and the Baseball Club owners— so what I am going to say is solely a personal and not an official point of view.

I honestly feel that it would be best for the country to keep baseball going. There will be fewer people unemployed and everybody will work longer hours and harder than ever before.

And that means that they ought to have a chance for recreation and for taking their minds off their work even more than before.

Baseball provides a recreation which does not last over two hours or two hours and a half and which can be got for very little cost. And, incidentally, I hope that night games can be extended because it gives an opportunity to the day shift to see a game occasionally.

As to the players themselves I know you agree with me that individual players who are of active military or naval age should go, without question, into the services. Even if the actual quality if the teams is lowered by the greater use of older players, this will not dampen the popularity of the sport. Of course, if any individual has some particular aptitude in a trade or profession, he ought to serve the Government. That, however, is a matter which I know you can handle with complete justice.

Here is another way of looking at it — if 300 teams use 5,000 or 6,000 players, these players are a definite recreational asset to at least 20,000,000 of their fellow citizens — and that in my judgment is thoroughly worthwhile.
With every best wish,

Very sincerely yours,
[signature] Franklin D. Roosevelt[9]

An interesting subtext to the exchange was the political antipathy between the two men. As Steven Bullock observes, Landis was a staunch conservative and not necessarily welcome in the White House. But Travis's boss, Clark Griffith, had gotten "somewhat close" to Roosevelt during the president's annual visits to Griffith Stadium, and Shirley Povich claimed that Griffith was influential in getting the president — the Senators' most famous fan — to approve the continuation of play.[10]

With the baseball season saved, Whitney Martin of the *Washington Post* pondered a major league season that would not feature many of its brightest stars and most interesting personalities, including Bob Feller, Hank Greenberg, and Ted Williams. Among the players he would miss, Martin cited Cecil Travis, whom he commented was "so quiet nobody knows he's around except the pitchers, who won't miss him too much." (The writer also said that he would miss Moe Berg — who would later reveal he had performed espionage work for the American military — because "in his smooth, confidential manner he would impart off-the-record information which gave you an idea of what was going on behind the scenes.")[11]

As Travis's old team gathered for spring training in Orlando in March, they voiced their dismay at the All-Star's absence. "I'll miss that Cecil Travis," George Case told a group of teammates as they lingered on the sidewalk outside the team's hotel. "Ever since I came into the league four years ago, Travis was my warm-up partner before every game." Bucky Harris added: "You'll miss Travis? How about me? Ever since I came back to Washington eight years ago, my best ball player was Travis. You can get yourself another warm-up partner but where am I going to get a guy who will hit .357 for me?"[12]

In early February, the major leagues decided to play not one but two All-Star games in the 1942 season, with proceeds going into a fund that would purchase bats, balls, and other baseball equipment to be used by members of the armed services. Major League Baseball hoped to raise $500,000 toward this goal. One proposal suggested an exhibition match to be played between major league All-Stars and a team of military All-Stars, but this was rejected.[13]

This did not rule out individual major league teams, facing service squads. With former major leaguers joining recreational teams at their military camps, the major league exhibition season provided ideal opportunities for such matchups. Leo Durocher's Brooklyn Dodgers went down to Georgia in early April to face Travis's new team, the Camp Wheeler Spokes. The Wheeler squad also featured three minor leaguers: Claude Corbitt, a shortstop from the Montreal Royals who had been slated to play with the Dodgers in '42; John Haley, a pitcher with the Kansas City Blues, and Tony Sabol, an infielder from Toronto.

On April 3, more than 10,000 soldiers watched the Dodgers beat the Spokes 7–5. Travis hit fifth and played third base, going zero-for-four while knocking in a run. The Dodgers started the game with staff ace Whit Wyatt. Although Brooklyn emerged victorious, the Wheeler team played respectably against the defending National League champs. The *Times* observed, "You couldn't convince any [spectators] that the Dodgers weren't lucky the contest didn't turn the other way."[14]

The drive to raise funds for armed services gave Negro League players an opportunity that they were otherwise denied — the chance to play against white players from the major leagues. Black players had been effectively banned from playing in the major leagues since the nineteenth century. Furthermore, commissioner Kenesaw Mountain Landis had banned the play of games between black teams and major league teams. But Landis softened slightly during the war and ruled that black teams could face "All-Star" teams of major leaguers, thought he limited the number of players that any one team could contribute to such contests.

As Brad Snyder notes in *Beyond the Shadows of the Senators*, Negro League teams relished the opportunity to prove themselves equal to major leaguers and gave their all in such situations. When both pitchers had been in their primes, Satchel Paige had triumphed over Dizzy Dean in exhibition matchups, and in 1934, Paige and the Pittsburgh Crawfords had taken three straight games from a team featuring Dean and members of the world champion St. Louis Cardinals. According to John Holway, teams of black players went 89–67 (with one tie) against major leaguers. Buck O'Neil explained: "We won the majority of those games — not because we were better. The major league ballplayers couldn't afford to twist an ankle.... We wanted to prove that major leaguers were not superior, and that Negro Leaguers were not inferior. So we'd stretch that single into a double."[15]

In May, Dean invited Travis, along with Zeke Bonura (who was stationed at Camp Shelby in Mississippi), to play with the Dizzy Dean All-Stars, against Satchel Paige and the Kansas City Monarchs at Wrigley Field on May 24. Proceeds from the game would go to the Navy Relief Fund. Dean, who had retired after the 1941 season, had been a star pitcher for the St. Louis Cardinals. During his first five seasons in St. Louis, Dean averaged 24 wins per season. In 1934, Dean won 30 games and led the storied Gas House Gang to a World Championship. In the 1937 All-Star game, a line drive off the bat of Earl Averill broke Dean's left big toe; his altered pitching mechanics led to a sore arm, and he would never again reach double figures in wins. In 1942, he was employed as a radio announcer for St. Louis while also spending time on the barnstorming circuit with a ragtag "All-Star" fleet.

Leroy Robert "Satchel" Paige was another legend that brought a marquee name to the exhibition. Paige had been a star in the Negro Leagues since 1927. In 1932, he had started 23 games for the Pittsburgh Crawfords, finishing 19 of them, and had led the league in wins (14) and strikeouts (109). Paige's talents on the mound were surpassed only by his showmanship and charisma. He named his pitches— the bat dodger, jump ball, hesitation pitch, Long Tom, the trouble ball, midnight rider, the four-day creeper — and taunted opposing hitters. He knew how to rise to the occasion, and in one 1934 exhibition game, he struck out the great Rogers Hornsby five times.[16]

An announced crowd of 29,775 watched the Dean All-Stars take on the Monarchs. Dizzy Dean started on the mound but pitched only one inning and was relieved by John Grodzicki, formerly of Columbus of the American Association. (Bob Feller had planned to be on hand to play but wired to say that he had been ordered to duty at Newport, Rhode Island.) Paige, whose durability was the stuff of folk legends, pitched seven innings. Kansas City outhit Dean's team 11–3 and won the game 3–1.[17]

Days before the game at Wrigley, Cumberland "Cum" Posey, owner of the Washington-Homestead Grays, announced the "completion of arrangements for Cecil Travis day" on May 31 at Griffith Stadium, when the Grays would face Dean's All-Stars. Feller reportedly would be on hand for this matchup, as would Paige.[18] Paige's popularity, due in part to a number of magazine stories that had profiled the pitcher and his legend, was phenomenal. He would regularly draw 20,000 fans in every city he pitched, and the Monarchs even loaned him out to other Negro League teams. As Buck O'Neil told Brad Snyder, "If Memphis needed to make a payroll, Satchel would pitch three innings for them."[19]

Private Travis secured a seven-day furlough from Camp Wheeler in order to face Paige at Griffith Stadium. In the days before the game, he went fishing with friends on Chesapeake Bay. Travis attended a Senators game to root for his old teammates and in the third inning drew an enthusiastic ovation from the home crowd when he was introduced by the public address system. He was also awarded a gold watch by the *Times-Herald* for being the Senators' best player in 1941.

Travis told *The Washington Post* that he could step right back into a major league lineup, but he told another source that "his timing was so off that he would be lucky to hit .100 in the majors."[20] He spoke about Paige, who was officially 34 but quite possibly much older. "He's powerful smart, and he's got good motion. He don't give you anything good to hit, and he gets hep to a batter's weakness quick." Of Dean, Travis said, "That ole Diz has got all the heart in the world, and still gives the fans a great run for their money."[21] Paige himself was characteristically blowing his own horn in anticipation of his rematch with the Dean All-Stars: "I was born with control and my fast one was working wonders for me against the All-Stars. It'll be doing the same in Washington on Sunday. This time I'll shut 'em out."[22]

In addition to Paige, the Grays would field six .300 hitters, including Buck Leonard and the great Josh Gibson. The game was eagerly anticipated in Washington, which was the Grays' home away from home. Since 1940, the Grays had played "home" games in Griffith Stadium while the Senators were on road trips, and the two teams had an intertwined relationship. Griffith allowed the Grays to play exhibition games at Tinker Field in Orlando, and Griffith also purchased batting equipment for the Grays:

> Buck Leonard recalled that if the Senators were ordering 800 bats, they would order an additional 100 for the Grays. Each Grays player, according to historian Donn Rogosin, found a Senator who used the same type of equipment: "Buck Leonard, a lifetime .355 hitter in the Negro Leagues, used Len Okrie's bat. Okrie batted a lifetime .218." Griffith's clubhouse man also purchased uniforms that said "Grays" rather than "Senators." The easiest way to spot a rookie or seldom-used member of the Grays was to look at his uniform — if the front of the uniform said "Grays," he was an integral member of the team; if the uniform had only a *W* on the left front, then the player never made it into league games because he was wearing an old Senators uniform.[23]

Grays players wanted the chance to face their fellow Griffith Stadium mates between the white lines of the diamond. But Clark Griffith refused to let his two teams meet. Grays pitchers Edsall Walker said, "We challenged them, but they wouldn't play us. They'd say, 'Hey, we ain't got nothing to win. If we beat you, that's what we're supposed to do. But suppose we lose?'"[24] Not surprisingly, the Grays were given little press coverage at

Travis (left, in his Camp Wheeler uniform), Dizzy Dean, and Satchel Paige participated in an historic exhibition game at Griffith Stadium on May 31, 1942. Paige's
striking out Travis was considered a triumph for black players and fans during seg-
regation. (National Baseball Hall of Fame Library, Cooperstown, N.Y.)

the time. (Even Travis would confess nearly 60 years later that, at the time,
he did not even know the Grays had played games at Griffith Stadium during Nats road games.) Poignantly, although the Grays were the *de facto*
home team for the game, they were given the visitors' locker room for the
game.

Dean's squad was, in truth, a far cry from the Washington Senators.

Most of the team wore "wretched, ragged uniforms with meaningless Ls" on their jerseys, the Ls standing for Lloyd Athletic Club, a sandlot team from Chester, Pennsylvania. The team's garb was somewhat fitting, as they were made up of sandlot players and career minor leaguers. Travis, who wore his Camp Wheeler baseball uniform, stood out as the team's one shining star. Despite the dubious level of Dean's "all-stars," the chance to face the Senators' best player offered an intriguing matchup for the Grays.

Nearly 10,000 people waited in the oppressive heat to get tickets. The mixed crowd of blacks and whites spilled from the Griffith Stadium promenade onto Seventh Street. Ticket windows opened at 11:00 A.M., but about 3,000 people were still waiting for tickets when the game began at 2:00 P.M. Black fans, who usually sat in the right field pavilion for Senators games, had purchased all those seats, and only bleachers seats were left for the late-arriving fans. According to the black newspaper *Afro*, scalpers were selling grandstand seats for $3.30 — almost three times face value.[25] Griffith called for additional police protection when ticket seekers began to get restless and even broke three windows in the clubhouse. According to newspaper coverage, though, only one fan had to be arrested for creating a disturbance. The last of the paying crowd of 22,000 — reportedly the largest non-major league crowd in Griffith Stadium history — did not file into the stadium until the fourth inning.

Dean gave up two runs and three hits to give the Grays an early lead. In the second inning, Travis stepped in the box for his first appearance against Paige. Paige delivered an offering, a curveball, and Travis sent it back up the middle for a single. Paige, who was notoriously bad in remembering the names of opposing players — and could remember hitters' batting stances but not their faces — would have to be told on the bench by Buck Leonard that it was Travis who had singled up the box. "So Cecil Travis got a single, eh?" Paige said. "He took advantage of that slow curve — it came right past me, too; could have knocked it down but was afraid I might have hurt my hand or something."[26]

Travis was stranded on first, and Paige — who pitched five innings that day instead of the usual three that he did in such exhibitions—carried a 2–0 lead into the fifth inning. Travis came to bat with Claude Corbitt standing on second base. Travis worked the count to three and one. Paige then threw an inside fastball, and Travis swung and missed. Paige's payoff delivery was another inside fastball, this time high in the zone. Travis swung and missed — Paige had struck out the Senators star.

The Griffith Stadium crowd — and especially the denizens of the right field pavilion — roared in recognition of the matchup they had just witnessed.

Francis Stann of the *Washington Evening Star*, displaying a touch of racial insensitivity common to many at the time, wrote:

> One had to go back nearly 18 years to find a parallel for the reaction ... back to that October afternoon when Earl McNeely's grounder hit a pebble and won Washington's first and only world championship. Negro blades in zoot suits stood and filled the air with "yippe," "yay," and "yea boy, yo' got 'im!" Darkies did flip-flops, those sitting close enough to vault over the low wall only the field. Strangers banged each other across sweaty backs.[27]

Back on the bench, Paige, who struck out seven batters in five innings, said Travis "went for two bad balls, fast ones inside, up against him." He also observed Travis "wasn't ready and steady—tried to make his mind too quick, at the last second. [One wonders if Travis was simply reverting to his natural, late-swinging technique.] He would have walked if he had looked at the last one." Later, Travis said, "I haven't seen good pitching in a long time.... I'm way off my timing. But Paige looked good to me. They say he's been pitching 17 years. I don't doubt [that] he was real good a few years ago."[28] Paige showed no doubt in his own abilities. Paige, the ultimate showman, proclaimed to the press that he could beat the Grays if he had Dean's All-Stars behind him. Later, though, he confessed to Wendell Smith of *The Pittsburgh Courier* on the train back to Pittsburgh that his best days were behind him.[29]

Both Paige and Travis left the game after five innings. In the end, the historical significance of the Paige-Travis surpassed its game's level of play, as the Grays rolled past Dean's team 8–1. But in contrast to most Grays games played at Griffith, which normally received minimal coverage, the May 31 exhibition attracted great interest in the local dailies and also the regional black papers. Along with a story on the game, *The Washington Post* featured a standalone photo of Travis as he was forced out a second base following his single.[30] Wendell Smith wrote:

> It was a great day for Washington's baseball fandom. They saw the great "Satch" at his best. They saw him uncork his blazing fastball and "blow" it past Cecil Travis in the only "test duel" of the game. They saw the Grays blast Dizzy Dean to the showers and make some of the most amazing catches ever pulled in this American league ball orchard.[31]

Art Carter wrote, "Satchel Paige is the Joe Louis of baseball. Perhaps it is more proper to say Joe Louis is the Satchel Paige of boxing, for Old Satch was tossing 'em plateward long before Joe cut his first wisdom tooth."[32] (Louis had defeated Baer in a heavyweight bout at Griffith the previous year.) Snyder summarizes that, although the Paige-Travis square-off recalled the Louis-Baer bout, it was even more significant because

> Griffith's refusal to hire black players suggested that black teams such as the Grays were inferior to white teams such as the Senators, that a Paige or a Gibson lacked the requisite skill to play on the same team as a Travis.... By striking out Travis, Paige refuted any notions of inferiority and gave people hope that the integration of baseball, as Griffith had prophesied in 1937, was not far off.

Robert McNeill, a black photographer who took a picture of Travis, Dean, and Paige before the game, recalled the jubilation of the black fans, who felt a sense of pride when their Negro League heroes showed that they could play as well as white players: "Even though they didn't feel that blacks would ever play in the [major] leagues, they sort of smugly got satisfaction out of knowing that this may be possible."[33]

Decades later, Travis, who like Paige had received "a few hundred dollars" plus travel expenses (though sans personal trainer) for playing with Dean's All-Stars, did not remember many details about the Grays. But he was notably impressed. "They didn't get too much publicity," he said. "They deserved a lot, but they didn't get it."[34]

They also would not get a second crack at Travis— or any of the other Senators. In June, *Tribune* sports editor Joe Sewell proposed that the Senators host the Grays for benefit game in the name of the Army and Navy Relief Funds. On June 19, Griffith replied that Major League Baseball had already staged a number of benefit games for the war effort, and he wrote, "It is my opinion that Negro organized baseball should step out in a program of its own to further the interest of war relief activities."[35] Even if Griffith had been in favor of such exhibition play, his good friend Judge Landis would not have been. Ric Roberts of the *Pittsburgh Courier* suggested that Landis even went as far as convincing Navy officials to deny Feller leave for the game. And Art Carter observed that the commissioner quashed plans for a third benefit game, scheduled for June 6 in Indianapolis, by convincing the army to pass a regulation forbidding its former baseball players from participating in such exhibitions; in addition to Travis, the law affected several members of Dean's All-Stars who were stationed at Jefferson Barracks in Missouri. Carter concluded: "Landis dislikes seeing those exhibitions outdrawing his major league teams."[36] (Indeed, the Travisless Senators had drawn only 5,000 fans to a Griffith Stadium night game on June 3 with the St. Louis Browns, just days after the sold-out exhibition between the Grays and Dean's All-Stars)[37] As Holway notes, "The Grays never received their showdown with the Senators; they settled for Cecil Travis."[38]

After the game, Private Travis returned to duty at Camp Wheeler. He would miss the Clark C. Griffith Testimonial Luncheon to be held at the Mayflower Hotel at June 10, but just before the May 31 game he gave an unidentified friend $2.50 with which to purchase a ticket for the luncheon and instructed said friend to give the ticket to a serviceman. Travis spoke flatteringly of his owner in words that exude more than simple "office" politeness. "Mr. Griffith has done everything for me a father could," he told the *Post*, "and he's treated me more like a son than a soldier, or a ball player, since I've been here this time. I'm sorry I can't be here for his luncheon and show how much I think of him."[39]

Travis's affection for Griffith was interesting given the Old Fox's reputation for being tight-fisted. Asked about Griffith in a 1991 interview, Travis said:

> Well, yeah, he had to be [tight-fisted]. He didn't have the money to throw away like they do now. In other words, he ran it as a *business*. In other words ... he couldn't pay salaries if you couldn't draw. That's how they got their money. They get that from TV now.... Yeah, he was tough. You had to produce. You had to produce and have one good year after another, and if you got any kind of raise at all, you were paid for the year back, no paying ahead of time like they get now. You get paid for the last year. If you had a good year, you might get a little raise. If you had a bad year, I guarantee you, you're going the other way.... He was tough ... I mean I liked him, but he was tough. I think he was generous enough for what he was, you know, the money he was taking in, and he helped around in Washington you know giving money and things that way. As far as I'm concerned he was a great fella. Shoot, many times I was invited out to his home and things. I guarantee you he would talk to you. He would call you up in his office ... chat with you and different things [about baseball]. He was there every game. He knew what was going on. I liked him. As far as I'm concerned, he was all right.[40]

Although Travis had to leave Washington behind once again, he would be back on the diamond soon enough. Lieutenant Mickey Cochrane, a Hall of Fame catcher and manager of the 1935 World Champion Detroit Tigers, was appointed to manage a team of service all-stars that would participate in an expanded version of the annual All-Star classic; one day after the July 6 All-Star Game, the Service All-Stars would face the winner from the previous day's contest. Cochrane named Travis to the team, along with fellow Army ex–major leaguers Hank Greenberg, Buddy Lewis, Ken Sylvestri, Hugh Mulcahy, Mickey Harris, John Grodzicki, Emmet Mueller, Johnny Berardino, Johnny Strum, Sam Chapman, Pat Mullin, Morrie Arnovich, and Joe Marty; and from the Navy, Bob Feller, Frank

Pytlak, Vinnie Smith, John Rigney, Fred Hutchinson, Benny McCoy, John Lucadello, Don Padgett, and Joe Grace.

Cochrane, taking his new job seriously, asked that his hand-picked All-Stars be given leave to report to the Great Lakes Naval Training Station 10 days before the game for practice. Feller, denied participation in the May 31 All-Star exhibition at Griffith, also looked forward to the game. He even announced his plans to debut a new pitch on which he'd been working. "I guess it came to me one night in my sleep," he explained to *The New York Times*. Feller called his new pitch a "slider" because of how it "slides from right to left just before it hits the plate."[41]

Travis was granted leave for his latest all-star duties and made the trip to Michigan. On the nation's 166th birthday and the first Independence Day of World War Two America, he and several other Army men played for Cochrane's base team, the Great Lakes Sailors, against a team from the Flint Amateur Baseball Federation. Travis struck a triple, as did Pat Mullin, hometown favorite as a former Detroit Tiger. Former A's outfielder Sam Chapman knocked a 400-foot home run and Russ Meers (who pitched for the White Sox before and after the war) threw a six-hitter to beat the Flint team 8–2.[42]

Travis (second from left) was a member of the 76th Division baseball team and faced other military teams in the northern Midwest, such as the vaunted Great Lakes squad.

Two days late at the Polo Grounds, the major league All-Stars faced off. Home runs by Lou Boudreau and Rudy York of the American League and Mickey Owen of the National League accounted for all the scoring in the 3–1 victory for the junior circuit. As a reward for their triumph, the American League All-Stars won tickets to Cleveland to face the Service All-Stars the following day. As with the May 31 Griffith Stadium exhibition, the game in Cleveland was notable more in billing than its excitement. The American Leaguers shutout the servicemen 5–0, although Travis did reach base on a double and a walk. Feller, having not yet perfected his new pitch, was touched up for three runs in the first inning; the *Los Angeles Times* said he looked "gaunt and 10 pounds under his pre-enlistment weight."[43] Ted Williams and Joe DiMaggio, two players not yet inducted into the military, contributed to the American League victory.

Travis returned to Wheeler, where he continued to play for the camp's team. During a pregame practice on August 13, Travis suffered a baseball injury that could only happen during wartime; he collided with a barbed-wire fence while chasing a pop foul and cut his face badly. A laceration under his jaw required six stitches, and the one around his right eye, five. But the freak injury did not keep him from joining the Wheeler team in a trip to Wichita, Kansas, for the national semi-pro tournament. In a game on August 18 against the entrant from Milwaukee, Travis drove in two runs and scored one to help his team to a 7–2 victory.[44]

Because of the enormous popularity of baseball at this time, and its perceived value in maintaining morale and physical stamina, major league servicemen such as Travis were afforded the opportunity to keep playing the game they loved throughout the war. One side benefit, it seemed, was that these players would stay in shape and thus be able to return to the majors after the war. Indeed, Travis played about 50 games a year on military diamonds from 1942 to 1944.[45] But some questioned how smoothly the postwar transition would be for professional ballplayers. Of the player returning from military service, Shirley Povich felt that such players as Ted Williams and Cecil Travis "could pass out of the big league picture if the war did not end within two years. A layoff of that length from baseball is virtually insurmountable. Their batting reflexes, honed to a fine edge when they were playing regularly, could be dulled to a point that wouldn't permit them to hit .250." He also suggested that the physical nature in military training could, in fact, be a detriment to a player's baseball physique. The player returning from way "may come out of the service bigger, stronger, tougher and withal a better physical specimen, but his new brawn won't help him to get his job back. In fact, it will probably be a distinct handicap." He recalled seeing Hank Greenberg playing in an exhibition game after 11 months of service time. After hitting three modest singles, the 1941 MVP commented that he was swinging as hard as he could but unable to drive the ball in the manner to which he was accustomed. Greenberg noted that although he had become more muscular during his military training and service, being "better off physically" could work against returning ballplayers after the war:

> I've got different kind of muscles, not the kind ballplayers need. I'm bigger around the chest from the work and training I've had, and that interferes with your swing. Honest, I couldn't bring my bat around today with anything like the snap I used to have.... Another year of this [and] I'm resigned to the end of my baseball career.[46]

If Travis's baseball future was up in the air in 1942, his personal life was just starting to take shape. In late August while playing in the Wichita tournament, Travis told his teammates that he was engaged to be married to Helen Hubbard, the daughter of Mr. and Mrs. Howard Hubbard. The couple planned a short engagement; the wedding was scheduled to take place on September 12 in Helen's hometown of Atlanta. When Travis returned to the Senators lineup, the papers would no longer be able to advertise him as single to the team's female admirers.[47]

In February of 1943, Travis was reunited briefly with Buddy Lewis, who was commissioned as a second lieutenant in the Air Force, when Travis got leave to visit Lewis at nearby Fort Benning. Travis, a buck private, had to give his old teammate and roommate a salute. "I brought it up sharply," Travis later said, "and then to get even with Buddy I slapped him on the back."[48]

Lewis had become fascinated with flying ever since taking a plane from his home state of North Carolina to Florida for spring training the year before. Fearing injury to his player in a plane accident, Clark Griffith had threatened to fine Lewis if the third baseman got back into an airplane. But Lewis had caught the flying bug, and he began to take flying lessons—unbeknownst to anyone except his roommate, Travis. Lewis became so adept at flying planes that he was assigned to the Air Commandos during the war. During the war, he would pilot a C-47 plane, a glider without weapon mounts, while transporting British-Indian troops into Burma, behind Japanese lines. In an affectionate taunt of Griffith, he christened his plane *The Old Fox*.

Soon, Travis himself began to ascend the ranks. He was promoted to corporal in March — and he was named manager of the Fort Benning Army team, for which he played shortstop and batted cleanup.[49] Later that spring, he was promoted to sergeant. And that summer, he became a father for the first time when Helen gave birth to Cecil Anthony Travis on July 4. Cecil, Jr., would be the first of three children for the Travis family.

In 1944, Travis was reassigned to Camp McCoy in Wisconsin. There, Travis became part of the 76th Infantry Division, nicknamed the "Onaway" division, after a rally cry once used by the Chippewa tribe that had once hunted in those parts.

As in Wheeler, Camp McCoy formed a baseball team, and Travis manned third base for the squad as it faced semipro and military teams throughout the region, including Cochrane's vaunted Great Lakes boys. Joining Travis on the McCoy diamond were second baseman "Bama" Roswell, who played six years in the majors as a utility infielder with the Braves and Phillies; pitcher Bill Cox, who played for both the former White Sox and Browns; and a number of prospects from the minor leagues. The team won 25 of its first 27 games, and the play of both Travis and Roswell stood out for McCoy as they won the Wisconsin state championship in the summer of 1944. Scouts described the McCoy nine as "a team any big league club would like to field."[50]

Meanwhile, Uncle Sam was planning to deploy the larger McCoy "team" into the larger and more dangerous fields of the European theater.

Elmer Gedeon, an outfielder who had played briefly with Travis as a member of the 1939 Washington Senators, had joined the Army Air Force before the 1941 season. Gedeon, like Buddy Lewis, had wanted to be a pilot. During his training, Gedeon and seven other servicemen were in a bomber that crashed during takeoff. Two of the crew perished. Gedeon got out of the plane safely but then reentered the plane to save a fellow crewmember who had suffered a broken leg and back. Gedeon suffered severe burns and three broken ribs but succeeded in saving his friend and himself. He was awarded the Soldier's Medal for his bravery.

After Gedeon's recovery, he completed his training and participated in bombing raids over France. In April 1944, German antiaircraft fire shot down his plane over St. Pol, France. Gedeon was killed in the crash, the first former major leaguer to die in World War II.[51]

10

World Champs

In Camp McCoy, Travis trained as part of the 76th Infantry Division. The 76th, which had been formed one month before the Bolshevik Revolution in 1917, had been the first National Army division to be drawn from civilian ranks. Also known as the Onaway Division — after a battle cry of the indigenous Chippewa tribe — it was first deployed in battle in the summer of 1918, near Bourges, France, and was deactivated in May 1919. It was reactivated on June 15, 1942, with an eye toward active duty in the Second World War.

In 1944, Travis and the rest of the 76th trained in the hills of Wisconsin, learning how to use special equipment for winter combat: skis, snowshoes, toboggans, snow tractors, snow goggles, winter camouflage suits, Eskimo parkas, arctic sleeping bags, individual stoves and cooking equipment, and more. Soldiers' rucksacks could weigh up to 90 pounds, and sometimes soldiers would sweat underneath them even in the dead cold. Veterans of combat in the African and the Pacific theaters trained the division. Finally, the announcement came: the 76th was going to war.

On Armistice Day, division units began to take trains to Boston, and in stages between Thanksgiving Day and December 10, troops sailed from Boston to Southampton, England. The 76th went to the resort town of Bournemouth, where they were housed in the same barracks as soldiers who had, decades before, crossed the English Channel to fight Napoleon at Waterloo. In exploring Bournemouth and the surrounding towns, American soldiers experienced local sites and customs such as warm beer at pubs, tea and scones at 4:30, the traffic of cyclists down Christchurch Road. In London they found such famous sites as London's Old Curiosity Shop, immortalized by Charles Dickens, and Piccadilly Circus. A local movie theater was showing Michael Curtiz's *Janie*, a screwball comedy about American teenage life. Local girls, the soldiers discovered, had taken to sweaters and the jitterbug just like the American bobby-soxers back home. English children followed the soldiers around as if they were Pied Pipers and asked them, "Any gum, chum?" Fittingly for a unit that included the gentlemanly Travis, the division earned a reputation among the English citizens as being well-behaved guests. The Office of the Commanding General issued a commendation to the unit for doing "little or no damage" to the requisitioned buildings and British Barracks Stores and leaving them in "highly satisfactory condition."[1]

There would be little time for sight-seeing in England for Travis and his mates. In late December, the 76th spent several days evacuating Bournemouth en route to the ports of Southampton, Portland and Weymouth, from where they would travel across the Channel into France. The English winter was bitter, and the troops had to maneuver over icy roads and march through snow to make it to their points of embarkation.

The channel crossing was conducted covertly, and no troops were lost to enemy attacks. Onaway landed in Le Havre, France, on January 12. There were no docks, so the troops landed in LSTs and then waded on shore. Travis and company proceeded inland on foot from Le Havre to the town of Limesy. Many of the men slept in open fields without bedding or shelter from the snow or wind. Onaway established headquarters in Limesy, and troops were quarters in nearby small towns. From Limesy, the 76th would proceed into the European Theater under command of the Fifteenth Army.

On December 16, Germany had launched a counterattack on Allied forces in the Ardennes Forest. The German counteroffensive, also known as the Battle of the Bulge, had been a last ditch effort on the part of Hitler, whose war machine had suffered key defeats in recent months. Hitler's goal for the attack was to advance his forces on to Antwerp, Belgium. Prior to and during the battle, German soldiers had sought to infiltrate Allied ranks by posing as Americans, wearing the soldiers of captured or killed troops. As Robert Leicke notes: "The Wehrmacht was combed for troops who spoke the American 'dialect.'"[2] After some German soldiers, Americans began to question unfamiliar soldiers by quizzing them on American popular culture. Such was the popularity of baseball in the United States at the time that soldiers would ask suspicious-looking men to recite the starting lineups of Major League teams.

One of the few men in the region who had first hand knowledge of baseball teams, moved eastward with the 76th between January 4 and January 26. Although it is often asserted that Travis fought in the Battle of the Bulge, in truth his unit arrived as the Germans were pulling back from the unsuccessful counteroffensive. Travis has been clear on this point: "I was in a 'mop-up' unit that followed behind the actual battle," he told the

USA Today Baseball Weekly.[3] He told another interviewer: "Well, we followed along behind. They [had] just had the battle and we followed right along the end there when the thing was over there."[4] They crossed into Belgium on the way meet to 87th Division in Champlon. The Belgian people kept fresh flowers on the altar of small roadside chapels, even in the dead of winter. In the Ardennes Forest, the landscape was a "portrait in white," and the snow itself was an enemy as it potentially covered mines laid by the retreating Nazis.[5]

While the 76th did not immediately see action, the east-moving troops faced another, ever-present enemy: the cold. When they could get bales of hay, they would use it as bedding for boxcars, where they slept. In the brutal Western Europe winter,

Travis, shown here playfully aiming the weapon of his prewar trade, had to exchange his bat for a rifle serving Uncle Sam in the European Theater. (FC Associates Museum Consulting & Appraisals)

the infantrymen sometimes found barns for shelter at night, but usually they had to settle for digging a hole in the snow. Travis would remember: "It was the cold that got to us.... You slept where you could, in a barn, any-place, but there was no heat. We just shivered all night long. At nights you just couldn't get warm. I'll never forget that cold as long as I live."[6]

Onaway reached Champlon and relieved the 87th in the late January. The battle-weary troops of the 87th greeted the 76th grimly. "You poor devils," they shouted. "You don't know what you're getting into up there. You'll learn."[7]

From there, the 76th crossed into Luxembourg and assumed defensive positions along the Sauer and Moselle rivers near Echternach, a burned out ghost town, facing the inverted bulge of German forces from the southwest. Beside the 76th were, on the left, the 4th Infantry Division, and on the right, the 2d Cavalry Group.

Luxembourg provided a tenuous base for the Americans. The Lux–embourg people were "closely linked to Germans in speech and habits," and the Grand Duchy of Luxembourg had been under German control for four years, so Allied Forces had to be on the lookout Germans looking to infiltrate their ranks while masquerading as Luxembourg civilians. But most of the local people preferred the presence of the Americans to that of their previous occupants. Luxembourg farmers went about their daily chores with smiles on their faces as they heard shells exploding over German lines, feeling "the calmness of assurance that the war had been chased from their cottage steps to the outhouses in the rear."[8]

The troops could see the mountainous terrain of Germany standing on the other side of the Sauer River. The men of the 76th had to hold positions for long periods of time in the coldest of weather. To make matters worse, infantrymen posted in snowy trenches had to restrict their movements for fear of becoming conspicuous targets from snipers on the other side of the line. Damp socks and combat boots that hindered proper circulation made conditions conducive "trenchfoot"—frostbitten feet that turned black as the soldiers lay in wait. "The thing about it, you'd sit there in those boots, and you might not get 'em off for days at a time. And COLD! You'd just shake at night. Your feet would start to swelling, and that's how you'd find out there was something really wrong. You'd pull your boots off and your feet [were] swelling."[9]

The Army did its best to rotate personnel and to deliver dry socks in ration shipments, but at the makeshift medical facilities, medics discovered many cases of trenchfoot. Travis himself developed the affliction; two toes on his left foot had developed frostbite. He kept moving with his unit but was limping so badly that he could barely keep up. Eventually, medics ordered him to a hospital in Metz, France, because they feared his toes would become gangrenous. Fortunately, Travis's foot healed, and he rejoined his unit within three weeks.

Onaway remained in defensive position until the early morning of February 7, when it launched a surprise attack-crossing of the Sauer River from the northwest corner of Echtenburg. While cold weather had been Onaway's enemy in January, slightly warmer temperatures worked against them now. "Ordinarily a meandering, slumerbsome stream, the Sauer River in February 1945 was a raging torrent fed by heavy rains and thawing snow. Swollen to a width of from 90 to 180 feet, its once graceful flow had developed a swirling current of 12 miles an hour."[10]

The 76th had to cross the Sauer, but first it needed to disable the counter-battery fire it was receiving from the Germans on the other side. The Americans shelled the far shore, dismantling key German artillery. Then planning began for crossing the river. All bridges over the Sauer in the sector had been destroyed, so the 76th would need to establish its own bridgework over the raging waters. Despite the shelling beforehand, their crossing attempts would not be unmet by enemy fire. In the dark, early morning hours, Onaway secured night cables to the opposite shore. Two of the cables were ripped out by boats as they careened downstream; the other two were pulled out when masses of soldiers from capsizing boats desperately grabbed onto them. But the infantrymen persisted. Onaway reached the far shore and, in 10 hours from the night of February 9 to the morning of February 10, it had established its first bridge over the river.

Lying in wait as a reward for Onaway's successful crossing of the Sauer was the vaunted Siegfried Line, a network of "pillbox" bunkers constructed into the German landscape. Camouflaged by natural vegetation as well as artificial means, these pillboxes formed strategic defense points by which German forces sought to slow attackers, making them susceptible to counterattack by assault forces stationed nearby. The Siegfried Line had as many as 40 pillboxes per square mile, one to every 40 yards. Each square mile contained no less than 100 other fortified positions, trenches, and ever-present minefields.[11]

The division spent seven days destroying the pillboxes with 90 mm artillery and inducing bunker after bunker of German soldiers to fly the white flag. They then advanced to the banks of the Prum River, where they assumed defensive positions, as they had while facing the Sauer earlier in the month.

Onaway enjoyed a brief respite on the banks of the Prum. The area was quiet; the fighting that left the landscape strewn with splintered trees and burnt earth had passed on. Men opened Christmas mail from home in weather that resembled early spring. Hundreds of soldiers were driven by truck back into Luxembourg to take showers at Quartermaster — their first since leaving England.

Liaison planes flew 15 missions over the far banks of the river to scout enemy locations. Then the Americans crossed the Prum and reached Holsthum, behind the Siegfried Line. At Holsthum, the 76th was paid a visit by General George Patton. Patton, donning a "parka, glistening helmet, spotless tan boots, and armed with the famed two pistols, drove up to the 76th Division CP, stroke brusquely into the inner sanctum, placed a huge fist on a map of Trier."[12] Patton ordered Onaway to march on to the north bank of the Moselle River and meet up with the XX Corps, to the ancient city of Trier, known for its extensive collections of Roman architecture.

Onaway forces drove to Trier, capturing 28 towns and more a 1600 prisoners.[13] By March 3, they had secured the entire region pocketed by the Sauer, Moselle and Kyll rivers. Three days later, Major Gen William R. Schmidt commended the 76th. He noted that his men had performed "valiantly, determinedly, aggressively, and skillfully" in clearing out more than 100 pillboxes and fortifications, taking 126 square miles of German soil—capturing 33 villages and 2,400 soldiers—and destroying Hitler's 212th Infantry Division.[14]

The 76th conducted another river crossing at night against enemy defenses, this time of the Kyll. Once across the Kyll, Onaway assembled near Priest and planned further movements eats, to the 850-mile Rhine.

Now under command of VIII Corps, the 76th moved from town to town in late March. The retreating Germans had left behind hand-painted signs meant to provide negative reinforcements: "Scenery Beautiful But Dangerous" ... "Many Roads Lead to the Rhine — More Lead to Death" ... "See the Rhine and Leave Your Skull There." Contrary to the bold messages of the signs, most of the German forces were disorganized and disillusioned, often resisting half-heartedly, often surrendering without a fight. Some SS troopers, though, organized rear guard units and fought desperately, and the 76th had to endure heavy mortar fire in taking the town of Kamberg.

As Onaway advanced eastward on Easter Sunday, they passed "truck after truck loaded with bedraggled, beaten German soldiers moving back to prisoner-of-war cages." Wherever possible, the GIs "crowded into German churches, sat in the ancient pews with their rifles and steel helmets between their knees, listened to the words of the chaplains, sang Easter hymns. Services were held in mess-halls, barns and in the field. And on Easter Sunday the 76th had reached its east boundary. All objectives attained. Another mission accomplished."[15]

At this point, as reports came from Austria of Nazi slave-laborers constructing a last-ditch fortress for Hitler, the Third Army was given a new mission: to blaze through central Germany and meet Russian forces approaching from the East. Four divisions of XX Corps would conduct the mission: the 76th and the 6th Armored divisions in the northern half of the sector and the 80th Divison and 4th Armored divisions in the southern half.

In its new assignment, Onaway advanced on the town of Helsa, a strategic point in the Nazi infrastructure. They were met with fire from artillery and tanks, and the men of the 76th hugged the ground until they were able to retreat under smoke screen. After pulling back, Onaway guns shelled the town, and then the infantry went in and cleaned out the area — a feat made possible when an Onaway bazooka specialist destroyed a German tank.

It was the first week of April. The division was now directed wind northwest from Gotha to Langensalza, where *Luftwaffe* planes made an ill-advised attack on the 76th and fell prey to the division anti-aircraft crews. From Langensalza they advanced northeastward to Kircheilingen, liberating slave laborers and Allied POWs in the process.

Once the Americans had secured the eastern shore of the Werra River, the 76th continued deeper into the fatherland. On April 10, the 76th seized the bridgeheads over the Gera River and then proceeded toward Zeitz. The city sat on a hillside across the Weisse-Elster River and formed a defensive strongpoint for the area; it also was home to an officer candidate school, and the colonel in charge had been left with orders to hold the city from the Allies at all costs. Accordingly, when he learned of the advancing American onslaught, he had issued arms to the local civilians and instructed them in sniper technique. He had also destroyed all bridges leading to Zeitz over the Weisse-Elster.

Onaway's military engineers formed a brilliant plan. Eight tanks were instructed to fire armor-piercing rounds into three stone pillars that stood as ruins from a broken bridge. The pillars came crashing down into the water — spanning the opposite shores of the river, instantly becoming makeshift bridges. The 76th proceeded across the deep, rushing waters. Tanks braved waters that reached over the bow guns before climbing the far shore. By the next day, most of Zeitz had been cleaned of its Nazi occupants. The Americans declared a temporary truce so that 200 German citizens could be evacuated from Zeitz.

The 76th then proceeded to the Mulde River, where XX Corps directed them to stay put. It was April 16, and the 76th had achieved the deepest penetration into Germany of any Allied forces on the Western Front.[16] Onaway assumed a defensive position while preparing to attack Chemnitz across the Mulde. Meanwhile, as Russian forces were making headway from the East, more and more German civilians surrendered to the authority of the 76th infantry. On April 20, Hitler's 56th birthday, the 76th symbolically launched 56 rounds of artillery into the SS barracks in Chemnitz.[17]

The next day, reports had the Russians only 22 kilometers to the east of the Americans. On April 22, Russian forces reached the outskirts of Berlin, and the men of the 76th division (which passed to the control of the First Army that day) followed the events on radio. The few remaining stations operating in the battle-torn country conceded imminent defeat but still quoted Nazi officials who claimed that Germany would not yield to President Roosevelt's directive of unconditional surrender.

The Russians fought for 10 days in Berlin. In that time, Patton's tanks had crossed into Austria, and the Allies learned that Hitler was dead. Only pockets of resistance in Czechoslovakia were all that remained of the once-formidable Nazi war machine.

On May 7, Major General Schmidt was informed that German high command had indeed agreed to terms of unconditional surrender. The 76th had seen 110 days of action. Elation began to set in. On a starry night on May 9, one Onaway soldier on duty told his buddy to take over his post for a moment, explaining, "I have some business attend to." The soldiers went over to a patch of bushes, "raised his M-1 into the air and shot a whole clip at nothing — nothing at all."[18]

On May 9, Maj. Gen. Schmidt and Brig. Gen. Francis A. Woolfley presided over the raising of the American flag in the downtown square of Limbach, Germany. Schmidt told the 76th that they were gathered to raise the stars and stripes "above defeated and conquered Germany."[19] It was a triumphant moment but one tempered by uncertainty and caution: "Where we will go next we do not know as yet. If we are to go to the Pacific, we will go fighting. If we are to remain here, keep on the alert. You are among enemies."[20] The flag was then lowered to half-mast in mourning; on April 12, President Franklin Delano Roosevelt, before whom Travis had played on eight opening days back in Griffith Stadium, had died in office, the victim of a cerebral hemorrhage.

Now under the command of Harry S Truman, the thirty-third president of the United States, American forces started the process of occupying conquered Germany. A task force from the 76th met Russian troops near Chemnitz. The division received a ceremonial flag from French forces at a formal retreat, with French forces recognizing the 76th as the first American division they encountered. The 76th was also the first American unit in Dresden.

Aside from ceremonial photo-ops, there was a lot of down time for the occupying forces. After V-E Day, it was time for Special Services to shine, providing recreation and entertainment for their fellow troops. This included shows written and produced by men of the 76th, USO shows featuring famous comedians and musicians of the day, movies, and clubs for the enlisted men. Baseball and softball tournaments were held. Sgt. Travis was named manager of the 76th Infantry Division baseball team. Travis's squad won 27 of 35 games, won the XV Corps championship, and made it to the final game of the ETO. In perhaps the closest thing to a "world series" to date, the 76th and 71st Infantry Divisions faced each other on a field in Nuremberg, the same city in which an Allied court would soon try Nazi war criminals. The 71st nine emerged victorious, 5–0.[21]

All the while, the men of Onaway anticipated their next battle assignment. The infantrymen had even begun to receive training in Japanese war tactics, in case the 76th was sent into the Pacific Theater, which was still engaged in combat. But on June 15, four years to the day that the Onaway Division had been reactivated in the States, its troops received unforeseen news. Maj. Gen. Schmidt, now serving as commander of the VIII Corps, directed that the 76th be dissolved.

The fate of Germany, along with notions of rebuilding and retribution, would be left to the diplomats and lawmakers. Sgt. Travis was heading home.

11

Going Home

Less than a week after the dissolution of Travis's infantry unit, friends told *The Washington Post* that Travis had accumulated enough service points to be eligible for discharge from the Army.[1] Speculation began that Travis might be rejoining the Senators within two months.[2] Washington baseball fans imagined Travis in the Senators lineup once again, belting line drives like he had during his historic 1941 season. But Travis remained in Germany with the occupying forces until early August. "I'd been in the service about as long as anybody. I'd been overseas for about nine months, and I knew my wife was pregnant and that maybe she'd already had the baby ... so I was anxious to get home, at least for a while."[3] He volunteered for assignment in Japan, in return for a 30-day furlough. When he got home, he was soon reunited with Helen, who introduced her husband to their second son, Michael, born in July.

The war in Japan was coming to a close. While historians have debated whether Japan was already headed to defeat, the dropping of atomic bombs on Hiroshima on August 6 and Nagasaki three days later effectively ended the war in the Pacific. On August 15, the Emperor Hirohito announced the surrender of Japan.

Soon thereafter, Shirley Povich reported what many Senators fans had longed to hear: "Cecil Travis will be getting out of the Army, and the Nats will be regaining one of the great hitters of baseball." Also due for honorable discharges were Sid Hudson, Jake Early, and Stan Spence. Buddy Lewis had already joined the Nats in July and was hitting well over .300. Povich anticipated: "The Nats will be one of the good teams."[4] In the dog days of August 1945, the Senators found themselves in a position that had been unfamiliar to the team and its fans for more than a decade: in pennant contention. Washington pitchers would give up the second fewest runs in the league in 1945. Roger Wolff (20–10) and Dutch Leonard (17–7) had sparkling seasons with ERAs of 2.12 and 2.13, respectively, while Mickey Haefner and Marino Pieretti would win 30 games between then. The Senators staff was aided by slick-fielding shortstop Gil Torres, who led the league in putouts. Washington bats were not as sharp; center fielder George Binks led the team with 81 RBI. The return of Travis, a 100–RBI man in 1941, was a much-anticipated event.

As August waned, Travis practiced on the baseball diamond at Camp McPherson in Georgia as he awaited his discharge to be finalized. "Sergt. Cecil Travis, one of the best ball players in the game, comes back to Washington this critical week," wrote Bob Considine of the *Post*.[5] "Travis is the man we need in this kind of a pennant race," announced team manager Ossie Bluege.[6] "Cecil Travis, brilliant Washington shortstop, [will] soon be filling that gaping void for the Senators," wrote Arthur Daley of the *New York Times*. If Travis can get into Washington uniform quickly enough, he can be of tremendous help for that homestretch drive."[7]

In a manner that seems to illustrate the type of military bureaucracy depicted in *Catch-22*, official announcement of Travis's discharge did not come until September 5. "This piece has to be all sweetness and light today, because you can't say anything unnice about Cecil Travis," the *Post* glowed about the team's returning hero. According to the article, Travis had accumulated 96 discharge points (16 more than the required total) and earned four battle stars in combat, including the Bronze Star, but still considered the Army very nice for approving his discharge.[8]

Much had happened in the years that Travis had been away. St. Louis had effectively served as the nation's baseball capital. The Cardinals won the National League in each year from 1942 to 1944. In the 1942 Series, St. Louis stunned the Yankees in five games, but New York beat them in five games the following October. The 1944 World Series was an all–St. Louis affair, with the Cardinals beating the surprising Browns in six games.

But the real story of wartime baseball might have been the number of players given a shot in the absence of the major leaguers who had gone off to war. In June 1944, 15-year-old Joe Nuxhall pitched two-thirds of an inning for the Cincinnati Reds. In 1945, the St. Louis Browns attempted to defend their league crown with Pete Gray, a one-armed outfielder. Gray wore his glove on his fingertips, and when he fielded a ball, he would switch his glove from his left hand to his armpit, take the ball out of his glove, and throw it back to the infield, all in one motion. Gray hit .218 in 77 games with the Browns that season. Also in 1945, a career minor league pitching prospect named Bert Shepherd returned to the United States on one leg, his right leg having been amputated after his fighter plane had crashed in Germany. Clark Griffith had signed Shepherd as a pitching coach in 1945, but on August 4, the right-hander became an inspiration to all Americans when he pitched five and one-third innings against the Red Sox, allowing only one run on three hits.

Meanwhile, the major leagues were under the guidance of a new commissioner. Kenesaw Mountain Landis had passed away on November 20, 1944, having served in his lifetime post for 24 years. He was succeeded by Albert "Happy" Chandler prior to the 1945 season. In the nation's capital, Bucky Harris had been replaced as Senators manager in 1943 by Ossie Bluege, the man whose job Travis had won 11 years earlier.

Travis finally rejoined his baseball mates on September 6 and, two days later, was written into the Senators lineup for the team's home game against the Browns. His old uniform number 5, which he had worn for seven seasons leading up to the war, was taken by first baseman Joe Kuhel, so he donned number 23. His debut was eclipsed somewhat by that of his most recent boss, Harry S Truman, who made his first visit the White House box at Griffith Stadium that same day. Truman, a native of Missouri — and who had accepted the Japanese surrender, symbolically, on the U.S.S. *Missouri*— was actually a fan of the visiting team.[9]

After Truman threw out the first pitch before 20,310 fans, Pete Appleton took the mound for the home team and registered a complete game win. Travis, playing third base, went hitless in four at bats but knocked in the team's first run on a groundout and fielded five chances cleanly at third.[10] The day after his game, the *Post* carried a photo of Travis taking his first swing in a game since 1941, with a caption proclaiming "After Three Years Travis Still Has the Same Old Swing: Apparently those three years Cecil Travis spent as an infantry Joe hasn't [sic] taken much from the veteran."[11]

Despite the ready-made headline, Travis did not find his return to major league play as smooth as he might have hoped. In his first nine plate appearances — eight with men on base — he failed to hit safely. His first big game came on September 12, when he went two for four and knocked in a run in a 5–1 victory over Cleveland. Then, one day after Washington's Walt Masterson outdueled Cleveland's returning war hero, Bob Feller, Travis again went two for four against the Tribe on September 14.

Still, Travis's legs weren't what they used to be. He was lifted for a pinch runner after providing a key hit in the winning rally. Travis, Washington's favorite son, drew the ire of fans when he failed to score from third on a potential sacrifice fly. Povich noted: "Those Washington fans who registered disgust when Cecil Travis failed to score from third base on a long fly to right field the other night were squawking at a guy who had his feet frozen in the Ardennes Bulge."[12]

Washington fans braced for a visit by the first-place Tigers on September 15. The players from Detroit were greeted in the locker room by 10,000 letters of support from fans, the result of a campaign by the sports editor of the *Detroit Free Press*.[13] The letters seem to have done the trick. By the end of the day, Detroit had a 2½-game lead, having swept a doubleheader from Washington 7–4 and 7–3. The next day the teams played another doubleheader, which they split. In the series finale, the Senators rapped out 16 hits against Detroit, with Travis going two for four.

The Senators finished play on September 23 by splitting a Sunday doubleheader with the Athletics. The split gave Washington a record of 87–67. They sat one game behind Tigers, who were 86–64 at that point but, through a fluke in scheduling, had four games left to play. The following Wednesday, Detroit split a doubleheader with Cleveland at Tiger Stadium, moving its record to 87–65. The Senators needed the Tigers to lose their remaining two games to force a playoff tiebreaker, but when the Tigers beat St. Louis 6–3 on the last day of September, Detroit clinched the pennant.

Even though Washington had thought enough of Travis to name him to the team's in the event that the team overtook Detroit, his return had not been statistically successful. He finished the 1945 season with a .241 average through 54 at bats, and he grounded into as many double plays as he had extra-base hits (three). Nevertheless, he did knock in 10 runs in just 15 games, and he provided glimpses of his past greatness that gave fans something to look forward to in 1946.

What position Travis would play for the team in the 1946 season remained unclear. Gil Torres had looked "played out halfway through" the previous season and had finished with a paltry .237 batting average — 120 points lower than Travis's in his last full season.[14] Speculation had Travis returning to shortstop and Lewis to third, but the organization also had Angel Fleitas, who had grown into the best shortstop in the Southern Association while playing for Chattanooga. In the December trade talks, the club explored the possibility of trading George Case for Red Sox shortstop Eddie Lake; instead, Case was sent to Cleveland in exchange for slugging right fielder Jeff Heath. Later that month, Clark Griffith projected Travis as the team's shortstop in '46.[15]

The upcoming season would be Travis's first full one in five years, and popular opinion held that the frostbitten feet he'd suffered in Europe had slowed him up in his brief return at the end of the 1945 season. (Travis always denied that frostbite was to blame for his postwar baseball struggles, instead pointing to a loss of timing that resulted from his time away from the game.) Griffith decided to send Travis, along with returning veterans Buddy Lewis, Stan Spence, Sid Hudson and Jake Early, to Hot Springs, Arkansas for three weeks in February to receive preconditioning treatment before spring training began.

While these players benefited from Griffith's gesture, veterans throughout the major leagues benefited from a unique application to the GI Bill of Rights, which guaranteed that returning servicemen would be able to get their prewar jobs back. "We're obligated to put our returned veterans back on the same jobs they held before they went into the service, and that's how we're going to start out," Griffith said. "If they fail, we'll have to make changes, of course, but those boys are going to get a good shot at their old jobs." The GI Bill, though probably not passed with professional baseball players in mind, provided sound insurance for returning stars such as Travis, but it also created interesting situations in other cases. What would managers do in the case of players who did not get drafted during the war and subsequently established themselves as everyday players for major league teams? For example, while Mickey Vernon missed the 1944 and 1945 seasons while serving for the Navy, Joe Kuhel had returned to the Nats and taken over the everyday first base job, scoring 90 runs in 1944 and knocking in 75 in 1945. Griffith vowed to stay loyal to the GI Bill and his returning vets:

> We're going to start out with the idea that Vernon is the No. 1 man.... Vernon was our regular first baseman before he went into the Navy, and he's entitled to take up where he left off. We bought Kuhel after Vernon left, and Kuhel did a great job for us, but until Vernon flops at it, the position belongs to him.

Vernon would reward Griffith's loyalty by having one of the best seasons in his fine, 20-year career, hitting .353 to win the American League batting crown in 1946.[16]

Griffith had no difficult decision in how to apply the GI Bill in Travis's case. The shortstop position had offered little production in the Washington lineup throughout the duration of the war, and the owner put great stock in Travis's return to form. "I won't know what kind of ball team it will be until Travis shows me," he announced, putting the hopes for the upcoming season on his soft-spoken star.[17] Encouragingly, word came from Hot Springs that Travis had regained much of his "old bounce."[18]

Travis traveled down to Orlando at the end of the month for spring training. This time, he was joined by Helen and their two sons. Travis was excused from practice one day while he sought quarters for his family. Once settled, Travis set about showing manager Bluege that he was ready to resume his shortstop position. "Four days after reporting to the Nats' camp, Cecil Travis has solved the shortstop problem to the complete satisfaction of the Washington club bosses. The job belongs to Travis, and it isn't a problem any more," the *Post* reported.[19] Travis looked his old self in the field, and he seemed to have found his trademark, line-drive stroke. Bluege commented: "The way he was hitting the ball [last year] he could have batted .500, with a little luck. I'm not worried about Travis' hitting."[20]

Travis had the opportunity to try out his swing as part of a 22-man squad that traveled to Havana, Cuba, to play seven exhibition games. The first game, on March 9 against the Boston Red Sox, drew 32,000 fans.[21] Travis went four for four in leading the Senators over Ted Williams and the Sox 10–9. Williams, who had won the 1942 batting title before going off to war, named Travis as his strongest competition for the crown in 1946: "He's too smart to try to pull the ball," Williams, the noted pull hitter, praised ironically.[22] Three days later, the Washington team faced a team of Cuban All-Stars, and Travis went three for five in a 6–3 Senators triumph. Washington won a rematch the following day, 13–6, and Travis made two nice catches of line drives off Cuban bats.

The trip was a successful one for the team both on and off the field (the team profited by $5000[23]) but the Senators players longed to get back to the States. Players found the turf of the Havana ballpark unbearably rough; Lewis took to playing the outfield in his bare feet. Newly acquired slugger Jeff Heath announced, "I don't like to hit in this park." (When he later made a two-base error in one of the contests, a Cuban fan voiced through a translator, "Maybe Heath no like to field in this park.") Griffith, the man who is credited with saving wartime baseball in the states, was sensitive to the importance of the Nats' "good neighbor" visit. "If we do come back, we won't play other big league clubs. We'll play Cuban teams. Those Cuban fans don't like the way our club and the Red Sox loafed in the two exhibitions here, and they get a bad impression of big league ball."[24]

As Griffith and his team looked forward to the trip home, Travis received an offer to bring his talents to more foreign baseball diamonds. On March 12, the Associated Press reported that Bernardo Pasquel, an official from the newly formed La Liga Mexicana, offered Travis a contract to play baseball in Mexico in 1946. Tensions had grown in recent years between the baseball cultures of the neighboring countries. Senators scout Joe Cambria even claimed to have been run out of Mexico at gunpoint in 1944 under suspicion of trying to "raid" Mexican teams. Millionaire brothers Bernardo and Jorge Pasquel intensified the tensions in 1946 when they attempted to launch a major league–caliber baseball association in Mexico. Pasquel had reportedly offered Roger Wolff, Washington's 20-game winner from the previous season, a three-year, $100,000-contract along with a $15,000 signing bonus.[25] Travis, for his part, stayed loyal to Griffith and refused the Mexican offer.

The Travis–Gerry Priddy double-play combination turned three double plays in the team's fifth straight win over the Cuban All-Stars on March 17. On March 18, Travis hit clean-up and went two for five in an exhibition victory against the Brooklyn Dodgers. Travis also forced in a run when Schoolboy Rowe hit him on the leg with a pitch.

After the game, the Senators' "A" squad returned to Orlando to resume its traditional exhibition season. Travis appeared back in the full swing of things. He collected four hits on March 23 against the Buffalo Bisons, went two for five and scored three runs a week later in a slugfest with the Dodgers, and slugged a deep home run over the right field wall of Tinker Field on April 2 against the Indianapolis minor league team. The next day, Ossie Bluege named Travis his new cleanup hitter. "Travis is the best hitter on my ball club, and he's going to be our cleanup man. He'll be all right too."[26] The Nats lineup for opening day — Travis's first in five years — had (in order) George Myatt at third, Buddy Lewis in right, Stan Spence in center, Travis at short, Jeff Heath in left, Mickey Vernon at first, Priddy at second, Al Evans behind the plate, and Roger Wolff on the mound. Perhaps seeking some good luck in his first full season after the war, Travis traded uniform numbers with George Binks, who gave Travis lucky number seven.

Washington, though, was unlucky at the start of the season. Boston won the season opener 6–3 and went on to sweep the three-game series. When the team traveled to New York for the Yankees' home opener on April 19, Bluege sought to shake things up and moved Travis down to the fifth spot. Babe Ruth was in attendance for the opener, and he signed autographs for flocks of fans before the game. Travis went two for four and Washington took a 6–5 lead into the bottom of the ninth, but the Senators' Johnny Niggeling gave up the tying run on a double to Joe DiMaggio and then the winning run on a sacrifice fly from John Lindell. Travis tallied another two-for-four the following day but took a back seat to Stan Spence, who hit for the cycle, and Washington won 7–3. The team lost 6–1 in the rubber match of the series but Travis went one for three, giving him an impressive .455 average for the series Yankee Stadium.

He brought a hot bat to Fenway Park and went two for four on April 22, a loss, and two for five on April 23, an 8–2 Nats win. All signs looked good for Travis in the early stages of the 1946 season. He seemed to signal his return for good in an historic game on May 5 at Griffith Stadium. Washington's shortstop went five for five, including a triple and home run, and knocked in four runs against Cleveland Indians hurlers, leading the Senators en route to a 12–4 rout. "Cecil Travis did all right," wrote Shirley Povich on the front page of *The Washington Post*.[27] Two days later, he rang up a single and two doubles in a 15-inning, 5–5 tie with the A's.

Despite Travis's hot hitting, the team was concerned with his lack of speed. Povich noted, "The Nats are a lumbering outfit, with Cecil Travis's slowness on the bases somewhat shocking."[28] This was a particular disadvantage in spacious Griffith Stadium, where speed was needed to compensate for the lack of home runs. The writing may have been on the wall when Washington acquired shortstop Billy Hitchcock from Detroit on May 16. With neither George Myatt nor Sherry Robertson producing at the plate, a move to third seemed inevitable for Travis.

Meanwhile, he remained focused on establishing his All-Star swing. After a brief slump in mid–May, Travis reentered the American League top 10 list at the end of the month, hitting .302 on May 28. Leading the league at a sparkling .405 was Mickey Vernon, who was emerging as the team's everyday first baseman, GI Bill or no GI Bill.[29]

Travis, Vernon, and the rest of the team were hot in late spring. After winning only five of 13 games in April, Washington went on a tear, raising their record to 27–19 after sweeping a Saturday doubleheader from the White Sox on June 8. The sweep came one day after Travis had doubled and scored the eventual winning run in the eighth inning. But even with the team's surge, they remained double-digits in games behind the Boston Red Sox, who were on their way to a 104-win season. Left fielder Ted Williams, second baseman Bobby Doerr, shortstop Johnny Pesky, center fielder Dom DiMaggio, and pitchers Mickey Harris and Tex Hughson — all veterans of World War II — had returned to lead Boston in the lopsided American League pennant race in 1946.

Meanwhile, the Senators fell off their pace quickly. After losing the nightcap to Chicago on June 9, Washington lost five in a row and fell into fourth place. The team hovered around .500 for the rest of the season. Travis began to cool off but provided a handful of highlights. In Detroit on June 16, his double with the bases loaded provided the margin of victory in a 6–3 win. In St. Louis on the first day of summer, he singled in two runs in a game-winning rally in the ninth. As a pinch hitter, he singled in the only run in a pitcher's duel between Bobo Newsom and Detroit's Dizzy Trout on July 24. He also knocked in the winning run in a 5–4 battle in Cleveland on July 26.

Travis still had some star power left in him, and (it would later come out) La Liga Mexicana persisted into June in their efforts to lure Travis southward. A New York agent under their employ posed as a Boston sportswriter who had forgotten his press credentials, and Clark Griffith unwittingly allowed the man into Griffith Stadium so that he could "interview" Travis. The man went to the Senators dugout and asked for Travis, who was taking infield practice. When Travis came off the field, Jeff Heath joked, "Hey, Cece! You're wanted down stairs. One of Pasquel's agents from the Mexican League wants to talk to you"— not knowing that the man was, in fact, an agent of the Pasquels.

The man got down to business with Travis and offered him a $15,000 check for signing with La Liga Mexicana. Travis asked the agent what the $15,000 would be for. The agent told him that it was for signing only, and that he would also be offered a five-year contract at $20,000 per year. Travis said, "I'll let you know."[30]

He never did. A few days later, the man found Travis during the Senators' road trip in Cleveland. This time, Travis gave the agent a flat "no" and asked that the Pasquels stop bothering him.[31]

The Pasquels' persistence did yield some early results. They succeeded in signing 18 ex–major leaguers to contracts, including the Dodgers' Mickey Owen. Dubbed the "Mexican jumping beans," the 18 players were banned from the major leagues by Happy Chandler (though some, including Owen, were eventually allowed back). But the most important long-term results of the Pasquels' efforts were its influences on Major League Baseball labor relations. The American Baseball Guild, a precursor to the Major League Baseball Players Association, used the Mexican League as leverage in its efforts to unionize professional ball players and be recognized by owners. Robert Murphy, labor relations advisor to the ABG, noted:

> Management almost always has refused to recognize labor at the outset.
> But actually our organization would help the clubs as well as the players.
> For example, we have just seen a lot of good players go over to the Mexi-
> can League. If they had been satisfied, they naturally would have
> remained in the United States. By improving salaries, player conditions
> and contracts, the guild would make the players satisfied. We would
> accomplish through arbitration what the players themselves now gain by
> jumping into Mexican baseball.[32]

Injury bugs circled Travis that summer. He left the game after colliding with Gerry Priddy's spikes on June 29, and in early July he broke a tooth and suffered bruises to his face after colliding with Joe DiMaggio at second base. Although he missed little time because of the injuries, he began to see time at third base. Billy Hitchcock took over as the team's shortstop, and it became clear that Bluege no longer viewed Travis as fit for the position. Ironically, at the same time, the *Post* reported that the Tigers, once familiar suitors, were inquiring about the possibility of acquiring Travis. Detroit was desperately trying to keep pace with Boston; with future Hall of Famer George Kell at third base but light-hitting Eddie Lake at shortstop, the Tigers apparently considered Travis fit for the shortstop job.[33] But, as with past rumors, nothing came to fruition and Travis remained in the nation's capital.

This would be good news to many of the hometown fans. A modest star, Travis had only earned more affection among fans as a returning war veteran. Among those rooting for Travis was one Jimmy Vinson, the 16-year-old son of Supreme Court chief justice Fred M. Vinson. In 1946, Jimmy dreamed of being a major league player like his favorite Senator. "Sure I'd like to be a major league ballplayer," he told Herb Heft of the *Post*. "Cecil Travis has always been my favorite player. But I might as well be a realist about the matter. I just don't have the physique," said the six-foot, 125-pound youth.[34]

Unfortunately for fans such as Vinson, though, Travis began to spend less time in the Senators' starting lineup. Travis experienced trouble in the field while his batting average dropped slowly but steadily. In August, the Veterans Administration invited Travis to an Army hospital in Washington to undergo treatment to restore proper circulation to his feet. They also gave him special orthopedic inserts for his shoes. Cautiously, Bluege inserted him back into the starting lineup at third base. Travis played steadily but not sparklingly. His last great game may have been in Detroit on September 15. The veteran Senator, now 33 years old, struck four hits in five times in the 15–5 beating of Dizzy Trout and the Tigers, knocking in four runs and also turning some key plays in the field at third. He also recorded two hits and an RBI in a 2–0 defeat of Philadelphia on September 26 — poignantly, Travis was thrown out while trying to go from first to third on a single by Jake Early — and three more in the team's final game of the season, a 7–0 win at Fenway that assured Washington of a "first division" finish in fourth place in the American League.

Overall, the 1946 season was a valiant disappointment for Travis. He finished the season with an average of .252 — his lowest average during a full season — with only 1 home run and 56 RBI in 465 at bats. In late September, Ted Williams had recalled thinking that Travis was Washington's best hitter but admitted that pitchers were now throwing fastballs by him. Williams also conceded the batting title to Vernon, who hit .353 to Williams' .342. "Let him lead the league for a year; he's a nice fellow," Williams said of Vernon.[35]

Williams, the Sox and the Senators would be further linked at the end of the regular season. As Boston awaited the end of the National League season and its World Series opponent to be decided, it arranged to play a series of exhibition tune-ups in Boston against a team of American League "all-stars." Washington players Travis, Stan Spence, Buddy Lewis, Jake Early and Mickey Haefner were invited to play against Boston. The first game took place on October 1, with fewer than 2,000 people turning out on the cold autumn day. The contest, won by Boston 2–0, was forgettable except for one one fateful matchup, in which Heafner hit Williams on the right elbow with a pitch; X-rays later revealed a contusion. Regrettably, he would not be the same player in the World Series, which pitted the Sox against the St. Louis Cardinals. The greatest hitter in the game managed only five hits in 25 at bats in the Series and knocked in only one run. The two teams, though, staged a classic battle. With the score tied in the eighth inning of Game Seven, Enos Slaughter scored all the way from first on a hit-and-run single by Harry "The Hat" Walker. Slaughter's now-famous "mad dash" proved to be the winning run for the Series champion Cardinals.

On December 10, the most famous of all Washington Senators and the team's strongest link to its one-and-only championship, pitching great Walter Johnson, passed away. He was 60. It was the end of an era in Washington baseball. Sadly, another ending was just around the corner.

After the 1946 season, noted columnist Furman Bisher wrote from Charlotte, North Carolina, to colleague Shirley Povich, stating his opinion that Bob Morem (a player in the Washington farm system who had tallied a record 23-game hitting streak in Class B Tri-State League play) and not Travis should be playing third for the Senators. "Folks down here think he's a sure-shot to be the Senators' third baseman in 1947," Burman wrote.[36] Morem never would catch on with the Senators (or any other major league team) but the gesture of Bisher (who would later join staff of the *Atlanta Journal-Constitution*) calling for Travis's replacement provided an early signal that 1947 would be the Georgia native's last in the majors.

Travis remained optimistic as he headed to spring training in 1947. "I feel like a different man," he said upon reporting to Orlando.[37] He returned to using a heavy, 36-ounce bat, and showed some uncharacteristic ability to pull the ball against batting practice pitching.[38] Bluege said, "I think Cecil Travis is ready for a big comeback at third base."[39] "If he doesn't come through for us, it will be my biggest disappointment, but I'm not worrying about that," he said in late March.[40]

Travis's preseason play was encouraging. He demonstrated some of his old flair and not only won the third base job but was installed into the fifth spot in the lineup for the home opener, his tenth in Washington.

In his postwar career, Travis (shown here in the Senators dugout at Griffith Stadium) was unable to regain his all-star form. (Transcendental Graphics)

President Truman, accompanied by first lady Bess and daughter Margaret along with Chief Justice Vinson and speaker of the house Joseph Martin, showed up to watch a starting nine of Joe Grace in left, Buddy Lewis in right, Stan Spence in center, defending batting champ Mickey Vernon at first, Travis at third, Gerry Priddy at second, ex–St. Louis Brown Mark Christman at short, Al Evans catching, and Buck Newsom pitching.

Washington's opponents for its home opener were the New York Yankees and Bucky Harris, in his first year as the team's manager. On April 18, Harris paid respect to Travis when he issued his former All-Star hitter an intentional walk in the first inning with two outs and two runners in scoring position; Allie Reynolds then induced Priddy into a harmless ground out. New York won 7–0.

Notwithstanding the respect he still commanded from opposing managers, Travis got off to a lukewarm start at the plate. He average hovered around .250 in mid–May, but he was playing well at third. His own manager maintained that he was playing the best hot corner in the league.[41] He showed some versatility as well, volunteering to serve as makeshift batting-practice pitcher before a game in late May; he was injured, though not seriously, when rookie third baseman Eddie "Ned" Yost sent a line drive that bounced off Travis's glove and hit him in the mouth. Travis would also play 15 games at shortstop in 1947 and — on the other end of the spectrum — even served as "sentry" duty in front of the presidential box in Griffith one game in June, protecting the First Fan area from foul balls.

Travis also moonlighted as an instructional journalist of sorts, provideding commentary as part of the "Walter Johnson memorial program for boys." Speaking to the *Post*, he outlined some key techniques in playing third base:

• Whereas a shortstop has to field balls cleanly in the whole, a third baseman has time to knock down balls and throw the hitter out, so he changed to a glove with "more stiffness in the fingers."
• Third basemen usually do not have to make long throws, so an accurate arm is more important than a strong one.
• A third baseman "who can't throw without a wind-up is no asset to his team"; he has to "master the snap throw."
• You need to have quick hands and usually don't have time to "scramble" after hard hit balls: "You get them with your hands, or usually you don't get them at all."
• Playing shallow at third "cuts down" the angle on the "territory vulnerable to a hitter."
• The third baseman is the "sole guardian" of his base; whereas first

or second base are sometimes covered by different players on plays such as bunts, relays, or steals, third base must always be manned by the third baseman during the course of a play.

• The third baseman should field any balls to his left that he can because he will have more time than the shortstop to throw and will have a shorter throw to make.[42]

• Though not playing to All-Star form, Travis still demonstrated through example, and the *Post* declared him the "defensive star of the game" against Cleveland on May 4.[43] The day before, he had knocked in the Senators' winning run against the Browns. The Red Sox looked into buying the services of Travis before the June 15 trading deadline, but as in the past, no deal was reached, and Travis stayed put.[44]

As the days of summer began, it was clear that Travis was entering in the autumn of his fine career. So in June, the Senators organization began plans for a Cecil Travis Day to be held in appreciation for all that Travis had meant to the team and its fans.

Originally scheduled for July 26, the affair was pushed back to August 15 — a good thing considering the enormous amounts of planning that went into the event. Cecil Travis Day became a major celebration. In the weeks leading up to it, the team set up special booths at the stadium entrances to accept contributions from fans for the event. Gerry Priddy headed the committee responsible for collecting contributions from ball players, and Clark Griffith added a contribution on behalf of the team. Representatives of local civic clubs, including the Reciprocity Lions, Kiwanis, Civitan, Executive, Chatter Box, and Optimist clubs also donated time and effort to the cause. Connie Mack's Athletics, Washington's opponent on the night of festivities, also contributed a check. Perhaps most tellingly, a group of American League umpires also volunteered to contribute to the pool of gifts that would be awarded to Travis. Throughout his playing days, umpires had appreciated Travis's respectful demeanor. He was regarded as perhaps the player least likely to complain about a call, and at one point in his career, the umpires had voted Travis their favorite player.

The umpires' favorite player and Washington's favorite son was honored in festivities that began 30 minutes before game time on Friday, August 15. It seems fitting that the team's game with Philadelphia was scheduled at night, as Travis had come up during an era when all games at Griffith Stadium were played by sunlight; the introduction of night baseball was one of the changes to the game that he had witnessed during his career, representing the approach of a new era. At 8:00 P.M., the Washington

Scottish Bagpipe Band opened the evening's ceremonies. Two girls danced the highland fling on the infield. Then, a float carrying Peggy Wilson, Miss Washington of 1947, proceeded to home plate, where two men steeped in baseball history, Clark Griffith and Connie Mack, preceded over the ceremonies. Joining them was a Veteran of Foreign Wars honor guard. Radio station WWDC covered the ceremonies for fans not present at the stadium.

Clark Griffith and Ossie Bluege uttered praise of Travis. Bluege, quoting a line from the poem "Abou Ben Adam" by Leigh Hunt, said, "Cece, may your tribe increase."[45] The crowd of 15,228 fans also heard congratulatory telegrams from Commissioner Chandler, American League president Will Harridge, and National League president Ford C. Frick, along with General Dwight D. Eisenhower of the United States Army. These dignitaries were joined by a representative "average fan," 15-year-old Clyde Holland, who called Travis a "great guy."[46] Holland contributed $2 toward Travis's gifts.

The list of gifts showered upon Travis that night included a De Soto automobile, a 1,500-pound Hereford bull for his farm, a two-ring neck pheasant, a Jeep trailer, an electric dishwasher, a power lawn mower, a hunting suit, an automatic 20-gauge shotgun, two thoroughbred English settlers, bird dogs, porch furniture, a coaster wagon, a leather chair, an electric oven, a portable radio, a necktie, a leather jewelry case, a baseball a scrapbook, a charcoal broiler, a four-wheel coaster bike and a tricycle, a sandbox and playpen, a combination swing-trapeze, two bedroom rugs, a six-piece bedroom set, a seven-piece cookware set, a lifetime fountain pen, a travel bag, a diamond ring, sterling silver kitchen ware, an electric percolator, a sport shirt, a smoking stand, a fishing rod and reel, a wristwatch, a diamond ring, two pairs of sunglasses, sterling candlestick holders, flowers, gift certificates for gasoline, a pair of shoes, and (fittingly) a baseball bat.

The famously bashful Travis stepped shyly to home plate and thanked all in attendance in a solemn voice. "I'll never forget this night," he said. "You've all been swell." Longtime friend Buddy Lewis, who worked hard in coordinating details that night, seemed especially pleased for his old roommate. One observer said, "You'd almost think it was Lewis night."[47]

After the festivities, the Athletics and Senators squared off. Travis played third base and bat fifth. Philadelphia pitcher Joe Coleman tossed a four-hit shutout and Washington lost 3–0. Travis, the .300 lifetime hitter, went one for three and walked once.

The next day, Travis looked back on the evening. Considering the cornucopia of gifts he had received, he joked, "I'll have to retire if I want to enjoy all these things they gave me."[48]

The 1947 season was not a good one for the Senators, who slipped back into the second division with a record of 64–90. Travis, reduced with dignity to a pinch hitter for the team in the final weeks of the season, finished with a season average of just .216, his lowest in any level of professional baseball. Morris Siegel of the *Post* reported that the veteran of 12 major league seasons had voiced his intention to retire from baseball and return to the family farm in Riverdale, though Siegel predicted that Travis would probably return in 1948 as "an active player to be used in a pinch hitting role."[49] On September 27, however, Clark Griffith announced that Travis had met with him and requested voluntary retirement.[50] Nearly 17 years after starting his career as a professional ball player, he was headed back to Georgia for good.

Epilogue: "I'm Not Sorry I Played"

Travis began his post-baseball life living in Atlanta with his wife and two sons, managing the affairs of his 250-acre farm. "I always have heard that it was tough leaving the game. Well, so far I haven't had the urge to get back and I don't believe I will," he told a reporter from the *New York Times*. He pondered his precipitous decline: "That was enough for me," he said. "I figured that if I couldn't regain my old form in two years I never would so I asked to be put on the voluntary retired list."[1]

"I tried for two years to get back to normal," he told *The Washington Post*. "I just don't have it anymore and I'm not going to try playing again," he said, noting, "I just don't have any more of that thing we call 'cat'.... I feel fine, as good as I've ever felt. But I can't react any more and I can't cover any ground."[2] He added: "I can't stand to go out there and stumble around."[3] He admitted that he probably could have received offers to keep playing for another two or three years, but his pride would not allow him to do so while he was unable to play at his old level. In fact, it soon came out that Travis had gone to Griffith the previous August offering to take a pay cut, saying, "I'm not worth the salary you're paying me."[4]

Griffith wrote Travis and asked him if he'd be interested in managing Charlotte, the organization's Piedmont League team. Travis declined. "I have a pretty good investment here and I want to stay home. The only kind of a job I'd be interested in now is a part-time scouting job and I may get that. But I don't even want to scout if it is going to take me away from home too much."[5]

Travis did accept a position as a scout — though as a part-time one — with the organization that spring. His assigned "beat" included Georgia and Alabama. "I'm going to spend a lot of time watching semipro teams in small towns like those I played in."[6]

Travis scouted for the organization until 1956. The job was a challenge given Washington's traditional lack of funds. He did have some success, though; among his signees was Gene Verble, a shortstop who managed to ascend through the ranks and play briefly with the Senators in 1951 and 1953. "I fiddled around for a while, finally got out of it all together," he said.[7]

After Cecil retired from scouting, the Travis clan retired to their Pine Crest Acres farm in Riverdale. Cecil and Helen had had a third son, Ricky, in 1955. On the land, Travis took to raising white-faced Herefords, much like the one he was awarded on his special Night back in 1947. In the 1960s, the Travises sold some of their acreage to developers, and new homes soon began to sprout up in the once-remote region. The family kept approximately 70 acres, and Travis had the property's lake stocked with bass and bream.

Travis, though, never entirely left the game. He became a fan of the Atlanta Braves, who became the local team after the franchise moved there from Milwaukee in 1966. (His old team, the Senators, had been reincarnated as the Minnesota Twins in 1961.) Atlanta had never been home to a major league team, and the club displayed good public relations sense in sending season tickets to Travis, Atlanta's local baseball dignitary. Cecil and his youngest son, Ricky, became regular fixtures at Braves home games, and Travis even appeared in "old-timers' games" at Fulton County Stadium. In 1972, Commissioner Bowie Kuhn invited Travis to attend the All-Star Game as his guest of honor, as did his first manager, Joe Cronin, who was serving as president of the American League. "I had to tell him Bowie Kuhn had already invited me," Travis remembered.[8]

While he remained a local hero, Travis became somewhat of a forgotten man to subsequent generations of baseball fans. In 1991, as the baseball world was celebrating the fiftieth anniversary of DiMaggio's streak and Williams' .400 season, an Atlanta-based attorney named John Clark consulted a baseball reference to see which player had recorded more hits that season. Imagine Clark's surprise at finding out that not only had Travis struck more hits than either player that year, but he was also a local boy! Clark told a reporter from the *Clayton News/Daily*: "On a lark I looked in the phone book." He found Travis's name still listed in the Riverdale directory. He called Travis, and they "chatted amiably for a while." Clark noted, "He seemed much younger than his age."[9]

During the 1991 All-Star game, as President George H. W. Bush joined Major League Baseball in commemorating the accomplishments of Williams and DiMaggio, Clark was inspired to pick up the phone and called Travis again. He found that Travis was watching the game, as well:

He thanked me for remembering, and, said, "Yea, we all occasionally have a good year" and we both went back to watching the game. If you want a down to earth, homespun, modest American who is glad to have what he has, glad to have served his country, you got Cecil Travis. He has no regrets.[10]

That same summer, the *USA Today Baseball Weekly* ran a feature that presented Travis as an answer to the quintessentially obscure answer to a trivia question: "He is not a familiar name to the casual fan. It's not preceded with 'Joltin'' or followed by 'Splendid Splinter.' He's not associated with a year, a record or a World Series heroic.... Few people remember his story." Recalling 1941, Travis told Jack De Vries, "To have a year like I had, everything had to go pretty good. You hit the ball good and everything else just falls in there. Oh, yeah, when I was playing that year, I felt I could do just about anything."

Asked how he wanted to be remembered by fans, Travis answered with the humility that had characterized him throughout his life. "That's for the fans to decide," he said. "I never think about things like that."[11]

People who saw him play continue to think about the Washington Senators' old sweet-swinging infielder. During the 1993 All-Star Game, Ted Williams paid a visit to the television booth. He was asked if he recognized his own swing in that of then–Toronto Blue Jays first baseman John Olerud, who was flirting with .400 that summer. "No," Williams said. "I had more of an uppercut swing. I was a power hitter. Olerud has this kind of whiplash swing. Now he is left-handed, but he reminds me more of Cecil Travis. Travis was a great hitter, used to play for the Senators— second in the league in hitting in '41, you know, ahead of DiMaggio. Contact hitter, like Olerud, they both ran faster than I did. He got hurt in the war and never played as well again."[12]

The tribute paid to Travis by the man considered by many to be the greatest hitter of all time sent baseball fans and buffs across the country scurrying to the latest edition of *The Baseball Encyclopedia*. The *Atlanta Journal-Constitution* paid Travis a call, seeking a quote from Travis. "I knew [Williams] well. We used to talk a lot about hitting," he remembered fondly.[13] He told *The Sporting News*, "Ted was always talking, always asking about pitchers: 'What they throwing you, Cecil?' 'How's so-and-so looking?'"[14]

Bowie Kuhn, who served as commissioner from 1969 to 1984, also remembers Travis well, and from a unique perspective. As a teenager, Kuhn worked as a batboy and scoreboard operator in Griffith Stadium from 1939 to 1943, and he holds fond memories of watching Travis play. "He was a wonderful ballplayer," he told Dick Heller of *The Washington*

Times in 2002. Kuhn—along with ex–major league dignitaries like Bob Feller and Ted Williams, as well as many fans—has campaigned to get Travis voted into Cooperstown by the Veterans Committee. Kuhn argues: "He has been hurt by the fact that his career was short and he played for the Senators at a time when they didn't win many games." Kuhn also observed that Travis's famous modesty—which precludes any self-promotion—also works against his chances at making the Hall of Fame. "He has never talked much in his own behalf, and nobody ever pushed for him like people pushed for the old Yankees, Giants and Dodgers," Kuhn said. "But there are a lot of legitimate reasons for him to get in."[15] Sportswriter John Holway examined the reasons in an article for *Baseball Digest*. Even though Travis's postwar years dropped his career average 13 points, his .314 mark still ranks third all-time among shortstops. (Honus Wagner is first at .329 and Arky Vaughan second at .318.) Travis's average compares favorably to such enshrined shortstops as Luke Aparicio (.262), Luke Appling (.310), Lou Boudreau (.295), Joe Cronin (.301), Travis Jackson (.291), Rabbit Maranville (.258), Phil Rizzuto (.273), and Pee Wee Reese (.269). But Holway argues Travis "put the right numbers in the book but the wrong letters on his cap."[16] The *W* that Travis wore on his cap for 12 seasons has had a similar effect as the *A* worn by Hawthorne's Hester Prynne: "too great a stigma to carry into Cooperstown." This is a feeling held by many who have examined Travis's career. If he had played for better teams and had the opportunity to show off his bat in publicized pennant races, or even in the World Series, he might have become a household name like a Williams, like a DiMaggio.

It's also likely that Griffith Stadium, the place where Travis played half of his games, worked against him. With its cavernous dimensions, the ballpark was not friendly to hitters. One may wonder quite fairly what kind of numbers Travis (who never reached double-digit home runs in any season and topped the 100 RBI mark only once) would have had if he had played, say, with the short porch at Yankee Stadium, especially when he was driving balls to right field in his best years.

Travis proponents sometimes overlook that although he was no leadfoot, he was no speed merchant on the bases. He never was the type of catalyst that a Reese or Rizzuto was, with 1338 and 877 runs scored, respectively, to Travis's 665. And to be fair, the ranking of his offensive numbers among the great shortstops of the game loses its effect when one considers that, while such players as Reese and Rizzuto stood as defensive stalwarts on their teams, Travis appeared at shortstop in only 710 of his 1328 career games. Many forget that he played almost 500 games at third base and 70 in the outfield. In addition, his cumulative fielding average of

.955 throughout his career falls far short of that for Reese (.962) and Rizzuto (.968); and Reese played more than 2000 games at the position, Rizzuto more than 1600. (In arguing that New York Yankees shortstop Derek Jeter was an overrated fielder, ESPN.com's Rob Neyer concluded that Jeter was "Cecil Travis with more power."[17])

Meanwhile, decades after Travis's retirement, a player named Cal Ripken raised the bar for shortstops forever. Baseball's all-time "iron man" played 2,302 games at shortstop, hitting 431 home runs and notching 1695 RBI while also compiling a sparkling .979 fielding percentage.

What does Travis have to say about speculation regarding his Cooperstown credentials? Very little. Travis has never promoted himself for Hall consideration. "I know some people say the war cost me a chance at the Hall of Fame," he has said, "but I don't think about that at all. Who knows what would have happened? Besides, there [are] already too many people in [the Hall]. I've always thought it should just be for great players. I was a good player, but I wasn't a great one."[18] Indeed, when pressed by interviewers, Travis's self-assessments with regard to Cooperstown have been consistently humble. He told Furman Bisher, "I always thought the Hall of Fame ought to be for people of an upper level, like Ruth and Gehrig and Cobb and Foxx, players who were great all their years."[19] When Bisher told him, "Ted Williams says you belong in the Hall of Fame," Travis thought for a moment and said, "I don't think that. There are a lot of players with records as good or better than mine who are not in it. I just don't think it would look right. Now, if I had had several seasons like 1941, then it might be different."[20]

Travis had reached his prime as a player in 1941, but unfortunately, he was denied the chance to build off that season when he was called to war. "You never think about what you lost," he told Marty Appel. "We had a job to do, an obligation, and we did it. I was hardly the only one."[21] Not only does Travis not bemoan his lost opportunities during the war years, but he refuses to blame his postwar failure to regain his stroke on his frostbitten feet, as many writers have done. "I lost something after the war," he told Todd Newville. "I don't know what it was. I got a couple of toes frozen but that never seemed to bother me as far as baseball goes.... My problem when I got back to baseball was my timing.... I could never seem to get it back the way it was after laying out so long. I saw I wasn't helping the ballclub, so I just gave it up."[22]

Meanwhile, Travis has been earned recognition nearer to his hometown. In 1975, he was inducted into the Georgia Sports Hall of Fame, along with another player well known to Atlanta-area fans, home run king Hank Aaron. In 1999, Travis was named to the Fayette County High School Hall of Fame, and the following year, the Fayette County Tigers' dugout was officially dedicated in his name.

Travis received another honor in 1993, though under humorous circumstances. The Hall of Stars Committee for RFK Stadium (then the home of the Washington Redskins) voted Travis into its ranks, which included such sport greats as Sammy Baugh, Joe Cronin, Walter Johnson, Sonny Jurgensen, Sugar Ray Leonard, and former Senators teammate Mickey Vernon. However, committee members were apparently under the impression that Travis had passed away; they sent a letter to his Riverdale address seeking a family member that could stand in for Travis as he was "posthumously" honored with the installation of a placard bearing his name in the stadium's mezzanine level. Travis wrote back: "I received your letter of July 29, 1993, regarding my induction into the Hall of Stars, but you made a mistake. The mistake is that I'm still very much alive at age 80." He told Morris Siegel of *The Washington Times*, "I got a little laugh out of it," and added, "My wife was shocked to read in that same letter that she was also dead."[23] Travis was honored in a ceremony at RFK during halftime of a November 28 game between the Redskins and the Philadelphia Eagles.

Fifty winters after the one Cecil Travis spent huddled in the cold in war-torn Europe, Dave Kindred of *The Sporting News* visited him at his farm in Riverdale, Georgia. As cows grazed on the thick grass around them, Travis sat in an easy chair looking at the pond on his property:

> A ripple of water flashes gold in the afternoon sun. In the old man you can see the kid shortstop who knew Ted Williams. He's wearing blue jeans and a ball cap. He is thin and strong and clear-eyed. When he talks vigorously about how small a ballplayers's glove was in his day, he raises his left hand with the fingers curved as if ready to take a ground ball. And then that hand moves back a half-inch or so, a shortstop's hands even at 81.

Travis spoke of the "soot and clang-clang" of road trips — back when teams traveled by train, not place. He recalled for the cold, the "durn cold" he endured in the European winter. He moved his hands across his thighs — the thighs that still carried him on his daily walk to the mailbox on Highway 138 one half-mile away — as he recalled the effects of injuries from his days with the Chattanooga Lookouts. "I can still feel the knots in the muscles," he said. But despite these hardships, Kindred encountered a man "happy to have done his duty, happy to have had his good years in baseball."[24]

Indeed, Travis is a man who carries fond memories of the game and the players of the time. "Imagine that, me, a farm boy from Georgia, and I got to play in front of presidents," he once said.[25] Travis still delighted in hearing that he was remembered by such men as Ted Williams and Shirley Povich, and he could still remember the excitement he felt during his major league debut in 1933. When oral historian Thomas Liley visited Travis's farm in 1991, the ex–Senator spoke in detail of his baseball days, even pointing out the copy of *The Baseball Encyclopedia* that he had recently consulted when looking up an old teammate's statistics. He noted that he and Helen still sent Christmas cards to the wife of Ossie Bluege, who had passed away in 1985. In a 2003 interview, Mickey Vernon noted that he and his wife had often visited the Travises while en route to Florida vacations, and that he still received a card from Travis every Christmas. "I admired the guy and still think an awful lot about him," Vernon said.[26] Summing up his feelings in the manner of an understated farmer from rural Georgia, Travis told Liley: "I'm not sorry I played."[27]

In August 2002, I called Cecil Travis, hoping to set an appointment to interview him. His number is still listed — something almost unimaginable in the current climate of high-profile players and the larger-than-life game. Earlier, I'd sent him a letter that informed him of my plans to write his biography and told him I would give him a call soon.

When I called that weekday afternoon, a younger man (one of Cecil's sons, I assumed, or perhaps even a grandson) answered the phone. I identified myself and asked for Mr. Travis. The man asked me to hold on, and after a few moments, I heard the voice of the 89-year-old Cecil Travis. I identified myself again and reminded him of the letter I had sent to him. He said that he had received it, but when I asked him what he thought about the possibility of my interviewing him, he said, simply and politely, that he was not fond of the idea. He then explained that he had been in poor health of late, and also that he had been overrun by interview requests in recent weeks. (Apparently, some people did still remember this once-great hitter.) I thanked him for his time, and we hung up affably.[28]

I imagine that a more practiced interviewer would have kept his subject on the phone, sycophantically praising his career and the importance of preserving his words in a book dedicated to his life, hoping to chip away at his resolve in order to gain the sought-after interview. But if writing a book on a player's life is one way to pay respect, perhaps allowing an 89-year-old man his well-deserved privacy is another.

Besides, Mr. Travis's lack of interest in being interviewed seems appropriate. In speaking with him briefly, I got the impression he just didn't care that someone was writing a book about his life. As a player and a soldier and, one may say, as a person, Travis succeeded without fanfare. He doesn't need the attention of others, doesn't need the fame, because he is content with his life and what he has done. And in the end, this might be the greatest thing that any major leaguer, or anyone else, can achieve.

Appendix:
Batting Statistics
of Cecil Travis

Minor League

Year	G	AVG	AB	R	H	2B	3B	HR	RBI	BB	K	SLG
1931	13	.429	35	7	15	4	0	0	0	n/a	n/a	.543
1932	152	.356[1]	570	88	203	27	*17*	3	88	n/a	n/a	.479
1933	129	.352	526	80	185	26	12	1	74	n/a	n/a	.452
Totals	294	.356	1131	175	403	57	29	4	162	n/a	n/a	.469

(**Bold italics** denote a league-leading mark.)

1. Although official team statistics credit Travis with a .362 batting average, his 203 hits in 570 at bats yield an average of .356. Tallying 206 hits in 570 at bats would have yielded a .3608 average, while 207 hits in the same number of at bats would have yielded a .3632 average. A total of 203 hits in 561 at bats *does* yield a .3618 average (which rounds up to .362) but for the purposes of the above chart, the number of at bats and hits officially recorded for Travis in 1932 are used.

(Major League Next Page)

Major League

Year	G	AVG	AB	R	H	2B	3B	HR	RBI	BB	K	OBP	SLG
1933	18	.302	43	7	13	1	0	0	2	2	5	.348	.326
1934	109	.319	392	48	125	22	4	1	53	24	37	.361	.403
1935	138	.318	534	85	170	27	8	0	61	41	28	.377	.399
1936	138	.317	517	77	164	34	10	2	92	39	21	.366	.433
1937	135	.344	526	72	181	27	7	3	66	39	34	.395	.439
1938+	146	.335	567	96	190	30	5	5	67	58	22	.401	.432
1939	130	.292	476	55	139	20	9	5	63	34	25	.342	.403
1940*	136	.322	528	60	170	37	11	2	76	48	23	.361	.455
1941*	152	.359	608	106	*218*	39	19	7	101	52	25	.410	.520
1942	Did not play												
1943	Did not play												
1944	Did not play												
1945	15	.241	54	4	13	2	1	0	10	4	5	.293	.315
1946	137	.252	465	45	117	22	3	1	56	45	47	.323	.318
1947	74	.216	204	10	44	4	1	1	10	16	19	.273	.260
Totals	**1328**	**.314**	**4914**	**665**	**1544**	**265**	**78**	**27**	**657**	**402**	**291**	**.370**	**.416**

(**Bold italics** denote a Major League-leading mark.)
+ Named to American League All-Star roster.
*Named to American League All-Star starting lineup.

Chapter Notes

Chapter 1

1. Shelby Foote, *Civil War: A Narrative, Volume 3, Red River to Appomattox*, pp. 391–392.

2. Ron Fimrite, "A Call to Arms," *Sports Illustrated*, October 28, 1991.

3. Qtd. in *NationMaster.com Encyclopedia* and *Wikipedia: The Free Encyclopedia* and Nation Master

4. Newspapers quoted in Steve Oney, *And the Dead Shall Rise: The Murder of Mary Phagan and the Lynching of Leo Frank*, p. 574; Ibid.; Ibid., p. 589.

5. *The Washington Post*, February 14, 1935.

6. 1930 Census.

7. *The Washington Post*, February 14, 1935.

8. Jack De Vries, "Travis was a silent hit in '41 season," *USA Today Baseball Weekly*, July 26–August 1, 1991.

9. Dave Kindred, "Memories Frozen in Time," *The Sporting News*, January 2, 1995.

10. Carolyn Cary, "Mr. Baseball in Fayette," July 10, 1968 (Georgia State Historical Archives).

11. *The Washington Post*, February 14, 1935.

12. Ibid.

13. Ibid.

14. Thomas Liley, interview with Cecil Travis, Riverdale, Georgia, January 29, 1991.

15. *Atlanta Journal-Constitution*, February 2, 1961.

16. Ibid.

17. Ibid.

18. *Atlanta Journal-Constitution*, July 11, 2000.

19. *The Washington Post*, February 14, 1935.

20. *The Citizen Online*, February 10, 1999.

21. *Atlanta Journal-Constitution*, February 2, 1961.

22. Ibid.

23. H. G. Salsinger, "The Umpire," May 22, 1934, Cecil Travis file, National Baseball Hall of Fame and Museum.

24. *The Washington Post*, February 14, 1935.

25. Thomas Liley interview.

26. Thomas Lavin, "Cecil Travis: Forgotten Star of Another Era, *Baseball Digest*, November 1983.

Chapter 2

1. "Senators Try Youth," date n/a, Cecil Travis file, National Baseball Hall of Fame and Museum.

2. "Senators Are Elated," September 15, 1932, Cecil Travis file, National Baseball Hall of Fame and Museum.

3. *The Washington Post*, January 7, 1932.

4. Wirt Gannon, *Your Lookouts since 1885.*

5. "Senators Are Elated."

6. "Griff Looks Ahead on Replacements," November 3, 1932, Cecil Travis file, National Baseball Hall of Fame and Museum.

7. Title n/a, Cecil Travis file, National Baseball Hall of Fame and Museum.

8. Ibid.

9. *The Washington Post*, January 22, 1933.

10. Ibid., February 9, 1933.

11. Ibid., February 28, 1933.

12. Nicholas Dawidoff, *The Catcher Was a Spy*, p. 84.

13. Ibid., February 28, 1933, p. 13.

14. Ibid., March 3, 1933.

15. Ibid.

16. "One Phenom Explodes," March 1933,

Cecil Travis file, National Baseball Hall of Fame and Museum.

17. Ibid., Mar 12, 1933.
18. Ibid., March 17, 1933.
19. Ibid., April 3, 1933.
20. Jack De Vries, "Travis was a Silent Hit in '41 Season," *USA Today Baseball Weekly*, July 26–August 1, 1991.
21. *The Citizen Online*, February 10, 1999.
22. *The Atlanta Journal-Constitution*, August 30, 1993.
23. *The Washington Post*, September 2, 2002.
24. Ibid., May 17, 1933.
25. Ibid.
26. Ibid., May 19, 1933.
27. Ibid., May 31, 1933.
28. Charles Alexander, *Breaking the Slump: Baseball in the Depression*, pg. 67.

Chapter 3

1. *The Washington Post*, "This Morning with Shirley L. Povich," c. 1934, Cecil Travis file, National Baseball Hall of Fame and Museum.
2. Ibid.
3. "...Threatens Bluege's Job," April 12, 1934, Cecil Travis file, National Baseball Hall of Fame and Museum.
4. Qtd. by Thomas Liley in interview with Cecil Travis, Riverdale, Georgia, January 29, 1991.
5. Marty Appel, *Yesterday's Heroes: Revisiting the Old-Time Baseball Stars*.
6. *The Washington Post*, May 1, 1934.
7. Ibid., May 3, 1934.
8. Ibid., May 6, 1934.
9. Ibid.
10. Ibid., February 14, 1935.
11. Ibid., May 6, 1934.
12. Ibid., May 7, 1934.
13. *The New York Times*, May, 7, 1934.
14. *The Washington Post*, May 6, 1934.
15. Clifford Bloodgood, "Cecil Travis, Coming Into Favor," *Baseball Magazine*, August 1934.
16. Ibid.
17. *The Washington Post*, June 26, 1947.
18. Ibid., May 18, 1934.
19. Ibid., May 19, 1934.
20. H. G. Salsinger, "The Umpire," May 22, 1934, Cecil Travis file, National Baseball Hall of Fame and Museum.
21. *The Washington Post*, June 16, 1934.
22. Ibid., July 18, 1934.

23. Ibid., July 19, 1934.
24. Ibid., July 28, 1934.
25. Ibid., August 2, 1934.
26. Ibid., July 28, 1934.
27. Ibid., August 13, 1934.
28. Clifford Bloodgood, "Cecil Travis, Coming Into Favor," *Baseball Magazine*, August 1934.
29. Henry F. Edwards, American League Service Bureau press release, December 30, 1934.

Chapter 4

1. *The Washington Post*, November 14, 1934.
2. Ibid.
3. Ibid., February 4, 1935.
4. *The Atlanta Journal-Constitution*, July 11, 2000.
5. Ibid., March 12, 1935.
6. Ibid., Apr 1, 1935.
7. Ibid., March 18, 1935.
8. Ibid., Mar 28, 1935.
9. Ibid., Apr 4, 1935.
10. Ibid., April 11, 1935.
11. Ibid., April 20, 1935.
12. Ibid., May 14, 1935.
13. Ibid., May 23, 1935.
14. Ibid., June 3, 1935.
15. Elden Auker with Tom Keegan, *Sleeping Cars and Flannel Uniforms*, pp. 41–43.
16. Ibid.
17. Thomas Liley, interview with Cecil Travis, January 29, 1991.
18. *The Washington Post*, March 18, 1935.
19. Ibid, July 3, 1935.
20. Ibid., July 5, 1935.
21. Ibid., August 7, 1935.
22. Ibid., August 9, 1935.
23. Ibid., December 16, 1935.
24. Ibid., Apr 16, 1948.
25. Liley interview.
26. Qtd. in Liley interview.
27. "A Natural National," September 26, 1935, Cecil Travis file, National Baseball Hall of Fame and Museum.
28. *Los Angeles Times*, October 13, 1935.
29. *The Washington Post*, October 21, 1935.
30. Ibid., December 16, 1935.
31. Ibid., December 18, 1935.
32. Ibid., February 3, 1936.
33. Ibid., January 8, 1936.
34. Ibid., January 18, 1936.
35. Ibid., January 22, 1936.
36. Ibid., January 26, 1936.

37. Ibid.
38. Ibid., February 3, 1936.
39. Ibid.
40. Ibid., February 26, 1936.
41. Ibid., February 27, 1936.
42. Ibid.
43. Ibid., March 25, 1936.
44. Ibid., April 5, 1936.
45. *Los Angeles Times*, April 7, 1936.
46. *The Washington Post*, April 13, 1936.
47. Ibid., April 19, 1936.
48. Ibid., May 9, 1936.
49. Ibid., May 21, 1936.
50. Ibid., May 25, 1936.
51. Ibid., May 21, 1936.
52. Ibid., February 24, 1936
53. Ibid., May 30, 1936.
54. Ibid., June 27, 1936.
55. Ibid., July 30, 1936.
56. Ibid., August 25, 1936.

Chapter 5

1. *The Washington Post*, January 23, 1937.
2. Ibid.
3. Ibid.
4. Ibid.
5. Ibid., March 3, 1937.
6. Ibid., March 5, 1937.
7. Ibid., March 27, 1937.
8. Ibid., March 25, 1937.
9. Ibid., March 31, 1937.
10. Ibid., April 9, 1937.
11. Bill James, *The New Bill James Historical Baseball Abstract*, pp. 611–612.
12. *The Washington Post*, Apr 18, 1937.
13. Ibid., May 25, 1937.
14. *Los Angeles Times*, June 19, 1937.
15. *The Washington Post*, July 29, 1937.
16. Ibid., July 31, 1937.
17. *Los Angeles Times*, August 8, 1937.
18. *The Washington Post*, August 8, 1937.
19. *Los Angeles Times*, November 3, 1937.
20. Ibid.
21. Ibid.
22. Ibid., January 11, 1938.
23. *The Washington Post*, January 12, 1938.
24. Ibid., February 3, 1938.
25. Ibid., April 2, 1938.
26. Ibid., April 3, 1938.
27. Ibid., April 10, 1938.
28. Ibid., April 14, 1938.
29. *The New York Times*, April 18, 1938.
30. *The Washington Post*, April 19, 1938.
31. Ibid., May 2, 1938.

32. Ibid., May 10, 1938.
33. Ibid., May 27, 1938.
34. Ibid., June 2, 1938.
35. Ibid., June 10, 1938.
36. *The New York Times*, June 27, 1938.
37. Arthur E. Patterson, "Lewis, Travis Rated Too Modest for Senators," Cecil Travis file, National Baseball Hall of Fame and Museum.
38. *The Washington Post*, July 14, 1938.
39. Ibid., August 12, 1938.
40. *Los Angeles Times*, August 15, 1938.
41. *The Washington Post*, August 14, 1938.
42. Ibid., August 22, 1938.
43. Ibid., August 30, 1938.
44. Ibid., August 30, 1938.
45. Ibid., November 17, 1938.
46. Ibid., October 30, 1938.

Chapter 6

1. Ethan Allen, "Batting-Grip, Stance and Swing," *Scholastic Coach*, April 1939.
2. *The Washington Post*, January 24, 1939.
3. Ibid., March 10, 1939.
4. Ibid., February 19, 1939.
5. Ibid., March 23, 1939.
6. Ibid.
7. Ibid.
8. Ibid., March 23, 1939.
9. Ibid., March 27, 1939.
10. Ibid., March 28, 1939.
11. Ibid., April 10, 1939.
12. Ibid., May 23, 1939.
13. Ibid., May 30, 1939.
14. Ibid., May 23, 1939.
15. Ibid., May 30, 1939.
16. Ibid., June 1, 1939.
17. Ibid.
18. Ibid., June 6, 1939.
19. *The Atlanta Journal-Constitution*, July 11, 2000.
20. *The Washington Post*, June 26, 1939.
21. *The New York Times*, July 5, 1939.
22. *The Washington Post*, June 27, 1939.
23. Ibid., July 7, 1939.
24. Ibid., August 8, 1939.
25. Ibid., August 7, 1939.
26. Ibid., August 10, 1939.
27. Ibid., August 20, 1939.
28. Ibid., August 29, 1939.
29. Ibid.
30. *Los Angeles Times*, August 31, 1939.
31. *The Washington Post*, August 29, 1939.

Chapter 7

1. *Los Angeles Times*, November 3, 1939.
2. *The Washington Post*, December 6, 1939.
3. Ibid., December 8, 1939.
4. Ibid., December 10, 1939.
5. Ibid., January 16, 1940.
6. *Los Angeles Times*, February 1, 1940.
7. *The Washington Post*, February 15, 1940.
8. Ibid., February 28, 1940.
9. Ibid., February 29, 1940.
10. Ibid.
11. Ibid., March 3, 1940.
12. Ibid., March 17, 1940.
13. Ibid., March 29, 1940.
14. Ibid., March 23, 1940.
15. Ibid., April 8, 1940.
16. Ibid., March 29, 1940.
17. Ibid., April 17, 1940.
18. *The New York Times*, April 18, 1940.
19. *The Washington Post*, April 17, 1940.
20. Ibid., April 28, 1940.
21. Ibid., May 5, 1940.
22. Ibid., May 20, 1940.
23. Ibid., May 21, 1940.
24. Ibid., May 26, 1940.
25. Ibid., May 25, 1940.
26. Ibid., June 22, 1940.
27. Ibid., July 7, 1940; July 9, 1940.
28. Ibid., July 18, 1940.
29. Ibid., August 6, 1940.
30. Ibid., August 5, 1940.
31. Ibid., August 6, 1940.

Chapter 8

1. *The Washington Post*, January 24, 1941.
2. Ibid., February 23, 1941.
3. Ibid., Feburary 25, 1941.
4. Ibid., April 4, 1941.
5. Ibid., April 12, 1941.
6. Todd Newville, "Remembering ... Cecil Travis," *Baseball Digest*, May 2003.
7. Ibid., April 7, 1941.
8. Ibid., April 13, 1941.
9. Ibid., April 17, 1941.
10. Ibid., April 18, 1941.
11. Ibid., April 7, 1941.
12. Ibid., April 15, 1941.
13. Ibid., April 16, 1941.
14. Ibid., April 28, 1941.
15. Ibid., April 16, 1941.
16. Ibid., April 28, 1941.
17. Ibid., April 19, 1941.
18. Ibid., April 25, 1941.
19. Ibid., April 28, 1941.
20. Ibid., May 2, 1941.
21. Ibid., May 3, 1941.
22. Ibid.
23. Ibid., May 3, 1941.
24. Ibid., June 1, 1941.
25. Ibid., June 2, 1941.
26. Ibid., June 15, 1941.
27. Ibid., June 10, 1941.
28. Ibid., June 13, 1941.
29. Ibid., June 13, 1941.
30. Ibid., June 16, 1941.
31. Robert Leckie, *Delivered from Evil: The Saga of World War II*, p. 226.
32. Michael Seidel, *Ted Williams: A Baseball Life*, p. 93.
33. *The Washington Post*, July 2, 1941.
34. Leckie, pp 250, 222.
35. "The 1941 All-Star Game," SportingNews.com. *www.sportingnews.com/features/allstar/1941.html*
36. Michael Seidel, *Ted Williams: A Baseball Life*, p. 99.
37. Ibid.
38. Dave Kindred, "Memories Frozen in Time," *The Sporting News*, January 2, 1995.
39. *The Washington Post*, July 9, 1941.
40. "History of the MLB All-Star Game," SportingNews.com
41. *The Washington Post*, July 15, 1941.
42. Ibid.
43. *The Washington Post*, July 27, 1941.
44. Ibid., September 8, 1941.
45. Seidel, p. 107.
46. Ibid.
47. "History of the World Series—1941," SportingNews.com. *http://www.sportingnews.com/archives/worldseries/1941.html*

Chapter 9

1. *The New York Times*, January 11, 1942.
2. *The Washington Post*, January 25, 1942.
3. *The New York Times*, January 8, 1942.
4. Ibid., January 12, 1942.
5. Ibid., January 24, 1942.
6. Ibid.
7. Qtd. in Steven Bullock, *Playing for the Nation: Baseball and the American Military during World War II*, p. 12.
8. National Baseball Hall of Fame and Museum *www.halloffame.org/exhibits/online_exhibits/baseball_enlists/a01_transcript.htm*
9. Ibid.

10. Bullock, p. 13.
11. *The Washington Post*, February 2, 1942.
12. Ibid., March 4, 1942.
13. Ibid., February 3, 1942.
14. *The New York Times*, April 4, 1942.
15. Brad Snyder, *Beyond the Shadow of the Senators: The Untold Story of the Homestead Grays and the Integration of Baseball*, p. 116.
16. Geoffrey C. Ward and Ken Burns. *Baseball: An Illustrated History*, p. 206.
17. *Los Angeles Times*, May 25, 1942; Snyder p. 114.
18. *The Washington Post*, May 23, 1942, pp. 23]
19. Snyder, p. 114.
20. Ibid., p. 118.
21. *The Washington Post*, May 30, 1942.
22. Ibid., May 27, 1942.
23. Snyder, p. 118.
24. Ibid. pp. 119–120.
25. Qtd. in Snyder, p. 115.
26. Snyder, p. 121.
27. Ibid., p. 122.
28. Ibid., p. 123.
29. Ibid., p. 122–123.
30. *The Washington Post*, June 1, 1942.
31. Qtd. in Snyder, p. 125.
32. Qtd. in Snyder, p. 122.
33. Snyder, p. 122.
34. Ibid., p. 123.
35. Ibid., p. 120.
36. Snyder, p. 117.
37. Ibid.
38. Ibid., p. 121.
39. *The Washington Post*, June 1, 1942.
40. Thomas Liley interview.
41. *The New York Times*, July 3, 1942.
42. Ibid., July 6, 1942.
43. *Los Angeles Times*, July 8, 1942.
44. Ibid., August 19, 1942.
45. *The Washington Post*, August 14, 1944.
46. Ibid., December 18, 1942.
47. Ibid., August 25, 1942.
48. Ibid., February 26, 1943.
49. Ibid., April 11, 1943.
50. "In the Service," *The Sporting News*, August 10, 1944.
51. Bullock, p. 123.; Gary Bloomfield, *Duty, Honor, Country: America's Athletes in World War II*, p. 81.

Chapter 10

1. Joseph J. Hutnik and Leonard Kobrick, eds., *We Ripened Fast: The Unofficial His-*

tory of the Seventy-Sixth Infantry Division, p. 47.
2. Robert Leckie, *Delivered from Evil: The Saga of World War II*, p. 801.
3. Jack De Vries, "Travis Was a Silent Hit in '41 Season," *USA Today Baseball Weekly*, July 26–August 1, 1991.
4. Thomas Liley, interview with Cecil Travis, Riverdale, Georgia, January 29, 1991.
5. Ibid., p. 56.
6. Qtd. in Gary Bloomfield, *Duty, Honor, Victory: American's Athletes in World War II*, p. 300.
7. Hutnik, p. 59.
8. Ibid., p. 67.
9. Bloomfield, p. 81.
10. Ibid., p. 73.
11. Ibid., p. 71.
12. Ibid., p. 102.
13. Ibid., p. 112.
14. Ibid., p. 114.
15. Ibid., p. 156.
16. Ibid., p. 173.
17. Ibid., p. 175.
18. Ibid., p. 180.
19. Ibid., p. 183.
20. Ibid., p. 184.
21. Ibid., p. 197.

Chapter 11

1. *The Washington Post*, May 13, 1945.
2. Ibid., June 10, 1945, pp. M6.
3. Ron Fimrite, "A Call to Arms," *Sports Illustrated*, October 28, 1991.
4. Ibid., August 16, 1945; August 17, 1945.
5. Ibid., August 28, 1945.
6. Ibid., September 6, 1945.
7. Ibid., September 7, 1945.
8. Ibid., September 6, 1945; September 7, 1945.
9. Ibid., September 8, 1945.
10. Ibid., September 9, 1945.
11. Ibid.
12. Ibid., September 16, 1945.
13. Ibid.
14. Ibid., November 7, 1945.
15. Ibid., December 21, 1945.
16. Ibid., February 18, 1946.
17. Ibid., February 21, 1946.
18. Ibid., February 18, 1946.
19. Ibid., February 28, 1946.
20. Ibid., February 26, 1946.
21. Ibid., March 10, 1946.
22. Ibid., March 17, 1946.
23. Ibid.

24. Ibid., March 14, 1946.
25. Ibid., March 15, 1946.
26. Ibid., April 5, 1946.
27. Ibid., May 6, 1946.
28. Ibid., May 22, 1946.
29. Ibid., May 28, 1946.
30. Ibid., September 24, 1946.
31. Ibid.
32. Ibid., April 20, 1946.
33. Ibid., July 28, 1946.
34. Ibid., July 31, 1946.
35. Ibid., September 22, 1946.
36. Ibid., October 18, 1946.
37. Ibid., February 28, 1947.
38. Ibid., March 7, 1947.
39. Ibid., March 10, 1947.
40. Ibid., March 22, 1947.
41. Ibid., May 8, 1947.
42. Ibid., April 24, 1947.
43. Ibid., May 5, 1947.
44. Ibid., June 1, 1947; June 8, 1947.
45. Ibid., August 16, 1947.
46. Ibid.
47. Ibid.
48. Ibid., August 17, 1947.
49. Ibid., September 21, 1947.
50. *The New York Times*, September 28, 1947.

Epilogue

1. *The New York Times*, January 10, 1948.
2. *The Washington Post*, January 11, 1948.
3. Ibid., January 10, 1948.
4. Ibid., January 18, 1948.
5. Ibid., January 10, 1948.
6. Ibid., March 7, 1948.

7. Thomas Liley, interview with Cecil Travis, Riverdale, Georgia, January 29, 1991.
8. *The Atlanta Journal-Constitution*, July 11, 2000.
9. *Clayton News/Daily*, August 17, 1991.
10. Ibid.
11. Jack De Vries, "Travis was a silent hit in '41 season," *USA Today Baseball Weekly*, July 26–August 1, 1991.
12. Qtd. on *SportsJones* (www.sportsjones.com).
13. *Atlanta Journal-Constitution*, July 22, 1993.
14. Dave Kindred, "Memories Frozen in Time," *The Sporting News*, Jan 2, 1995.
15. *The Washington Times*, April 22, 2002.
16. Ibid., April 5, 1992.
17. Rob Neyer, "Don't believe that Jeter's defense has improved," ESPN.com. *espn.go.com/mlb/columns/neyer_rob/1415695.html*
18. *Atlanta Journal-Constitution*, October 3, 1999.
19. Ibid., October 30, 1993.
20. Ibid., July 11, 2000.
21. Marty Appel, *Yesterday's Heroes: Revisiting the Old-Time Baseball Stars*, n.p.
22. Todd Newville, "Remembering ... Cecil Travis," *Baseball Digest*, May 2003.
23. *The Washington Times*, September 18, 1993.
24. Kindred.
25. Appel, n.p.
26. Rob Kirkpatrick, phone interview with Vernon interview, February 13, 2003.
27. Thomas Liley, interview with Cecil Travis, Riverdale, Georgia, January 29, 1991.
28. Rob Kirkpatrick, phone interview with Cecil Travis, August 13, 2002.

Bibliography

Alexander, Charles. *Breaking the Slump: Baseball in the Depression*. New York: Columbia University Press, 2002.

Allen, Ethan. "Batting-Grip, Stance and Swing." *Scholastic Coach*. Volume 8, Issue 8, April 1939.

Appel, Marty. *Yesterday's Heroes: Revisiting the Old-Time Baseball Stars*. New York: Morrow, 1988.

Auker, Elden, with Tom Keegan. *Sleeping Cars and Flannel Uniforms: A Lifetime of Memories from Striking Out the Babe to Teeing It Up with the President*. Chicago: Triumph, 2001.

The Baseball Encyclopedia: The Complete and Official Record of Major League Baseball, 8th ed. New York: Macmillan, 1991.

Bisher, Furman. *The Furman Bisher Collection*. National Books Network, 1989.

Bloodgood, Clifford. "The Leading Socker of the Senators." *Baseball Magazine*. Vol. 60, Issue 4, March 1938.

Bloomfield, Gary. *Duty, Honor, Victory: America's Athletes in World War II*. Guilford, Conn.: Lyons, 2003.

Bullock, Steven. *Playing for the Nation: Baseball and the American Military during World War II*. Lincoln: University of Nebraska Press, 2004.

Cecil Travis file, Fayette County Historical Society. Fayetteville, Georgia. (Carolyn Cary, county historian.)

Cecil Travis file, National Baseball Hall of Fame and Museum. Cooperstown, New York.

Ceresi, Frank, Mark Rucker and Carol McManis. *Baseball in Washington, D.C.* Charleston, S.C.: Arcadia, 2003.

Dawidoff, Nicholas. *The Catcher Was a Spy: The Mysterious Life of Moe Berg*. New York: Pantheon, 1994.

Deveaux, Tom. *The Washington Senators, 1901–1971*. Jefferson, N.C.: McFarland, 2001.

DeVries, Jack. "Travis Was a Silent Hit in '41." *USA Today Baseball Weekly*. Volume 1, Issue 17, July 26, 1991.

Edwards, Harry F. American Leagues Service Bureau press release. December 30, 1934.

Fimrite, Ron. "A Call to Arms." *Sports Illustrated*, October 28, 1991.

Finoli, David. *For the Good of the Country: World War II in the Major and Minor Leagues*. Jefferson, N.C.: McFarland, 2002.

Foote, Shelby. *Civil War: A Narrative; Volume 3, Red River to Appomattox*. New
     York: Vintage, 1986.
Gammon, Wirt. *Your Lookouts from 1885*. Chattanooga: Chattanooga Publishing, 1955.
Holway, John B. "Does Cecil Travis Belong in the Hall of Fame?" *Baseball Digest*.
     Volume 52, Issue 5, May 1993.
Hutnik, Joseph J., and Leonard Kobrick, eds. *We Ripened Fast: The Unofficial History
     of the Seventy-Sixth Infantry Division*. Frankfurt: Verlag Otto Lembeck, 1944.
James, Bill. *The New Bill James Historical Baseball Abstract*. New York: Free Press, 2001.
Kashatus, William C. *One-Armed Wonder: Pete Gray, Wartime Baseball, and the
     American Dream*. Jefferson, N.C.: McFarland, 1995.
Kindred, Dave. "Memories Frozen in Time." *The Sporting News*, January 2, 1995.
Lavin, Thomas. "Cecil Travis: Forgotten Star of Another Era." *Baseball Digest*.
     Volume 43, Issue 11, November 1983.
Leckie, Robert. *Delivered from Evil: The Saga of World War II*. New York: Harper
     & Row, 1987.
Newville, Todd. "Remembering ... Cecil Travis." *Baseball Digest*. Volume 62, Issue
     5, May 2003.
Oney, Steve. *And the Dead Shall Rise: The Murder of Mary Phagan and the Lynch-
     ing of Leo Frank*. New York: Pantheon, 2003.
Palmer, Pete, and Gary Gillete, eds. *The Baseball Encyclopedia*. New York: Barnes
     and Noble, 2004.
Patterson, Arthur E. "Lewis, Travis Rated Too Modest for Senators." n.d. Cecil
     Travis file, National Baseball Hall of Fame and Museum.
Povich, Shirley. *The Washington Senators*. New York: Putnam, 1954.
SABR Oral History Project. Interview with Cecil Travis, Riverdale, Georgia, Jan-
     uary 29, 1991, by Thomas Liley.
Salsinger, H. G. "The Umpire." May 22, 1934. Cecil Travis file, National Baseball
     Hall of Fame and Museum.
Seidel, Michael. *Ted Williams: A Baseball Life*. Lincoln: University of Nebraska
     Press, 2000.
Snyder, Brad. *Beyond the Shadow of the Senators: The Untold Story of the Home-
     stead Grays and the Integration of Baseball*. New York: McGraw-Hill, 2003.
Walton, Tubby, as told to James Quillian Maxwell. *The Life Story of Tubby Wal-
     ton*. 1968: self-published.
Ward, Geoffrey C., and Ken Burns. *Baseball: An Illustrated History*. New York:
     Alfred A. Knopf, 1994.

Newspapers

Atlanta Journal-Constitution 1961, 1993, 1999, 2000
The Citizen News (Fayette County, Georgia) 1999
Clayton/News Daily (Clayton County, Georgia) 1991
Los Angeles Times 1935–1940, 1942
The New York Times 1934, 1939, 1940, 1942, 1945, 1947, 1948
The Sporting News 1944, 1995
USA Today Baseball Weekly 1991
The Washington Post 1932–48, 1992–93
The Washington Times 2002

Online Resources

Ancestry.com
  www.ancestry.com

Baseball Almanac
  www.baseball-almanac.com

The Baseball Index
  www.baseballindex.org

BaseballLibrary.com
  www.baseballlibrary.com

The Citizen News (Fayette County, Georgia)
  www.thecitizennews.com

ESPN.com
  espn.go.com

National Baseball Hall of Fame and Museum
  www.halloffame.org

The Society for American Baseball Research
  www.sabr.org

Southern League of Professional Baseball
  www.southernleague.com

The Sporting News
  www.sportingnews.com

SportsJones
  www.sportsjones.com

Index